RENAISSANCE

IN THE SOUTH

Renaissance in the South

A CRITICAL HISTORY OF THE LITERATURE, 1920-1960

by John M. Bradbury

THE UNIVERSITY OF NORTH
CAROLINA PRESS · CHAPEL HILL

PRINTED BY THE SEEMAN PRINTERY, DURHAM, N. C.

Manufactured in the United States of America

To Anne

ACKNOWLEDGMENTS

I wish to acknowledge the aid afforded me in the form of grants by the Trustees of Union College and President Carter Davidson, as well as by Helmer Webb, Head Librarian at Union College until 1962. In addition, the Union College Library staff, including especially Miss Ruth Ann Evans, Mrs. Philip Stanley, Charles Wilde, Edward Elliott, H. Eugene Wine, and Wayne Somers, have been most cooperative and resourceful.

Though I have avoided as far as possible reliance on other critics, I am indebted to more of them than I could hope to list here. If any are to be singled out, they must be Louis D. Rubin, Jr. and Robert D. Jacobs, who have ably anthologized modern Southern criticism. Mr. David James Harkness's series of Literary Profiles done in the University of Tennessee *News Letters* have supplied many leads to obscure or obscured Southern authors. Professor Richard Walser of North Carolina State University has extended excellent hospitality, along with helpful information. Many research librarians in Southern states have contributed data. In particular, I have enjoyed the valuable cooperation of Mr. George Logan of the New Orleans Public Library and Miss Betty Service of the Sarasota Public Library.

CONTENTS

RENAISSANCE
IN THE SOUTH

INTRODUCTION

To a Kentuckian growing up to literary consciousness during the 1910's and 1920's, the state of Mississippi was an enduring comfort. As long as Mississippi survived, he felt statistically assured that his own backward Commonwealth could never effectively challenge her perennial status as forty-eighth among forty-eight in national literacy. The surprise was disproportionally great, therefore, when at the outset of this study came the discovery that in the 1950's Mississippi had taken the lead, on a per capita basis, among American states in the production of creative literature. The state does not yet read or attend its artists as it should, but perhaps it cannot take time from its writing. Incontrovertibly Mississippian are America's most honored novelist, her most successful playwright, her most renowned Negro writer. In addition, a high percentage of her finest poets, short story writers, and novelists prove to be natives of the Magnolia State.

But Mississippi's case is symptomatic rather than unique in the recent literary history of the South, for the general revival of Southern letters since the First World War has been the major literary phenomenon of our time. North Carolina and Georgia have produced even more prolifically. Louisiana, Alabama, and South Carolina have been rivalled nationally only by Virginia, Tennessee, East Texas, and, indeed, Kentucky. There have been important contributions, too, from Maryland, from Florida, though much of that state has become a Northern province, from Eastern Arkansas, and from the Shenandoah Valley in West Virginia.

What has now for some years been recognized by literary critics and historians as the Southern Renaissance includes, in addition to one winner of the Nobel Prize for literature, eleven recipients of Pulitzer Prizes for fiction, which constitutes a full third of those awarded since 1929; four for drama and five for poetry. Since 1940-41, seven of the seventeen awards made by the New York Drama Critics Circle have gone to Southern playwrights. Three Bollingen Prizes, representing "the highest achievement in American poetry," have been taken by Southerners since 1950, and thirty-five Southern authors have been granted Guggenheim Fellowships to work in fiction, poetry, and drama since 1927. The National Book Awards, offered since 1950, have gone three times to Southern novelists and three times to Southern poets. In sum, the South which was offering almost nothing to American letters before World War I has since been earning a considerably larger share than its population warrants of the literary kudos.

In attempting to deal adequately with this amazing outburst of activity, I have been first concerned to establish proper limits for the South and to qualify individual authors as proper "Southerners." I have already indicated the territory which culturally and economically constitutes for me the South. A Southern author is, generally speaking, one who was born and has lived his formative years within this area. There must be, however, a number of exceptions to this rule. Lettie Rogers, for example, born in China of a Southern missionary family and coming to Virginia for her schooling, is certainly Southern, not Chinese. On the other hand, Julian and Anne Green, of Virginia and Georgia parentage, were brought up Parisians and remain so.

From Texas, much of which is Western plateau, I have included those authors who have grown up in a culture allied to that of their trans-Mississippi neighbors. For Arkansas, much the same rule holds, and I have, in particular, excluded the special breed of Ozark Mountain local colorists. Though I include Marylanders as dwellers below Mason and Dixon's line, natives of the District of Columbia can be allowed only in the special circumstance of family ties and interests. Washington belongs to everyone and to no one. (Marjorie Kinnan Rawlings, born in Washington, settling in Florida, and using the latter all but exclusively in her fictional settings, belongs to the South. A daughter of Calvin Coolidge born in the White House would not.) West Virginia is attached culturally to Pennsylvania and Ohio, rather than to Virginia. However, Jefferson County, the northeastern tip through which flows the Shenandoah River, both historically and by predilection belongs to the South.

A number of anthologies of recent Southern literature and collections of essays about it have appeared since the Renaissance became a recognized phenomenon. None of them has done justice to the variety and scope of the literature produced. Something of a canon has been established, with the result that a quite limited number of authors have been credited with total responsibility for the South's modern contribution to American letters. The canon includes almost exclusively that group which I have called the "new traditionists," those whose work fits the pattern prescribed by the South's New Critics. Thomas Wolfe has certainly been acknowledged, but often, too, has been dismissed critically, while a few popular local colorists, like Jesse Stuart and Erskine Caldwell, have been allowed to represent the remaining bulk of Southern production.

The more one reads in the modern literature of the South, the more compelling becomes the desire to redress the critical balance. A strong and wide-spread liberal wing, covering both urban and rural subjects, has been largely ignored. Problem novels have proliferated; those dealing with industry and the farm are matched by a similarly diverse group centering on the family and group relations. A highly significant area of this development has been the serious Negro point of view story, chiefly written by white Southerners, a sub-genre which has exhibited remarkable growth and maturity. The South boasts its "tough school," its realistic, as well as romantic, historical novelists, its humorists, even its existentialists.

In order to facilitate discussion of this huge mass of material, I have been forced to set up rather arbitrary categories. A serious writer does not, as a rule, set out to produce a type of novel, but only a good novel. The historian, however, has no choice but to group and classify; only so can he display the range and depth, the larger trends and individual deviations within the movement. I have expressly excluded for obvious reasons the categories of the detective story and juvenile literature, though the South has produced some of the most successful authors in both fields. Scant attention has been paid to the popular entertainers, the light humorists, and the slick purveyors of romance, though all of these abound.

In attempting to do justice to all the real talents among the writers of fiction, I have made a number of virtual rediscoveries, authors whose enduring qualities have been buried in the avalanche of more recent writing, their graves all but unmarked through critical neglect. At the same time, I have felt it time to shuffle up and down a few established reputations. Popular novelists like Ben Lucian Burman, Jesse Stuart, and Erskine Caldwell I have thus relegated to the pulpy limbo where I am convinced they belong. Isa Glenn, Frances Newman, Anne Winslow, Edwin Granberry, and others I have restored to positions of honor which I feel they deserve. These are to me acts of simple justice which I trust the future will confirm.

1

THE AWAKENING

The Southern Literary Renaissance, some forty years old but still maturely vigorous in 1963, is a phenomenon unparalleled in American history. The country has experienced significant creative revivals in the past, principally in New England and the Midwest, but never before has a region so suddenly, so widely, and so effectively burst into literary activity as has the South since 1920.

This renaissance can be dated with unusual precision. As late as 1917, H. L. Mencken in *The Smart Set* was quite justifiably attacking the artistic aridity of the South under the title, "The Sahara of the Bozarts." Five years later, when the soldiers of the American Expeditionary Force of World War I had settled back into a changed environment and begun to voice their own viewpoints, Mencken's remarks were already out of date. Little literary magazines had been established, poetic movements were under way, dramatic workshops were producing, novels and short stories from every part of the region were commanding the attention of publishers.

The "causes" of a renaissance are subjects for interested speculation rather than for strict determination. History would seem to indicate, however, that a prime requisite must be a sense of challenge that stirs the minds of men simultaneously and stimulates a new awareness of the values by which they have been living. Whether the challenge is primarily intellectual or social, it must extend sharply into both spheres. The South had experienced a primary challenge in the 1860's, but the social upheaval attending the war was accompanied by no intellectual ferment, only an emotional response that demanded expression in action. Literature could act only as a camp follower while the action proceeded and as a mourner of the lost cause after defeat.

The Southern situation in 1920 called for reassessment, not for

regrets and recriminations. The war action had been successful but
disillusioning both for soldiers and for those who had manned the
home front. Their personal values had been shaken, and their home
towns, farms, and jobs had been largely transformed. There had occurred, as several Southern analysts have insisted, a new kind of
invasion. The movement of industry into the South, begun around
the turn of the century, had been tremendously accelerated by war
demands. The prosperity brought by new factories and high prices
had encouraged a wholesale recruiting of the invaded themselves in the
cause of a "New South," industrially organized and dedicated to
"Progress." New orbits of power, centering about financial control,
enlisting highly vocal boosters, and encouraging demagogic politicians,
were forcing the leading old conservative elements into the peripheries
of influence.

When Southern youth returned from Army experiences, their old-
fashioned provincial prejudices had already been shaken by new
associations, new environments, and the widespread malaise of a
"lost generation." The home situations to which they returned did
not encourage settling back into old grooves, but rather exploration
and expression. There was, to stimulate them, a considerable literary
excitement in the air and the Menckenite challenge of cultural backwardness. The American poetic revival of the 'Teens had reached its
climax; the Midwestern school of social realists was shocking the
country with exposures of small-town hypocrisies. Particularly relevant
to their own backgrounds were two much discussed books of fiction:
Sinclair Lewis's *Main Street* and Sherwood Anderson's *Winesburg,
Ohio*. Especially Lewis's mordant exploration into the bigotries and
blatancies of small-town America struck a responsive chord in Southern minds and offered a popular form in which to channel their
observations. In 1921 the new literary magazine established in New
Orleans editorialized: "We are sick to death of the treacly sentimentalities with which our well-intentioned lady fictioneers regale us.
... We have our Main Street here as elsewhere."

These challenges can be documented over and over again in the
fiction and poetry that have issued in a wide stream from the Southern
states. The old order, decayed like Faulkner's Compsons or stiffly
idealistic like Warren's Stantons, meets the new opportunistic Snopeses
and Starks. Wolfe's lost hero wanders bewildered because he "did not

understand change." Others are indignant, ironic, or militantly hopeful as they face the challenges. They come back to a familiar scene no longer familiar; or their eyes are opened to the strangeness of a world long taken for granted. Intently, they go about the exploration of their native streets and farms.

The South was not quite the artistic desert which Mencken described in 1917, but his account was close enough to the truth to cause rankling discomfort among Southern apologists. There were two novelists, neighbors in Richmond, Virginia, who had achieved national recognition. Ellen Glasgow's bold, liberal-minded interpretations of Virginia's social problems had convincingly established her reputation, though she had yet to publish her masterpieces. James Branch Cabell's vogue as sophisticated romantic ironist had not yet run its full course. There was also the prolific Upton Sinclair of Baltimore who had won a broad following for his thinly disguised social tracts—and who most surprisingly was to win a Pulitzer Prize for fiction. In addition, there remained a handful of local colorists and popular sentimental fiction writers whose prime was well passed: Mary Johnston, Cora Harris, Alice Hegan Rice, James Lane Allen, Marie Oemler, and their imitators.

Many poets of local reputation and slight talent there were, but only one of importance, Lizette Reese of Baltimore, who in her retiring way had made a substantial contribution to the poetic revival of the early years of the century. Cale Young Rice of Kentucky had earned some reputation, but more of it in England than in his own country. Several Southern playwrights had made their way on Broadway, among them Rida Johnson Young, popular author of such musicals as *Naughty Marietta* and such dramatic hits as *Brown of Harvard* and *Glorious Betsy*; and Frederic Kummer, who had done *The Brute* and *The Painted Woman*.

A few of the major poets who belong to the Southern Renaissance had published first books prematurely, as it were, during the war years. But the movement proper opened on a self-conscious note in 1921 with the establishment of *The Double Dealer* in New Orleans under the antitraditionalist editor, Julius Weiss Friend; and *The Reviewer* in Richmond under Emily Clark, whose policy was explicitly a desire "to develop young Southern writers." In the same year, *The Lyric* of Norfolk began to print local and regional poets, and the

Poetry Society of South Carolina, featuring the work of Dubose Heyward of Charleston and that of transplanted Northerner, Hervey Allen, issued its first *Yearbook*. Early the next year in Nashville, Tennessee, the remarkable and influential poetry magazine, *The Fugitive,* appeared, with Vanderbilt teachers and students dominating the editorial staff. At Chapel Hill, North Carolina, under the leadership of Frederick Koch, The Carolina Playmakers, a group established in 1918, made its first tour with original student dramas in 1921, and published its first volume in 1922.

Inevitably, many of the early Southern Renaissance figures are to be found loosely grouped around these early centers of literary activity. But the 1920's were hte era of exiles as well, of Pound and Eliot, of Joyce and Hemingway and Stein. For young artistically-minded Southerners, the North offered the same lure that Europe suggested to Fitzgerald and to the already disillusioned group of expatriates. Young Thomas Wolfe, an original member of The Carolina Playmakers, fled to New York and finally Europe, proclaiming his sense of exile. Max Bodenheim escaped Mississippi to become a spokesman of Bohemianism in New York's Greenwich Village. Brilliant young Frances Newman, stifled in her native Atlanta, moved off to New York and Paris. Evelyn Scott fled Southern bellehood in Tennessee and New Orleans for a precipitous affair which took her to Brazil and finally New York. Allen Tate, choked in the coal business, left Kentucky for a free-lance career in the metropolis, and John Gould Fletcher deserted Arkansas to shine in the Imagist firmament of Amy Lowell.

The exiles, like Joyce, eventually found their most congenial literary material in the regions they had left. Like Joyce, too, they tended to treat their deserted heaths in a highly critical spirit. Some, however, like Tate, were able to reassimilate their heritages and base their careers on a new understanding of Southern traditions. Only a few, like Bodenheim, could discard their traditions as if they were outgrown clothing and concentrate their energies on interpreting their new environments.

The native centers soon began not only to attract ambitious young writers, but to stimulate indigenous talents who might have gravitated to more lucrative callings. New Orleans developed an artistic coterie as well as a little magazine. With regionalist Lyle Saxon and Midwesterner Sherwood Anderson on the spot, the new Bohemia drew

Faulkner from Mississippi and Roark Bradford from Tennessee, while it encouraged the talents of natives like Hamilton Basso and E. P. O'Donnell. The Nashville center, where John Crowe Ransom alone had published, encouraged such faculty and student talents as those of Donald Davidson, Allen Tate, Robert Penn Warren, Merrill Moore, Ridley Wills and his brother, Jesse, Stanley Johnson, and such business men as Alec Brock Stevenson. Shortly after the original *Fugitive* period, novelists Andrew Lytle, Caroline Gordon, and Jesse Stuart, poet Randall Jarrell, and critic Cleanth Brooks were drawn into the Nashville orbit.

Charleston's Poetry Society primarily gave Dubose Heyward an early opportunity for publication; it aided, too, in drawing out the talents of later novelists Josephine Pinckney, Robert Molloy, Herbert Ravenal Sass, Katherine Simons, C. S. Murray and Richard Coleman. Richmond's *The Reviewer* encouraged such aspiring writers as Julia Peterkin, Frances Newman, and Mencken's wife, Sara Haardt; but the Poetry Society of Virginia, founded somewhat later, succeeded more extensively in bringing out local talent across the state. Many excellent poets, including Carlton Drewry and Virginia Moore, have been associated with the Society.

The University of North Carolina and its Playmakers, dedicated to regional drama, proved the most magnetic of pioneer literary centers. The University had already produced Hatcher Hughes, who was teaching drama at Columbia and writing plays, one of which, *Hell Bent for Heaven,* won a Pulitzer Prize in 1923. Thomas Wolfe, the first Playmaker to have a drama produced, Paul Green, a Pulitzer Prize winner in 1927 with *In Abraham's Bosom,* and Jonathan Daniels, journalist and author of a novel, were early students of Professor Koch. Later Playmakers include fiction writers Bernice Kelly Harris, Frances Patton, Foster Fitz-Simons, Joseph Mitchell, Noel Houston, and LeGette Blythe; poets Frank Borden Hanes and Charles Eaton.

As the literary movement continued, Southern colleges and universities, like those in other sections of the country, followed Carolina's lead and developed their own creative writing programs. The University of Alabama, in particular, under Carl Carmer, who was followed by Hudson Strode, drew into its program a number of promising young writers. Among these were Edward Kimbrough, who has returned to teach at the University, Robert Gibbons, William

Bradford Huie, Thomas Hal Phillips, Carlyle Tillery, Frances Tillot-
son, Alice Fellows, Harriet Hassell, Borden Deal and his wife, Babs
Deal. At Lincoln Memorial University in Tennessee, novelist Harry
Kroll pioneered writing courses, helping to develop Jesse Stuart and
James Still. From 1928, William Blackburn at Duke University was
a stimulus for such students as R. P. Harriss, Mac Hyman, Frances
Patton, Ovid Pierce, and more recently, William Styron and Reynolds
Price.

Still other universities sponsored literary magazines to provide
outlets for Southern writers and offer intellectual stimulation: *The
Southern Review* at Louisiana State University, *The Southwest Review*
at Southern Methodist University, *The Virginia Quarterly* at the University of Virginia, *The South Atlantic Review* at Trinity College
(later Duke University), *The Agora* and *The Carolina Playbook* at the
University of North Carolina. Before 1935 a host of little magazines,
chiefly of poetry, had been established to flourish briefly: *The Nomad*
and *The Gammadion* in Birmingham, Alabama; *The Buccaneer* and
The Kaleidoscope in Dallas, Texas; *The Circle, Interludes,* and *The
Adolescent* in Baltimore, Maryland; *Verse Craft* and *Bozart* in At-
lanta, Georgia; *Will-o'-the-Wisp* in Suffolk, Virginia; *The Journal of
American Poetry* in Charlotte, North Carolina, and *Contempo* at
Chapel Hill; *Sonnet Sequences* in Landover, Maryland; *Blues* in
Columbus, Mississippi; *The Scepter* in Franklin, Tennessee; *The
North Carolina Poetry Review* in Gastonia, North Carolina; *The Ob-
server* in Memphis, Tennessee; *Shards* in Augusta, Georgia; *The
Calithump* in Austin, Texas; *The Cycle* in Homestead, Florida; and
The Dragon-Fly in De Land, Florida.

Writing schools in the North also attracted a number of young
people with literary ambitions, particularly Columbia University in
New York, where the creative and journalistic writing programs were
firmly entrenched, and where publishers and agents kept their eyes
open for new talent. A few chose Chicago where the Midwestern
school was still promoting a congenial realism. For those who insisted
on more direct experience and needed financial support, the field which
offered at least a minimum of security with the opportunity for writing practice was that of journalism. Approximately one-third of the
new novelists who developed during the first decades of the Southern
Renaissance began working as reporters. Some of these authors moved

later into publishing firms, some into radio and public relations after their first novels. A small percentage were able to make of creative literature a life occupation.

None of the early writers who produced the new movement had the benefit of formal training in advanced composition courses. Neither were they vitally concerned with winning a popular audience. They were most often poets, for the Southern Renaissance, like most such literary movements, began with its major emphasis on lyric poetry. Poetry had indeed provided the chief intellectual excitement of America's 'Teens in every section except the South. It offered the most immediate challenge, therefore, if not the most lucrative, for the aspiring Southern writer. Many of the young men and women who were to make their marks primarily in fiction published initially in verse. William Faulkner's early work was poetry; Elizabeth Maddox Roberts, Dubose Heyward, Robert Penn Warren, Josephine Pinckney, Evelyn Scott, and James Agee, to mention only a few, printed volumes of verse before they turned to fiction.

Fiction and, on a smaller scale, drama experienced remarkable rejuvenation from the outset of the Southern Renaissance, but poetry was in the air and Mecken's indictment had been explicit: "Down there a poet is as rare as an oboe player." The response was amazing. By the end of the Twenties every Southern state had produced little magazines and/or poetry societies; local groups organized less formally and independent poets came out of the towns, the hills, and the bayous. Most importantly, the Nashville Fugitive group, with John Crowe Ransom at its center, developed the talents of Robert Penn Warren, Allen Tate, Donald Davidson, and Merrill Moore. South Carolina's Poetry Society produced Dubose Heyward and Josephine Pinckney among others. John Gould Fletcher of Arkansas and John Peale Bishop of West Virginia came out of European apprenticeships to add their voices. Florida produced the early Pulitzer Prize winner, George Dillon; Kentucky, the sonnet-master David Morton; Maryland, the bold E. Merrill Root; Mississippi, William Alexander Percy and Maxwell Bodenheim; Alabama, the prolific Clement Wood; Louisiana, Negro poet Jean Toomer; North Carolina, Leigh Hunt; Virginia and Texas, a host of competent minor poets.

In the later years of the movement, poetry has never lacked a firm place, but it has not, like fiction, developed a new, specifically

Southern tradition. Though a minor strain of faded romanticism has persisted, the more important poets have developed their variations on what may be called the symbolic irony of the Eliot school or sought in surrealism, neoclassicism, the hill-country ballad, or more experimental forms a voice that speaks for their modern sensibilities. Tate and Warren, unlike their early colleagues, have continued to expand their range without, however, deserting the basic attitudes and diction which they absorbed and adapted from Eliot and Ransom. The most illustrious of their followers in the later decades, Randall Jarrell, had added new tones and idioms, but his accent on wit, irony, and reference keeps his poetry well within the neo-metaphysical tradition. Other considerable poets like Hubert Creekmore, Kathryn Worth, and Ben Belitt belong primarily to this continuing tradition.

Variety, however, has been the rule in the work of modern poets. Karl Shapiro, a Pulitzer Prize winner from Baltimore, is unique in his reversion to the meters and intellectual propensities of Pope and Dryden. Charles Henri Ford and Parker Tyler display all the pyrotechnics and illogic of the European surrealist heritage. The mountain ballad has strongly influenced the effective verse of Byron Reece and George Scarbrough, while a back-country naïveté colors the work of James Still and dominates that of Jesse Stuart. More recent poets of considerable talents are proving that the manners and idioms of the past are capable of new extensions. Adrienne Rich, George Garrett, William Jay Smith, Eleanor Ross, Donald Justice, Marion Montgomery, and James Dickey have already exhibited originality along with mature command of their medium.

In contrast to the early poetry of the Renaissance movement, the early drama remained largely preoccupied with regional interests. From its center in Chapel Hill, home of The Carolina Playmakers, one major dramatist, Paul Green, emerged to conquer Broadway. Green, as well as Thomas Wolfe, who produced several one-act plays, and others of the group, concentrated exclusively on folk drama, drawn from the hills or from the backwoods Negro settlements. The influence of this group, reinforced by that of Hatcher Hughes, an earlier Carolina graduate and Pulitzer Prize winner in 1924, led to a preoccupation which was quickly outdated. Since no other theatre center existed in the South and Broadway was only a distant gleam to the beginning writer, only an occasional dramatist from other sections of the South made an impression on the stage world. Drama critics Stark Young and Ward Morehouse had single successes; Robert Wilder, Frank Elser, and Robert L. Buckner appeared briefly; but only Laurence Stallings, who collaborated with Maxwell Anderson on the great hit, *What Price Glory?*, went on to make a career as playwright.

After the early Thirties, few Southern writers wrote plays. Only Lillian Hellman from New Orleans succeeded in galvanizing the attention of Depression-weary audiences on Broadway. Over the years Miss Hellman has proved the most effective of American dramatists dealing with the clash of ideas. A liberal critic of Fascist doctrines and the new South, she has known better than her less adept liberal rivals how to dramatize her conceptions and eliminate overt propaganda. The other great exception among later Southern playwrights is, of course, Tennessee Williams, recipient of more theatrical awards than any other American of his generation. Williams, a rarely poetic dramatist in his early hits, has gradually hardened and harshened his vision, but he retains his mastery of dramatic technique. Only John Patrick of the other potential Southern playwrights on the contemporary scene has conspicuously made his way on Broadway, finally winning a Pulitzer Prize with his comedy, *Teahouse of the August Moon*. Meanwhile, the old Chapel Hill group, with Paul Green as leader and with recruits added, has created a new American genre, the outdoor historical spectacle.

The novelists and short story writers, who comprise the core of the Southern Renaissance, have been highly conscious literary artists. From their first important volumes of fiction, Katherine Anne Porter, Faulkner, Warren, Caroline Gordon, Tate, Lytle, and others of the first generation conceived of the story not, like Thomas Wolfe, as a medium for self-expression, nor as vehicle for the promulgation of ideas, but as an art form. For them, as for T. S. Eliot, art was an autotelic activity, and they wrote in the conviction that fiction could aspire to the artistic unity, finish, and ultimate effect normally associated only with poetry. Some more consciously than others sought models or exemplars in the work of earlier writers. The critics among them, when they turned their attention from poetry to fiction, soon uncovered the primary sources of the practice already established.

For critics Tate, Gordon, Warren, and Cleanth Brooks, it is clear that Flaubert stands as the progenitor of modern fiction and Henry James as his primary heir. Conrad, Chekhov, Joyce, and Stephen Crane appear at various positions in the succession. In these critics' analyses, aesthetically conceived and executed fiction involves certain basic structural and textural elements in some proportion: a carefully detailed or "naturalistic" surface, irony, symbolism, a strict and consistent handling of the point of view. For convenience this practice will be labeled "symbolic naturalism"; it becomes the new tradition of the Southern novel and short story. The major writers of the first Renaissance generation—and I include here Isa Glenn, Elizabeth Maddox Roberts, the reanimated Ellen Glasgow, and Stark Young—practiced with rare unanimity their personal variations of this technique. Furthermore, a majority of their ablest successors, from Eudora Welty and Carson McCullers to Flannery O'Connor, William Styron, Elizabeth Spencer, Leo Leatherman, Wesley Ford Davis, Peter Taylor, and Madison Jones, have written in this established tradition.

By no means all of the important novelists of the first generation can be neatly catalogued under the label of symbolic naturalism. Thomas Wolfe exhibits no slightest affinity to the technique, and other prime portrayers of youth in revolt, like Frances Newman and Evelyn Scott, show little more. The pioneer social realists, like Edith Summers Kelley and Dubose Heyward, regional colorists like Edwin Granberry and Marjorie Kinnan Rawlings, write substantially outside of the developing new tradition. On the other hand, competent novelists in other genres began in the first decade to adopt elements of the technique, whether consciously or no.

While the distinguishing mark of the founders of the new tradition in Southern fiction was artistic control of the medium, certain philosophic, social, and economic doctrines gradually assumed prominence among them. Here again, as in poetry and criticism, the Nashville group is central. John Crowe Ransom's "unorthodox defense of orthodoxy" in *God without Thunder* (1930), essays by Tate echoing Eliot's "classicism," the poetic concerns of the whole group, set the major philosophic tone. The thinking of these men, starting from Ransom's ironic dualism, soon began to reflect ideas remarkably close to those projected by the English philosopher T. E. Hulme in his essay, "Romantic and Classic," a piece which had directly influenced Pound and Eliot. Hulme spurned the romantic doctrine of man's perfectibility and embraced the classic view, recognizing human frailty, "original sin" or natural corruption, and the need for restrictive discipline and ordering authority. The central Southern spokesmen took, in Hulme's sense, the classic position, which is fundamentally that of religious orthodoxy.

The corollary social and economic doctrines, as they developed in the late Twenties among the Vanderbilt group, stressed preservation of the traditional Southern order and return to the solid values deriving from a land-based economy. Tate, Ransom, Warren, Davidson, and Lytle contributed to the Agrarian manifesto of 1930, *I'll Take My Stand,* a volume which contrasted the responsible, code-ordered life of a landed society with the chaotic and predatory irresponsibility introduced by finance capitalism. In fiction, these agrarian doctrines spread their influence chiefly through the novels of Faulkner and Warren, Gordon, Tate, and Lytle.

Beginning, however, with Katherine Anne Porter, a contrary orientation has developed. Miss Porter's explicit rejection of a typically Southern heritage, in her Miranda stories, can be found in the work of many writers who follow the artistic canons of symbolic naturalism. Most of this heterodox group imply a selective, rather than a wholesale rejection, but the social criticism which pervades other types of fiction has consistently made headway here as well. The problems of race relations, caste privilege, agrarian reform, and the rest seldom occupy the novelists directly, but since they are the ineluctable realities of everyday Southern life, the writer can scarcely avoid expressing attitudes towards them. Among the younger formalists, emphasis falls largely on the decadence of the surviving aristocracy. Modern materialists and their political representatives fare even worse. However, the Negro and the liberal champion of the underprivileged receive increasingly sympathetic fictional treatment by this group of novelists.

While the early formulators and the later practitioners of the new tradition in fiction make up the central and most influential group of writers produced in the Southern Renaissance, a much larger number of the novelists have been occupied on other literary fronts. The greatest sociological significance attaches to the liberal, or self-critical, wing of the movement. Here the clearest historical development has occurred. In the early Twenties newly stimulated writers were beginning to take closer and more sympathetic looks at the sharecropper, the Negro field hand, the city laborer, and the social patterns of small-town life. In 1922 Edith Summers Kelley opened a new fictional vein with her study of a cropper's daughter in *Weeds*. Shortly afterward, Elizabeth Maddox Roberts and Ellen Glasgow took up the theme. Also in 1922, three novelists from three separate states brought into the open the Negro's social and economic problems, as plantation worker, city dweller, and small-town reformer. Before the end of the decade, Dubose Heyward, Julia Peterkin, Robert E. Kennedy, Roark Bradford, and others had assumed the Negro's point of view to explore a variety of conditions and attitudes in Southern communities.

Though the social views manifested by the authors of these books with Negro orientation were by no means uniformly liberal, or even critical of white prejudice, the curiosity and observation of the authors suggested new forces at work. The same type of exploratory interest is evident in the critical genre initiated by Emanie Sachs' *Talk* of 1924. Described by critics as a Kentucky version of *Main Street*, this novel of gossip and class patterns indicated the possibilities for satire and serious social analysis on the Southern small-town level. T. S. Stribling was soon following this lead, as were a host of others.

Only with the Depression Thirties and early Forties, however, did radical and militantly liberal fiction appear in the South. In stories centered on Negroes and poor whites, as well as in novels of industrial strife, a substantial number of Southerners joined the national trend, enlisting their full sympathies with the exploited, the uprooted, the deprived. Paced by avowed radicals of the industrial scene, like Myra Page, Grace Lumpkin, Leane Zugsmith, and Olive Dargan, and reinforced by staunch liberals adopting Negro and red-neck points of view, this group attacked the traditional prejudices and hypocrisies which an economic collapse had exposed.

By the late Forties militancy had died away; the era of the sweeping panacea gave place to one of individualized humanism. In the novel oriented about the Negro, men like Jefferson Young and Peter Feibleman, young women like Lucy Daniels and Charlotte Johnson substituted for the polemical sympathy of the Forties a new kind of empathic understanding. Social and family problems began to replace economic dilemmas as thematic material. The poor white figured less in the later novels as exploited worker, more as political, racial, and religious bigot. Stories of industrial strife were succeeded by novels featuring the new tycoons of business and banking or conflicts between decadent aristocracy and new bourgeoisie.

Often closely related in ideology to the liberal wing, but more exclusively preoccupied with the dissatisfied individual, is the considerable group of young Southerners who focus on the frustrations and revolts of sensitive youth. Fiction of this type, commonly autobiographical in tone if not in fact, invariably attracts the beginning writer, and especially the beginner who grows into a society experiencing rapid changes. Even before the dramatic appearance of Thomas Wolfe, this genre possessed a considerable history in the South. Sensitive girls like Evelyn Scott, Frances Newman, and Carmen Barnes; men like Fulton Oursler, Frank Elser, and John Fort had begun careers in the Twenties with stories of youthful idealism and rebellion. Wolfe, who never truly emerged from his period of sensitive youthfulness, wrote an early climax for this development, and comparatively few have attempted to rival his scale or intensity since. On a more modest level, however, the semiautobiographical novel of youth has held its attraction to the present. The most notable example in later years, Robert Gibbon's *The Patchwork Time* (1948), has yet to receive the attention it deserves.

In such categories as the historical romance and the local color story, the South has long been a heavy producer. However, serious historical realism, as well as regional realism, have been largely Renaissance developments. The early period offered not only such solidly done historical novels as Elizabeth M. Roberts' *The Great Meadow* and Carolina Gordon's *Green Centuries,* but three Pulitzer Prize volumes, by T. S. Stribling, Caroline Miller, and Margaret Mitchell. The popularity of this genre has lured a constantly growing number of novelists, historians, journalists, and even poets into the field. But popular appeal can hardly account for the high quality of both research and writing which so many of these novels demonstrate. Southern pride in family once led to the romanticization of history; since the sweeping changes of the Renaissance period have begun to have their effects, family consciousness has demanded painstaking reassessment of heritages. The result is the mature historical novel.

The term, "local color," suggests an attitude toward environment, rather than simply interest in it. The earlier portrayers of the local scene, both before the Southern Renaissance and during its first decade, tended to look upon their subjects and the particular features of setting as curiosities to be exploited for their novelty. Only gradually do the delineators in fiction of the mountaineer, the hillbilly, and the back-country Negro overcome this "color" approach: the highlighting of dialect, quaint custom, and unfamiliar scenery. Exceptions do appear in the first era, heralding a transformation from local color to a new atmospheric realism, in which realistic portraiture and the universal problem supplant the sensational. Fiswoode Tarleton's terse, graphic stories lift the mountain tale into significant literature. At the same time, Edwin Granberry draws both highly charged romance and effective realism from his Florida settings, while Marjorie Kinnan Rawlings makes tragic human drama from the neighboring scrub and hammock country.

In later years, sound fiction has been drawn from bayou and river, swamp, island, and secluded valley, as well as from hill and grove. No part of the South remains undescribed, no type of colorful native, from Cajun to Sea Island Negro to "red-bone" or shanty boat-dweller has escaped detailed interpretation in fiction. Too often still the popular sensational approach prevails, as in the lurid and sentimental stories of Erskine Caldwell, or in the sentiment-cum-humor tales of Jesse Stuart, Ben Lucian Burman, and Cid Ricketts Sumner. But the more recent years have offered solid fare as well: the mountain novels of Harriette Arnow and the Cajun stories of E. P. O'Donnell, for example.

In other fictional areas, such as hard-boiled naturalism of the post-Hemingway school, social satire, humor and farce, the psychological study, novels of war, religion, and politics, the South has at least kept pace with other sections of the country. Perhaps only in the more experimental forms and in exploitation of philosophies associated with the literary avant-garde does the South seem to retain a kind of conservative provincialism. It must be remembered, however, that Faulkner's progressive techniques in such books as *The Sound and the Fury* have been accorded major credit for inspiring the modern French *anti-roman*. More recently, also, two Southern novelists, John Barth and Walker Percy, have written very able novels which are existentialist in theme and style. And to judge from the magazine fiction being produced by a number of Southerners still unpublished in books, one may predict that the day of conservative technique, like that of conservative attitudes in literature, draws to a close.

The large view which a perspective of forty years offers can present the Southern Renaissance in at least two major aspects. The common approach of Southern critics has been what may best be visualized as a centric, high-level perspective. That is to say that the most influential critics of the movement have set themselves in the center of a very broad literary development and trained their eyes on the peaks and ranges which excite their artistic imaginations. Here are seen in detail the central massifs: the poetic heights of the early period, the monumental productions in fiction which make up the new tradition, and the three tall figures in drama. Legitimate as it is, this view has left unexplored some heights which the more obvious projections have obscured. Furthermore, the bases from which the peaks spring are neglected.

Equally legitimate is the panoramic view, with the observer moved back from the center to a post where he can observe mountains, hills, plains, and valleys as aspects of a single landscape. From the centric focus, for example, the English Renaissance becomes the high artistic achievements of Marlowe, Shakespeare, Jonson, Webster, Spenser, and Sidney. For the literary historian of the period, however, there are Middleton, Dekker, Tourneur, Ford, Massinger, Chapman, Drayton, Nashe, Deloney, Greene, and Lodge, none of them negligible talents and all of them eminently representative of the age and its cultural accomplishments. So to assess the Southern Renaissance solely by reference to Faulkner, Wolfe, the Fugitive group, and their eminent lineage is to characterize the United States by its Rockies and Appalachians. These are, indeed, impressive, but they do not fully represent the country. So much of the Southern movement has been concerned with a critical-liberal reassessment of the social landscape at a below-summit level that no Parnassian view can properly evaluate it. To examine the whole sweep of modern Southern literature is to alter the common judgment of its essential character. This process in no way diminishes the artistic heights; it serves well, however, to establish a solid base beneath them and sometimes also to disclose long unnoticed ranges.

2

THE FIRST PHASE:

POETRY AND DRAMA

As a self-conscious movement, the Southern Renaissance opened immediately after World War I with the establishment of literary magazines and societies conceived to encourage the development of new writers in an area which had signally failed to participate in the American poetic revival of the previous decade. The editors of *The Double Dealer, The Reviewer,* and *The Fugitive* openly deplored the state of letters in the South and hopefully envisioned the day when their section would assume its place in literary America. Though only *The Fugitive* was specifically dedicated to poetry, the assumption was widespread that poetry was the proper medium in which to demonstrate a revival of creativity. Verse issuing from the East, the Midwest, and even the Far West had enjoyed an unparalleled popularity before the war and a host of new little magazines had been born to publish it. The Imagist movement and the Chicago school of neo-Whitmanism continued to flourish during the war years. Meanwhile, fiction had not fully established its respectability as an art form in America, despite the efforts and insistences of Henry James, William Dean Howells, and Stephen Crane. With such new authors as Sinclair Lewis and Sherwood Anderson, it was beginning to enjoy a popular role as conveyor of social criticism, with its chief target the provincial small town. The drama, under the hand of Eugene O'Neill, had just begun to take itself seriously, but it too leaned in the direction of social criticism. Disinterested literary art remained the province of poetry.

The South of 1920 could boast of only one poet of established national reputation, but several who were to bring honor to the Renaissance movement had already published first volumes during the war years. John Gould Fletcher, in fact, had issued five little volumes in the single year of 1913 while he lived in London, and he offered his first Imagist collection, *Irradiations,* two years later. Apprentice volumes by John Peale Bishop and John Crowe Ransom appeared in 1917 and 1919. In addition to these major figures, lesser luminaries like Maxwell Bodenheim, William Alexander Percy, Olive Dargan, Clement Wood, Karle Baker, and James Weldon Johnson had anticipated the Renaissance proper with wartime volumes.

Recognition came first to Fletcher, a native of Little Rock, Arkansas, but an emigré to Massachusetts, then to Paris and London. Through his association abroad with Pound's group and his meeting with the ambitious Amy Lowell, the young poet became one of the founders of American Imagism. Fletcher's early verse, unlike that of Pound and H. D., owed its form and inspiration rather to impressionism than to French *symbolisme*. With Amy Lowell, he preferred undisciplined free verse and the extended catalogue of impressions to the terse, sharp evocations of the *symboliste* tradition. *Irradiations* exhibited a facile, fluent talent intoxicated with color and prodigal of images, but almost wholly lacking in critical restraints. Like most of the young rebels of his Bohemian and Dadaist generation, he sought freedom from the traditional disciplines, novelty, and expressive form. The Imagist association, however, and particularly the influence of the Japanese *haiku* form, to which Pound had introduced the circle, led him shortly to abandon his "color symphonies" and to concentrate his effects in a kind of elliptical impressionism. His free-form *haiku* poems lack the pungency and classic clarity of Pound's and H. D.'s adaptations of the form, but they illustrate well his thesis that "style and technique rest on the thing conveyed and not the means of conveyance."

The war years changed Fletcher as they changed so many of his compatriots. Abandoning his Imagist affiliations, he began a long search for new and tougher modes of expression. Working alone and finally, after 1933, in his native Arkansas, he sought through many experiments to find a proper voice for his developing pessimism. He achieved his few hard-won successes in philosophic lyrics, employing stark imagery in disciplined patterns. As his chronic illness grew upon him, he probed farther and farther into his inner darknesses, but at the same time sought to attach his personal emotions to the regional

scene. In the *Epic of Arkansas* (1936) and *South Star* (1941), he dug
into the legends, traditions, and customs of his native area in an attempt to relate them to his private dilemma.

No final synthesis of Fletcher's work is possible, for his poetic
career was a continual and largely unsuccessful attempt to discover a
unified vision and a personal idiom. Only the mystic overtones and the
sense of evanescence relate the Imagist to the later regionalist and
tragic philosopher. When the Pulitzer Prize Committee in 1939
granted him an award for his *Selected Poems,* it was recognizing his
early fame and his long devotion to his art rather than a distinctive
poetic achievement.

John Peale Bishop, another of the early expatriates, spent eleven
years abroad after his graduation from Princeton. His youthful volume
appeared in 1917, but, like the other pioneers, he did not mature
poetically until after the war years. In fact, his first considerable book
of verse, *Now with his Love,* was published only after his return to
Charles Town, West Virginia, from his stay in France, where he had
thoroughly absorbed the French *symbolistes* and their successors. His
"influences," beginning with those of his Princeton associates, Edmund
Wilson and Scott Fitzgerald, through the French, Yeats, Eliot, and
Tate, are too extensive to demonstrate. His quality as a poet remained,
however, basically symbolist—a compounding of the concrete with the
allusive, sharp observation with wit and irony, metaphor with slanted
statement.

Bishop's concern was primarily formal, and thus he stands more
intimately allied with the Fugitive group than with his fellow expatriates. "The ceremony must be found / Traditional," he says in
the fine poem, "Speaking of Poetry." Ceremony his verse always preserves, even in the erotic poems—perhaps the nakedest in American
literature to his time. He is conservative of poetic tradition despite the
considerable variety of his poetic forms. Meticulous in craftsmanship
and rich in reference, he nevertheless sacrifices nothing in immediate
sensuous appeal. Often his poems are paintings with movement,
though the implications extend unobtrusively beyond the graphic
detail. His effort, like that of Ransom, is to yoke once again the
"world's body" and the intellect, the real with the imagined: "The
ceremony must be found/ That will wed Desdemona to the huge
Moor."

Bishop's brilliantly exact diction and his colorful, sometimes surreal, surfaces do not disguise a drab view of the modern world. In concert with his Fugitive friends and with Eliot, he sees the loss of a stable tradition as the dissociating force in our society. With the progressive substitution of finance capitalism and rootless urbanism for individual ownership and attachment to the land, he finds man directionless and degraded, moving toward self-destruction, or surviving only as the proletarian crab, "all belly but his sword a tail." He concludes "Colloquy with King Crab":

> But his shell
> Affords no edifice where I can creep
> Though I consent like him to go on claws.

There is in Bishop nothing of the nightmarish emotional strain so evident in the early Tate and Warren, though often images close to those of the surrealist painters dominate his poems. Nor is there any of their arid abstraction of the same years. Bishop remains a poet of eye and ear, though always disciplined in his most sensuous moments. A number of his lyrics, too often neglected by anthologists, are among the finest the Southern Renaissance has produced.

The third among the pioneers of the new poetry and the most influential was John Crowe Ransom of Tennessee. Though he too had his sojourn overseas (as a Rhodes Scholar), Ransom possessed nothing of the "lost generation" temperament. Like the others, however, he matured poetically only after the war when he returned to his native soil. Settling to teach at Vanderbilt, he proclaimed himself an alien, not from Tennessee or America, but from "this my generation." Ransom's flavored brand of wit, his dualistic philosophy, and his example as a published poet were instrumental in stimulating the remarkable poetic burst in Nashville. His influence continued both at Vanderbilt and at Kenyon College, where he served as editor of the distinguished quarterly, *The Kenyon Review*. However, Ransom's career as a major poet—he received the coveted Bollingen Award in 1951—barely survived the Twenties. Only a handful of poems testify to a lingering creative urge once he committed himself to theoretical and practical criticism.

In the congenial surroundings of Vanderbilt University with his "seven of friends," Ransom's poetic talents flowered rapidly. *Chills and*

Fever (1924) and *Two Gentlemen in Bonds* (1927) represent the bulk of his poetic achievement. They exhibit a unique blend of wit and elegance, archaic and modern diction, observation and philosophy. Ultimately Ransom delivers in these volumes a graceful, sophisticated elegy for a past way of life, at once gay, mannered, and stricken. Its successor, life in the twentieth century, offers an "unseemlier world," where "man cannot fathom nor perform his nature." Ransom's blue ante-bellum South was doomed by the nature of things, like his "Blue Girls," and by its own excesses; his autumn-graying modern world is grown desperate through its inability to integrate its dual nature. Beyond the mind-body division, Ransom projects his dualistic dilemma into the heart of the human condition. Man, born to die, seeking ideals in a real universe, finds a beautiful but indifferent nature inevitably thwarting his romantic dreams of harmonious possession. Ransom as poet is able to reconcile the dilemmas, as he is able to reconcile the incompatibilities of his diction. He makes precarious equilibriums out of his conflicts, and sustains them through a delicate balance of tones.

Of the other Southern poets who anticipated the postwar surge of creativity, William Alexander Percy, publishing first in 1915, demonstrated a consistently high level of lyrical talent through four volumes of nature verse. Though he never ventures far from patterns derived from Housman and Masefield among others, and develops no original vision, his observation of the Mississippi countryside, of field hands and country folk are always perceptive and sometimes moving. Olive Dargan of Kentucky struggled with pain out of an early Keatsian romanticism to a more disciplined expression of stoic acceptance before her leftist leanings drew her into the novel form. From Alabama, the fluent and finally overprolific Clement Wood (also a novelist) achieved a considerable success with love poems, both lyric and narrative, in his youth when he sought beauty single-heartedly. His *Glad of Earth* (1917) and *Earth Turns South* (1919) are fully sustained paeans to love and natural beauty. In Wood's later volumes, however, a penchant for philosophizing in increasingly abstract language and a failure to hold under discipline his facile flow of thought and diction dull his effectiveness.

Maxwell Bodenheim, a refugee Mississippian who became almost the symbol of Greenwich Village bohemianism of the Twenties and Thirties, attracted considerable attention as early as 1918 in such volumes as *Minna and Myself, Introducing Irony* (1922), and *Against This Age* (1923). His highly colored, image-packed impressions of city life and his off-beat judgments caught the ear of a rebellious generation. Bodenheim's wide-ranging eye often catches effectively the neglected aspects of country as well as city, and he decks them out with unusual flamboyant metaphor. He progresses from observation to irony to the sardonic, always in undisciplined free verse and always by a sort of lively free association. A brilliant juggler with words and images, he seldom manages to gather his props together for the finale. A former Little Rock neighbor of Fletcher's, Karle Wilson Baker, began in 1919 with *Blue Smoke* a long career dedicated to poetry. Though she is often content with conventional sentiments, particularly religious ones, she is capable of graceful and poignant lyrics. Finally, James Weldon Johnson from Florida became the first published Negro poet of the Southern Renaissance with his *Fifty Years and Other Poems* (1917). It was ten years, however, before he discovered his true effectiveness in a series of richly imaginative folk sermons, *God's Trombones*. The only other early Negro poets, Georgia Douglas Johnson of Atlanta and Joseph Cotter, Jr., of Louisville, produced largely conventional lyrics, though Cotter's ballad pieces are lively and colorful.

The Poetry Society of South Carolina began, like the Fugitive group, with meetings among friends to discuss poetry, and it managed to beat *The Fugitive* to press with its *First Yearbook* in 1921. However, among the founders of the Charleston Society, only one, Dubose Heyward, was born a Southerner; the others, Hervey Allen and John Bennett, brought their enthusiasms and talents from colder climates. The following year Heyward and Allen combined their talents to produce a volume of *Carolina Chansons*. Though he was hardly a natural lyricist, Heyward brought a clear eye to his descriptive pieces from seacoast and mountain, a sympathetic spirit to his vignettes and narratives depicting Negro roustabouts and poor whites scrabbling their livings out of the hills. Soon, however, he discovered a more effective medium for his social attitudes and his descriptive powers in the novel.

Perhaps the most talented of the poets associated with the Society was Josephine Pinckney, still another who went on to make a reputation as a novelist. A group of her free verse vignettes appeared in

Poetry as early as 1921, and her first volume, *Sea-Drinking Cities,* was published in 1927. Like Heyward, Miss Pinckney excelled at description of scene and character. Her verses, however, evoke moods, rather than express attitudes, so that her pictures lack the force of social criticism, as well as the suggestion of philosophic depths beneath the clear surfaces. Within her narrow range, she has a sure touch and a compelling power of evocation. Others in the immediate circle of the Society—members were admitted from other areas as well—included a number of graceful minor poets: Beatrice Ravenel, Katherine Simons, Ellen Magrath Carroll, and Elizabeth Durham.

The Carolina group welcomed generously the appearance of *The Fugitive* magazine in April, 1922, though the astringency of its flavor doubtless irritated some of the more genteel Charleston tastes. More than commonly in such a group undertaking, *The Fugitive* of the early issues reflected one man's tone and attitudes—Ransom's—even to an extent his forms and diction. Soon, however, Allen Tate was showing his excitement over T. S. Eliot's *The Waste Land,* and other undergraduates, Robert Penn Warren and Jesse Wills, caught the fever. Donald Davidson, both more musical and more nostalgically romantic than his colleagues, for a time retuned his measures to the ironic pitch of Ransom, and most of the other contributors adapted to or absorbed Ransom's style. Instructor Stanley Johnson followed most closely in the mentor's path, while Alec Brock Stevenson was close in mood and form to Davidson, and Jesse Wills to both Ransom and Eliot. Only Merrill Moore, of the innumerable sonnets, exhibited a complete independence from the beginning. Moore's hastily scribbled fourteen-liners, which he continued to produce throughout his life as a psychiatrist, are built on the odd observation or errant fancy. He draws out or compresses the inspiration into the inevitable pattern with no regard to any other form of discipline. His inability to take his talents seriously leaves him an anomaly among his dedicated colleagues in Nashville.

Before the magazine had run its full four-year course, it was evident that at least two major poets, in addition to Ransom, could develop from the Fugitive group. Both Tate and Warren exhibited attitudinal, as well as verbal, excesses. Tate's prematurely cynical poses and Warren's metaphorical violence betrayed the young poet's straining for effect. But both quickly mastered a variety of forms and managed to

blend intellectual and emotional components in strong images. Like
Ransom and Eliot, as well as the French poets whom Tate was led
to study, they concentrated on the modern human dilemma, rather
than on the natural world or the passing show. They eschewed
regional preoccupation and lyric grace, preferring the poetry of wit
and irony and allusion which was developing into an international neo-
metaphysical style.

The third poet of promise, Donald Davidson, absorbed only superficially the intellectual toughness, the wit and compression of the
leading Fugitive spirits. His first volume, *The Outland Piper* (1924),
suggests an uneasy and shifting equilibrium between the conservatively
romantic lover of nature, music, and fantasy, and the disillusioned
satirist. Proud of his Tennessee heritage, uneasy in modern city life,
Davidson escapes to an enchanted world of the imagination or turns
sadly or bitterly on "the world's deceit," on the "wolves" who crouch
over their money, and the hypocritical "Ecclesiasticus."

In his later volumes, *The Tall Men* (1927) and *Lee in the Mountains* (1938), Davidson completely abandons Ransomic diction, as well
as his conventional quatrain forms, for a less constrictive conversational
blank verse. Like others of the group who turned back to their
Southern traditions in the late Twenties, Davidson in these books re-
examines the past he came from and himself as its inheritor. *The Tall
Men* harks back to pioneer long-riflemen, carries forward to the poet's
childhood, his postwar city life, his marriage, and to an apocalyptic vision of the future. Fundamentally integrated neither in concept
nor in imagery, the poem betrays typical romantic weaknesses and
indulgences, provincial prejudices, and rhetorical extravagances. Despite his conspicuous faults, however, Davidson possesses considerable
narrative and descriptive power. These abilities stand him in good
stead in several scenes from *The Tall Men* and in the lyric and dramatic poems of his final volume. Even here, however, his biases obtrude,
and he does not always avoid romanticizing his subjects. Davidson's
retreat into comfortable traditionalist positions from which he can only
fire diatribes against the modern order has left little challenge for his
creative talents. Since the handful of new poems in *Lee in the Mountains,* Davidson has ceased to publish verse.

Allen Tate, despite his long friendship with Davidson, has very
little poetically in common with him. Tate began with a concept of his

art derived first from Ransom, then from Eliot, a highly nonparochial
and classic view. He read deeply in the later French poets while he
continued to follow British and American developments as a reviewer
and essayist. Furthermore, he established an intimate association with
Hart Crane. His early poetry is inevitably derivative, but by the time
he was ready to publish his first volume, *Mr. Pope and Other Poems*
(1928), he had evolved his own variation of the new metaphysical
style. Though he was led, like several of his former colleagues, to re-
explore his Southern heritage in the wake of the Scopes trial, he continued to find in Eliot his prime preceptor. Eventually he followed
Eliot into a fruitful study of Dante and into the acceptance of
Catholic doctrine.

The poetry which Tate has thus far produced in some seven
volumes is notably intellectual, compressed to the point of ellipsis and
even of obscurity, referential, bold in imagery, and often desperate
in tone. Tate accepts Eliot's "waste land" metaphor for life in the
twentieth century and even identifies himself with Eliot's figure of
the Fisher King. Out of his dilemma as a man who has been unable to
recover his heritage, rendered impotent by the loss and powerless to
gain sustenance from his sterile age, Tate derives his sometimes nightmarish, often luridly harsh imagery. Whether he begins with the concrete image and works toward the abstract conception or reverses the
process, he builds his tension consistently from modern man's desperate
plight. The poems uniformly offer a bleak, dry, baroquely wrought
surface, despite their constant involvement with human dislocations
and moral issues. Similarly, the emotion which courses through them,
often fiercely, is unrelievedly cold in its intensity. Nature is frequently
invoked, but the natural images arouse no warm response from the
poet: "the splayed leaves," "the blind crab," "the cold pool," "the hound
bitch/ Toothless and dying," "the gray lean spiders," "the bleak sun-
shine," "one peeled aster," "the cold dusk," "the dreary flies." Often
he boldly mixes metaphors in order to compress several images of darkness and bleakness together with abstraction: "We are the eyelids of
defeated caves."

Tate achieves his variety in form, rather than in tone or concept.
He manages the free form derived from Eliot, as in "Ode to the Confederate Dead," strict quatrains, as in "The Mediterranean," heroic
couplets, blank verse, trimeter stanzas, and other patterns with equal

mastery. There is little effect of monotony, therefore, in a volume of his verse. A number of his poems gain their effects not only with precision but with strong emotional impact. It is only at the end of reading that the limitations of his talent become apparent. He has finally only one subject on which he plays variations, and basically only one sort of emotion to express. The experience of his poetry leaves us longing for the warm pulse of human blood and the feel of flesh.

Robert Penn Warren began to write, as an undergraduate, under the same influences which inspired Tate, and his early verse often reaches the same desperate pitch. Beginning with Ransom's philosophic dualism and Eliot's diction for the most part, Warren sought less in the past and more in nature for an adjustment to the modern world. His progress led him first into the mountain rocks, his first stoic preceptors, then into "The Garden," where the innocent retreat of Marvell's "green thought in a green shade" no longer serves; but where, through and beyond the damning guilty knowledge, a sacramental post-Edenic innocence may be won, beyond desire. By the time he published his first volume, *Thirty-Six Poems,* in 1935, Warren had established his basic attitudes and matured his own diction. There are still the brute realities to which the ideal-hungry mind must reconcile itself, but reconciliation is possible to the man, "instructed of what ripeness is," who has learned not to covet but to enjoy the world's richness.

Many of Warren's middle period poems, collected in *Eleven Poems on the Same Theme* (1942), parallel and concentrate the concerns of his novels: the tragedy of romantic idealism, the shock of discovery, the escape from reality, and the hard responsibility of knowledge. In ballad form and in compressed philosophical narratives, often violent in incident and in image, he displays the errors, the catastrophes, the fears, the frustrated escapes which succeed on the discovery of the world's recalcitrance.

Warren's latest poetic phase began with the fine long narrative poem, *Brother to Dragons* (1953), ostensibly the story of Thomas Jefferson's family and the tragedy of romantic idealism, but also the story of "R.P.W." discovering the autumnal "joy" at which "The Garden" hinted. In *Promises: Poems, 1954-1956,* for which Warren won both a Pulitzer Prize and a National Book Award in 1958, and in *You, Emperors, and Others* (1960), the theme of joy continues, though it is a joy "terrible" with precariousness and responsibility.

These late volumes, however, break sharply with the dense, cerebral style of the middle period. *Promises,* centering on the two children of the poet's late remarriage and on memories of his own childhood, reads like fragments of a diary, with reflection and recollection summoned up by moments of observation, moments of happiness too pure for safety. For the most part, these are inconclusive poems, simple records set down because they seem to matter, not necessarily to mean. The diction is as simple as the key word and the structures simply sequential (if the ironically amusing fantasy, "Ballad of a Sweet Dream of Peace," be excepted). In the main, *You, Emperors* continues this late strain, with its long free lines flowing over experiences from the Kentucky past or the farther past of Roman emperors in whose land the poet sojourns. There is less of the unalloyed joy in this volume, more philosophic acceptance of meaningless tragedy, which forces man to face "the lonely fact of humanness we share." Again Warren exhibits his brilliant narrative powers in recollected scenes of violence. Of all the Southern writers who turned from poetry to fiction, Warren alone has returned to establish himself as one of America's major poets.

All of the Southern states participated in the poetic revival of the Twenties and early Thirties, often with local groups sponsoring creative activity, but more often with isolated individuals developing their own talents and enthusiasms. No poetic nucleus grew around *The Double Dealer,* though Faulkner and the Fugitives published there, for the magazine quickly deserted its original regional emphasis and gained fame by encouraging new authors from other sections: Ernest Hemingway, Hart Crane, Thornton Wilder, and Kenneth Fearing among others. In Virginia, however, *The Reviewer* and *The Lyric* gathered about them a considerable group of native talents. Emily Clark, herself a poet, edited the Richmond magazine and devoted much of her time and energy to stimulating others. Most of the Virginia poets, however, published first in the Norfolk journal, which concentrated on poetry, and they continued to find it their chief outlet. A few, like Virginia Moore, Lucia Trent, Sally Bruce Kinsolving, and Lawrence Lee, moved North and published most often in journals of national circulation. All three editors of *The Lyric,* John R. Moreland, Virginia McCormick, and Leigh Hanes, were accomplished and dedicated poets who succeeded in attracting to their magazine a native group, including Virginia Tunstall, Josephine Johnson, and Julia

Johnson Davis, all of whom published volumes of verse. These are minor poets certainly, but minor poets displaying considerable skill and variety.

A belated and often disillusioned romanticism haunts much of *The Lyric's* poetry. The bulk of it is inspired by the natural world, but some of the stronger poems by Moreland, Miss Tunstall, and Miss McCormick reflect a sharp awareness of the human scene in its tragic absurdity. The most original of the Virginia-born poets is Virginia Moore, whose often strident, colloquial tones speak clearly for the postwar era. She writes with little discipline but with a new verve and wit, which she can turn on herself as well as on the observed world about her. She reaches her peak of intensity in lyrics detailing love's caprices.

Richmond-born Sally Bruce Kinsolving, who moved to Baltimore, was instrumental in founding there the Poetry Society of Maryland. Her initiative in the citadel of H. L. Mencken was matched by that of a native Marylander, James William Price, who established the Verse Writers' Guild of America in 1922 and the verse magazine, *Interludes,* two years later. In 1924 also The American Poetry Circle founded its journal of verse, *The Circle,* in Baltimore, under the editorship of Leacy Green-Leach and Marcia Lewis Leach. The most interesting of the Maryland poets, however, joined none of the societies and published in neither of the magazines. After studying with Robert Frost at Amherst, E. Merrill Root took a teaching position at Earlham College and became one of the large board of directors for *The Measure,* a New York poetry journal founded in 1921. Root's rugged verse is a continuous affirmation of man's potentialities. He storms, sometimes bombastically, against the world's injustices—"the skin diseases of the planet"—indignant, scorning compromise in his Whitmanesque insistence on the sheer quality which life offers. There are no bounds to Root's romantic vision of possibilities; defying man's despoliation of his Eden, he counsels,

> Build on waste and desolation
> Your green towers of affirmation.

In Texas, scattered groups established the Poetry Society of Texas, the verse magazine, *The Buccaneer,* and finally *The Kaleidoscope,* whose press in Dallas has issued a long list of volumes by poets from Texas and points east. Though no poets of national reputation have emerged from the Texas groups, a high level of competence has been fostered by the press and appreciation has spread widely through the state. Alabama, which produced two short-lived little magazines, *The Nomad* and *The Gammadion,* in the Twenties, sent out into the world of letters not only Clements Wood, but also Sara Henderson Hay, whose sensitive lyrics and criticism made her a considerable name in the East. In Atlanta, Georgia, Ernest Hartsock taunted Mencken by naming his poetry magazine *Bozart.* Around the Atlanta center grew up a considerable group of Georgia poets, among them Daniel Hicky, Arthur Crew Inman, James Stuart Montgomery, Roselle Montgomery, and Anderson Scruggs, all of more than average competence. Hartsock himself displayed a boldness and breadth of view which secured his place as the leading spirit of the Georgia awakening.

While Kentucky developed no group or magazine of its own, its natives made enviable reputations on other fronts. Tate and Warren went South to become Fugitive leaders; David Morton, Sara Litsey, and Jesse Lemont established themselves in the East; and Elizabeth Maddox Roberts won prizes at the University of Michigan. Of these, Morton, a teacher at Amherst, best illustrates the high level of technical ability, as well as the latent nostalgic romanticism, of the early Southern poets. His lucid, gently melancholic sonnets and quietly musical nature lyrics earned him a modest national fame, which faded only gradually as the less melodious, bolder modern voices won away his audience. Miss Roberts, before she turned to the novel, tested herself in verses of a naive childish appeal, *Under the Tree* (1922), and went on to absorb the language and forms of native Kentucky ballads and songs.

Among the early poets from other Southern states, George Dillon of Florida, an editor of *Poetry* magazine at nineteen and a Pulitzer Prize winner at twenty-six, was certainly the most spectacular success. Dillon's first volume, *Boy in the Wind* (1927), while a remarkable achievement for an undergraduate, has no surprises; it demonstrates a fine sensibility, however, under notable control in various traditional verse forms. Its successor, *The Flowering Stone* (1931), though it continues motifs and themes from the first volume, presents a matured talent coping with the mysteries of life and death and establishing a stance against the brute facts it discovers. In supple blendings of simple nature imagery and bold abstraction, Dillon works through the death of love to the conclusion:

> We come to dust. Yet while that dust endures
> The earth is young, and amorous, and yours.

The voice remains level, unharried in its tempered pessimism as in its youthful affirmation. Then it falls strangely silent. Dillon, chosen editor of *Poetry* in 1937, has published only translations since.

Early Southern Renaissance drama, most of it issuing from The Carolina Playmakers of Chapel Hill, was heavily slurred with mountain and Negro dialect, as well as spiced with the new liberalism which Frank Graham, Howard Odum, and Frederick Koch brought with them to the University. An earlier graduate, however, was the first playwright to bring distinction to the University. Hatcher Hughes won a disputed Pulitzer Prizer in 1924 for a stark drama of the Carolina mountains, *Hell-Bent for Heaven,* in which a hypocritically religious young man attempts to revive an old feud in order to eliminate his veteran rival in love. The play moves rapidly, with realistic dialogue and sharply delineated, if somewhat implausible, characters, but it hardly displays the dimensions of significant drama. Hughes, who had studied drama at Columbia University and returned to teach there, had collaborated with Elmer Rice on his first successful play, *Wake Up, Jonathan,* in 1921, a story of a cold-hearted captain of industry who tries to recover his alienated family. Four other of his plays, including *Ruint* (1925), an attempt to exploit the mountain scene once more, failed rather dismally. Another Tarheel, who migrated to the big city without benefit of training and made her way on Broadway with mountain dramas, was Lula Vollmer, daughter of a traveling lumber man. Her first two plays, both of them hits, were produced in the same year, 1923. Both *Sun-up* and *The Shame Woman* are melodrama, rather heavily sugared with sentiment, and their success, like that of *Hell-Bent for Heaven,* seemed to reflect the era's sociological bent, certainly not its sophistication. Like Hughes, Miss Vollmer continued to exploit her successful vein, but none of her later plays, during the Twenties and Thirties, had more than a seven-week run. She found her niche finally, however, as a writer for radio.

The star pupil of Professor Koch's Playmakers classes was Paul

Green, later a teacher of philosophy and of drama at his alma mater. Others, including young Thomas Wolfe, wrote effective one-act dramas of the hills, but none of them went on to establish stage careers. Like Wolfe, the talented graduates discovered in the novel a more satisfactory medium for expression. Green, however, after an initial prize-winning success with a Negro one-act play in the national Little Theatre contest of 1925, achieved a quick fame on the New York stage. Unlike his predecessors, Green was not content to exploit the brief popularity of mountain characters or to rely on local color. His plays range all over the diverse North Carolina country, from coastal cotton fields, to isolated mid-country villages and hill settlements. His major interest is not color but social problems. In particular, he pioneered in the drama with serious treatment of the Negro. His volume of 1926, *Lonesome Road: Six Plays for a Negro Theatre,* set him in the vanguard of those new Southerners who not only appreciated the Negro's economic and social plight but attempted the difficult feat of identifying with his point of view.

Green's first full-scale play dealing almost exclusively with Negroes won him a Pulitzer Prize when it was produced at the Provincetown Theatre in 1926. A tragedy in seven scenes, *Abraham's Bosom* details the futile attempts of a mulatto turpentine worker to raise himself and his people against the stubborn hostility of the whites, the recalcitrance of his Negro friends and relatives, and his own mistaken marriage. The play has power and true feeling, though the later scenes do not always avoid the pitfall of melodrama. Green's only other attempt to produce a Negro play on the New York stage failed. *Roll, Sweet Chariot,* a "symphonic play" with chorus and orchestra, relieved its sordid picture of a decayed village and its deteriorated inhabitants with music. A bold and honest attempt, the play fell down particularly in its attempted symbolism. This symphonic vein, however, combining drama, music, pageantry, sometimes dumbshow and even cinema, has since the early Thirties proved Green's major preoccupation in the theatre. The success of his huge outdoor spectacular, *The Lost Colony* (1937), established the new genre in the United States and led to commissions for six other historical pieces of the same kind.

Only once in later years did Green return to Negro subject matter, this in a successful collaboraton with Richard Wright, adapting the latter's novel, *Native Son,* for the Broadway stage. But Green's artistic stature as a playwright does not depend primarily on his Negro plays nor on his symphonic spectacles. Of his three full-scale dramas dealing with rural white families, two deserve to stand among the most impressive of their era. *The Field God* (1927), a powerful study of an independent, virile farmer run afoul among religious bigots, failed in New York as much for the dramatic shortcomings of its later sequences as for the starkness of its tragic conflicts. *The House of Connelly* (1931), however, has no dramatic lapses. Employing a theme which would be later elaborated by both Lillian Hellman and Tennessee Williams, Green contrasts the decadent aristocracy with a tough-fibred young tenant girl, who is able and willing to restore the land as well as to rehabilitate the weak-willed heir. The plays lacks the cumulative tension of Miss Hellman's social dramas and the psychological penetration of Williams' earlier pieces, but its picture of a changing society carries conviction.

Johnny Johnson (1936) exhibited Green's liberalism in quite a different form. With the addition of Kurt Weill's music, this fantastic satire on militarism runs a wide range from slapstick comedy to gory tragedy and propagandist harangues. Its verve and dramatic ingenuity carry it over a number of structural and conceptual weaknesses to a Chaplinesque conclusion. This Depression-era play demonstrates all of Green's talents as a playwright, but it also underlines his limitations. The critic and social reformer is never far below the surface in any of his dramatic works. Though he reaches for poetry and introduces music to enhance his effects, it is the broad issue, the panorama, which excites him. The telling detail, the psychological subtleties are not his forte. As in most artists with deep ideological commitments, Green's grasp of the immediate is comparatively weak. He can produce the dramatic situation admirably, but the density and texture of life itself is too often wanting. Green remains, however, the pioneer social realist of the Southern theatre, and the most effective spokesman for Southern liberalism in his era.

Other areas of the South produced only an occasional playwright during the first fifteen years of the Renaissance, though they contributed two of nation's finer dramatic critics in Stark Young and Ward Morehouse. Both of these men had their fling on the stage, and each had his single success. Young had been writing romantic closet drama in verse since 1906, but did not achieve his first major production till

1924. The Provincetown Players put on his *The Saint,* about a Texas cowboy turned ascetic and his girl, for a run of seventeen performances. Two years later, *The Colonnade* ran for twenty-six performances in London. But his one hit came only in 1938, when his version of Chekhov's *The Sea Gull* was well received on Broadway. Morehouse from Savannah, Georgia, joined the New York *Sun* in 1926 and presented his first play, *Gentlemen of the Press,* two years later. An immediate hit and one which has held its popularity, *Gentlemen of the Press* poses the problem of integrity versus monetary success in a realistic portrait of a newsman turned plush public relations expert. A hard-hitting play, it animates the critical spirit which fills so many of the Southern intellectuals of the postwar generation. Morehouse tried Broadway once again with *U. S. 90* and failed before he settled down to criticism and theatrical biography. Less successfully than Morehouse, his fellow columnist on the *Sun,* Robert Wilder of Virginia and Kentucky, made his brief foray onto Broadway during the early Thirties before he found a more lucrative medium in the novel.

The earliest of the new playwrights to exploit Southern regional themes on Broadway was the Kentucky producer-director of Portmanteau Plays, Stuart Walker. His repertory of dramas without scenery appeared first on the New York stage in 1916, then again in 1919. In between, he put on his own full-length play, *Jonathan Makes a Wish,* for twenty-three performances. Walker's importance has little to do with his original one-act or longer plays; he performed a considerable service, however, by bringing a sampling of new and old plays to theatres all over the country and thereby indirectly stimulating the Little Theatre movement.

Other Southern playwrights, like Frank Elser of Texas, appeared for a time on the Broadway scene—Elser achieved a moderate success with *The Farmer Takes a Wife* (1934), an adaptation of Walter Edmonds' novel, *Rome Haul.* But only two natives of the South made careers in the New York theatre. Robert L. Buckner from Arkansas, actor and playwright, had only one prime success as a dramatist with *The Primrose Path* (1939), a play on which he collaborated with Walter Hart. He wrote five other plays between 1930 and 1940 in addition to acting on Broadway and in stock companies.

The greatest triumph of the early period, however, was reserved for a Georgian, Laurence Stallings, who collaborated with Maxwell Anderson on *What Price Glory?* (1924). The play, largely reflecting Stallings' disillusioning war experiences, became a major rallying document for the pacifist groups of the Twenties. Following up his success, Stallings, again with the collaboration of Anderson, produced two historical plays, *First Flight* and *The Buccaneer,* neither of them a literary or box-office success. For twenty years thereafter Stallings continued to work on Broadway and in radio, collaborating in musicals and adapting novels, including *A Farewell to Arms,* for the stage. But the Coolidge and Hoover era of optimism and theatrical triviality, followed by the Depression, never again inspired him to sound true emotional depths.

3

THE NEW TRADITION

The supporters of "symbolic naturalism" in fiction were slow in establishing their critical primacy during the first fifteen years of the Southern Renaissance. But by 1935, when Porter, Faulkner, Gordon, Tate, and Warren had written books that could stand as exemplars and the Southern critics had clarified their position, the technique could be seen as a distinct and important element of the literary movement. With the founding of *The Southern Review* under Brooks and Warren, the publication of major critical books by Ransom and Tate, and the final crystallization in 1943 in Brooks and Warren's textbook, *Understanding Fiction,* all the major elements that were to fix the new Southern tradition had been fully discussed and disseminated.

Several important writers had independently assimilated and practiced the technique, at least in part, before the critical canon had been established. In particular, two older women, one of them newly widowed and beginning to write in the Twenties, the other a novelist of long distinction as a social historian in fiction, Isa Glenn of Georgia and Ellen Glasgow of Virginia, were pioneers in the new school of fiction.

Miss Glenn, a follower of Henry James's theory of fiction, has been neglected by critics and literary historians, but her fine ironic novels belong in the mainstream of twentieth-century literary development. A native of Atlanta and cousin of James McNeill Whistler, with whom she studied art in Europe in her youth, Miss Glenn began her career in fiction only after the death in 1921 of her husband, General Schindel, whom she had accompanied on tours of duty in the Philippines, the Orient, and the South Pacific. Between 1926 and 1935, she produced eight novels, set in Saigon, Manila, Brazil, Georgia, Washington, New York, and on the high seas. Only two of her books are completely

Southern in flavor, but often the situations in foreign settings imply parallels with current social problems in the South.

In theme, organization, and technique, Miss Glenn' major novels are astonishingly Jamesian. Her style, however, is distinctly her own, sharp, pungent, often barbed with wit and satire, and she saturates her stories, particularly her foreign ones, with an atmosphere that is an individual achievement. *Heat* (1926), her first novel, is oppressive, not only with humid air, but with the tropical odors and Spanish-walled mysteries of Manila. The lush precipitousness of "purple" Rio complements the romantic impulsiveness of the mismated mother in *Little Pitchers* (1927), and *Transport* (1929) squeezes its Army cargo on the Pacific under a merciless sun until the malicious juices of officers and wives ooze out poisonously on one another.

Miss Glenn normally employs James's prime technical device, the use of narrative blocks viewed from a single limited vision which can on occasion broaden out into objectivity or narrow to introspection. *Heat* uses three eager young newcomers to Manila to focus the dilemma of Lt. Tom Vernay, newly out of West Point. The romantic lieutenant himself, captive and victim of Manila's old world charms, provides the major perspective, but his view is supplemented by that of the forthright girl who tries to save him for herself and that of the businessman friend who sees the situation from his conventionally objective view. Miss Glenn exploits fully the ironies which her partial viewpoints afford, and her ending, thoroughly Jamesian, finds the eminently moral Charlotte, in her attempt to rescue Tom, herself compromised.

Another Jamesian technique lends poignancy to the story of an incompatible marriage in *Little Pitchers* (1927). The story unfolds gradually to the comprehension of the viewpoint character, a child who develops from the age of three to a precocious fifteen. Without sacrific-ing the sensitive boy-view, Miss Glenn is able to exhibit, around him as well as through him, the stage-struck, irresponsible, but often lovable mother, and the dogged engineer father whom she manages to destroy. As the couple's violent quarrels move from Saigon to Brazil and New England, the reader is constantly offered a double focus: on the parents whom the boy is learning to understand and evaluate, and on the mental life of the imaginative protagonist himself. Dramatic irony is thus constantly sustained until the final moment of enlightenment.

In *Transport,* a constantly shifting multiple viewpoint enables Miss Glenn to expose the tensions, suspicions, and secret guilts that harry the Army officers, wives and nurses aboard. The heat and confinement of a three-week voyage across the Pacific so afflict the passenger-narrators that the picture they present comes out heavily tinged with their jaundice. Despite the wit and sharp satire which enliven the gossip and clandestine meetings, *Transport* begins to pall long before it reaches harbor. Lacking compassion, the book affords no relief from its relentless exposures.

In 1933 Miss Glenn offered her version of *The Ambassadors* under the title, *Mr. Darlington's Dangerous Age.* Adopting the theme of James's book, as well as his techniques, she sends her impeccable middle-aged banker to rescue a younger brother from a life of easy depravity in Manila. The book develops its inevitable ironies as the languor and free morals of the East cement their hold on Darlington. Only in tone and in the lavish display of atmosphere does Miss Glenn depart from James's model. She handles her characters with a light, deft touch, never far from satire, even when the implications are tragic.

Her two Southern novels represent Miss Glenn's control of her medium at its surest. *Southern Charm* (1928) confines its setting to a New York apartment, its time to three evenings, and its cast to six people, five of whom are Georgians. The major point of view character, Mrs. Habersham, living with the daughter she trained to become a spoiled man-trapping belle and with her successful, doting Northern husband, is objective enough now to see her daughter's shortcomings and tired enough to accept her. When her younger daughter, long disowned for an unmaidenly slip, turns up chic and capable from Europe to denounce her early training in "charm" and to open the husband's eyes, Mrs. Habersham has her moment of weakness. Slow in developing, the story moves briskly and brightly to its Jamesian ironic conclusion.

A Short History of Julia (1930) does a more thorough and consistently delightful job of exposing traditional Southerners living limited lives behind their box hedges and deep-set Georgian façades. Taught proper feminine reticence by her marble-surfaced mother, Julia de Graffenreid loses out in her two great passions and adjusts to spinsterhood. As counterpoint to her own story of frustration, she hears constantly and enviously of the Negro lives about her, full of passionate intensity. The Negroes are fundamentally unapproachable for Julia's set, but the suspicion grows on them that their servants know more about living than they will ever learn.

Miss Glenn's other novels, *East of Eden* (1932), set in New York, and *The Little Candle's Beam* (1935), set in Washington, are less successful. Though the earlier book exhibits her Jamesian control fully, its mordant examination of a self-centered, cold group of successful writers and its pitiless picture of a marital war of nerves notably lack the saving note of human sympathy. *The Little Candle's Beam,* a tired, loose book, has little to recommend it but a few uncharitably sharp delineations of society matrons.

The wit and irony which Isa Glenn brought to her examinations of Southern society are rivaled only in the late novels of Ellen Glasgow. Before 1925, Miss Glasgow had produced a dozen novels, all of them in the vein of "social realism." In that year, after a romantic disillusionment and a suicide attempt, she wrote *Barren Ground,* the best of her realistic novels. She followed this success the next year with a new sort of novel, *The Romantic Comedians,* which places her among the pioneers of the new school of Southern fiction.

The militantly democratic attitudes that had disguised a traditionally sentimental sensibility in her novels before *Barren Ground* drop out of the late books. A more congenial tone of satire and light irony replaces the heavy drive of idea in *The Romantic Comedians* and *They Stooped to Folly* (1929), both set in a thinly disguised Richmond. Built on paradoxes and characterized stylistically by a constantly paradoxical wit, these novels turn up to tempered ridicule the romantic gentility which survives in a ungentle age. Her themes are those most typical of the Southern Renaissance. She juxtaposes aristocrat and new bourgeois, older generations and experimental youth, conventions and sex deviations, romantic tenets and modern realism. If out of these oppositions she makes high comedy rather than Isa Glenn's tragicomedy, it becomes her sharp and aloof femininity far better than the serious realism into which her ideas of social history had projected her in the past.

Miss Glasgow never exhibits the artistic control of her medium which Miss Glenn learned from her reading of Henry James. Like most satirists, she is too prone to inject her own comments and to expose her manipulation of characters. She preserves her tone beauti fully, however, and her eye is as sharp as her tongue. In *The Romantic Comedians* she chiefly observes respectable sixty-four-year-old Judge Honeywell, suddenly widowed, committing the folly of marrying a poor girl of twenty-three. The deluded, sexually reanimated Judge occupies the center of the stage, but his actions are assessed realistically through the eyes of his new mother-in-law (ten years his junior), of his romantically attached and disappointed contemporary, Amanda Lightfoot, and, more clinically, of the author herself.

The author is too much present in *They Stooped to Folly,* but the satire is sharper as it cuts into traditional Southern patterns of moral behavior. The novel's chief observer is a chivalric lawyer of the old school, Virginius Littlepage. Virginius' shrewd observations about his contemporaries often belie his character and suggest his creator, but he has ample material for comment in his own last-gasp lust for one of the "fallen women" of the title, his absurdly messianic daughter's attempt to reform her husband, and his "fallen" secretary's attempt to rehabilitate herself.

Following her two comedies, Miss Glasgow returned to tragedy in *The Sheltered Life,* but her basic theme and setting is the same. The folly of the human male in particular absorbs her. Through the eyes of a young girl and those of her grandfather, again with overt assists from the author, *The Sheltered Life* details the failures of the genteel tradition in the early twentieth century. Symbolic images of the hunt and blood dominate the story and reach their apotheosis with the opening salvos of World War I. The "sheltered life" of Queensborough's belle, as she tries to maintain the style of the Victorian ideal through poverty and her husband's infidelity, ends in her own insanity and her husband's death. Concomitant with the theme, "men like to destroy beauty," appears the sense of lives wasted by the imposition of an uncongenial pattern of manners and morals.

Such sceptical attitudes toward the classic past of Southern society as those of both Miss Glenn and Miss Glasgow are highly characteristic of the whole literary movement, but not of the central symbolic naturalist tradition. Other liberally-minded practitioners in the mode appear from time to time, but the large majority share the traditionalistic convictions of Faulkner and the Fugitive group. This view of tradition, however, took form only in the second decade of the Renaissance. Properly speaking, Miss Glenn and Miss Glasgow, together with Elizabeth Maddox Roberts and Stark Young, are pre-cursors of the new tradition, in one or more ways atypical.

Miss Roberts, though she is generally considered with the generation of Miss Glasgow and James Branch Cabell, belongs as an artist entirely to the Southern Renaissance era. After a long crippling illness, the Kentucky girl recovered sufficiently to take a Ph.D. degree at the University of Chicago in 1921, and the following year published a volume of poems, *Under the Tree*. Her first novel, *The Time of Man* (1926), a pioneer poor white story, established her as a sensitive and compassionate writer of fiction, and she consolidated her reputation four years later with a realistic historical novel, *The Great Meadow*. Between these two landmarks of her career, she wrote two less successful novels, and later added three more, in addition to a second volume of poetry and two collections of short stories.

None of the latter novels is a complete artistic success, but they contain elements which relate them to symbolic naturalism. Miss Roberts, rather a student of poetry than of the art of the novel, seldom achieves the unity of tone or the proportion which a complete work of fiction requires. One of the books is pure fantasy, *Jingling in the Wind* (1928), and three of the others contain strangely unintegrated and unbalanced sections of fantasy. *Jingling in the Wind* incorporates broad elements of satire aimed at large-scale advertising and megalopolises in general, but its wandering story involving male and female rainmakers completely lacks focus. Though evidently a seriously intended stylistic experiment, *He Sent Forth a Raven* (1935) includes a set of highly fantastical characters—the dominant violent grandfather who builds an aerial bridge from house to barn roof in order to manage the farm and still live up to his bitter vow never to set foot on God's earth again, the wildly eccentric carpenter-philosopher, and the odd repetitive itinerant preacher who can't be ousted from the house.

The attempt to tell this story of a girl's growing up through a series of impressions of farm life and school, a succession of moods, overheard conversations, and fragments of action, comes off well at times. Miss Roberts is expert at conveying the poetry of the countryside and the play of mood in the girl's mind; however, she manages the girl's emotional crises so peripherally and gingerly that no formed character ever appears. Though Jocelle finally marries a pacifist county agent, her creator seems all the time to be looking another way. There is no story, only a sort of impressionistic memoir.

The other three more conventional novels display Miss Roberts' very considerable talents for poetic speech, for evocation of place and development of character, and the powerful use of symbols to create mood and meanings. Still, each of the stories contains curious breaks in tone, technique, and style so that no one of them fully accomplishes its promise.

A Buried Treasure (1931) provides the most startling example of Miss Roberts' unevenness. Through more than half of the book, this is her finest performance in control of point of view, in development of effective symbols and in character revelation. Then the novel breaks wide open. The ironic inevitability of the early chapters turns suddenly to sentimental optimism. Happy accidents and impossible changes of character solve all the potentially tragic situations; the symbolism and the control of viewpoint are simply abandoned.

The story revolves about the discovery by a poor, aging farm couple of a treasure cache buried on their place during the Civil War. We watch the couple progress from initial scepticism and joy through suspicion of their neighbors to distrust and fear as the valuable burden forces out their weaknesses. Their surprise announcement party turns into a nightmare of suspense as Philly sits planted over the newly reburied treasure.

A supplementary viewpoint is introduced through young Ben Shepherd, who has come to the village to unearth gravestones of his ancestors—an additional buried treasure—and who happens to witness the momentous discovery. Through Ben's rooting among stones and bones, the invasion of his food supply by voracious, flesh-devouring ants, as well as through Philly's early preoccupation with woodlice, Miss Roberts establishes a strong symbolic complex, related both to buried treasure and to man's furtive life ending in untreasured extinction. Sex, too, becomes involved with the insect symbolism and its bitter tone. Abruptly everything changes to pulp fiction. Real robbers appear and are happily thwarted, Ben disappears, a sharp character change solves the marriage problem, and in place of insects we have childish romantic dance games under the moon. Miss Roberts seems to have given up on herself or on her public.

My Heart and My Flesh (1927), an introspective novel, is somewhat more successful on the whole but still curiously broken into tonally separate sections. Again the story of a girl brought up in town and country, the novel begins with a strange Prologue in which Theodosia's family are introduced through the views of a child, who does not appear in the novel proper, and those of several town Negroes. A typical slowly paced section dealing with Theodosia's childhood and young womanhood is followed by a series of abrupt tragedies, among them the discovery that her father had produced three mulatto children, one of them after marriage, by a half-witted Negro wench. Turning to her rival suitors for escape, she loses one to a new girl while the other is burned to death. Her father deserts her and she haunts the cabin of her half-sisters, hating them and perversely trying to establish a sisterly relation with them, until she has prodded the elder sister to murder her faithful lover. Finally she collapses, loses her house, and is shipped off to an impossibly penurious aunt in the country. After the violence, all of it underplayed and indirectly presented, Miss Roberts returns to her quiet, introspective and often poetic style. As she is slowly starved by Aunt Doe, Theodosia listens to inner voices of guilt and hopelessness until she is rescued to a hope of resurrection through agrarian interests and an agrarian suitor. The book ends weakly after the long bout with guilt, as if again Miss Roberts' powers of concentration had failed her.

In contrast to *My Heart and My Flesh,* the last novel, *Black is My True Love's Hair* (1938), frames a calm, poetic center section, again of a girl's recuperation in a Kentucky farm village, between two violent sequences. At the opening of this Brontean romance, the renegade Catholic heroine is fleeing wildly from the truck driver with whom she had run away. She escapes again from gypsies who try to exploit her as a whore to a sister's home, where she lives under a cloud of scandal and her lover's threat to kill her. After the central idyll, presided over by earth-bound figures, but again with fear and guilt intruding, the story erupts again into melodrama. The lover's evil, violent sexual passion is frustrated after he shoots at her, and she escapes to her sound earthy miller's son. Like the Brontes' melodramatic romances, this appears finally a frustrated maiden's story, in which sex attraction is violently etherialized, then equally violently transformed into lurid evil.

Like many of her Southern compatriots, Miss Roberts found the short story a more congenial medium generally than the novel, where her concentration too often lapsed. The limited range of the short story allowed her the compression of poetry and natural limits in which she could focus her powers. Some of her stories like the overtly bitter sharecropper tale, "The Haunted Mirror," with its effective central symbol representing a past that must be destroyed by the Snopes-like invaders, or the bloodily symbolic "The Betrothed" (both from *Not by Strange Gods* [1941]); and "Death at Bearwallow" or "Chicken of Earth" (from the *Haunted Mirror* [1932]) demonstrate a fine poetic sensibility in mastery of environment, mood and symbolic extension.

Miss Roberts never achieved greatness in the novel form largely because she could not, like Henry James, compensate for the limitations of her experience with a sustained and constantly refined analysis of the novelist's art. At heart a lyric poet, she was able often to transfer her poetic virtues to short fiction. In the novel, without a steady vision of the art form, she could concentrate her energies to produce fine sections, but could seldom sustain them to produce a unified and fully satisfying work.

As a pioneer of the Renaissance, Stark Young of Mississippi made his influence felt only after he had published a volume of verse, two plays and a set of travel sketches in the decades between 1906 and 1926. A college teacher for seventeen years and later one of America's most distinguished drama critics, he turned his attention to prose fiction only in middle age. There is little to distinguish Young's first two novels, *The Heaven Tree* (1926) and *The Torches Flare* (1927), except a quiet authority in dealing with the New York theatre, Greenwich Village life, and a few perceptive glimpses of Southern backgrounds. In *River House* (1929), however, Young takes precisely the step which Faulkner and members of the Fugitive group were taking at the same moment: he initiates a fictional exploration of his peculiarly Southern heritage. The surface story in *River House* is modern, but the basic problems underlying the still mannered and aesthetically arranged life in a Mississippi plantation house are those stemming from a typical old family quarrel, which finally extends its sinister influence into the younger generation as they insist on probing it. There are many virtues in this novel, particularly in the dialogue which catches the special flavor of the relatives who represent various aspects of the family past, as well as in the evocation of a life which preserves so many outmoded dignities. Unfortunately, the immediate story of the young couple whose experience essentially repeats the pattern their elders have set is a pallid one, carrying little of the conviction which the background characters create.

So Red the Rose (1934) has proved the enduring public favorite among a myriad of Southern novels dealing with the War Between the States. More than any other single book, it re-established in critical grace the Civil War genre which had for so long been bogged in the "treacly sentimentality" of crinolines and trailing banners, of magnolias and darky banjos. *So Red the Rose* is not entirely free of the nostalgic idealisms, the chivalries and heroisms of its gross predecessors; otherwise, it could hardly have achieved its immense popular success in the South. The novel does, however, in the hands of a skillful and cosmopolite author, avoid the intense partisanship, the romantic gallantries, and the sacrificial absurdities which had characterized earlier "lost cause" fiction. Furthermore, Young's book represents a serious attempt to apply to the historical novel some of the major principles of symbolic naturalist technique.

This application primarily involves historical accuracy in detail, an objectivity which precludes author intrusion, and a sense of symbolic extension. For Young, the naturalist basis of *So Red the Rose* derives directly from personal family history and supporting documentation, with particular attention paid to period speech and manners. At the symbolic level, the Bedfords and the McGehees, roughly the English and Scotch traditions as they had developed through several generations of plantation life in the South, are pitted against the representative Northerner, General Sherman, who had run a military school in the Natchez neighborhood and accepted the local hospitality. The pattern developed in the novel becomes substantially that which characterizes Ransom's poetry, Tate's poetry and his novel, *The Fathers,* Warren's early fiction, and Davidson's poetry and essays. (Young had joined these Fugitive writers in contributing an essay to *I'll Take My Stand* several years earlier.)

The ante-bellum planters stand for an agrarian ideal, based on land ownership and responsible moral codes. Opposed to them and their agrarian ideal, stands General Sherman, an example of Eliot's "dissociation of personality," an essentially kind, gentlemanly individual and loving father, who, for lack of an integrated, land-based tradition, can turn under stress into a vindictive and ruthless leader of a conquering army. If the author strains somewhat, as Southern novelists of the conservative persuasion are like to do, the one-to-one relationship between land-management and integrated personality, he has nevertheless created in his General Sherman a modern type which has been most effectively dramatized in Charlie Chaplin's Monsieur Verdoux, the cold-blooded uxoricide careerist whose tender family life is touchingly feckless.

It must be admitted, however, that *So Red the Rose* fails in several respects to meet the highest standards of symbolic naturalist fiction. Young's overidealized and incompletely realized young heroes and heroines and his almost wholly sexless treatment of their love affairs recall too vividly the romantic tradition of Sir Walter Scott's fiction. As in Scott, this unrealistic reticence comports badly with the realistic accuracy accorded the details of setting and of manners. Furthermore, Young's confusing shifts of point of view and his run-on sentence style, both evidently deliberate, not only contradict the best practices of his narrative mode, but contribute annoying distractions for the reader.

The new tradition of symbolic naturalism in fiction was properly inaugurated at the time of the Great Depression by William Faulkner of Mississippi and the Fugitive group of Tennessee. It is tempting to assume a mutual influence between Faulkner and the Fugitives, for Ransom, Tate, Warren and Davidson were publishing poetry in the sprightly New Orleans little magazine, *The Double Dealer,* while Faulkner lived in the Crescent City and was printing verse and sketches in the same magazine. All of these men began at the same period to explore anew their Southern heritages, as did Caroline Gordon, who had married Tate in 1924. In the absence of direct evidence, however, it is safe only to see in operation the more general influences which were leading others as well to reassess the South. The mode of symbolic naturalism was simply that which, with considerable variations, had been established by the greater novelists and short story writers of the age.

William Faulkner developed slowly into a novelist after a heterogeneous early experience, which took him from his native Oxford,

Mississippi, to the Canadian Air Force, and to New Orleans, where Sherwood Anderson was holding court. Faulkner lived and drank with Anderson, consorted with the new artist colony centered about the Spratling studio, and wrote undistinguished bits, later published in *Salmagundi* (1932). His first novel, *Soldiers' Pay* (1926), an uneven, but original and interesting book, displays a talent for tragedy as well as for comedy, and a rich command of metaphor. The story of an aviator returned to the South, going blind and all but insensible, *Soldier's Pay* includes one grotesque woman-chaser, a few wild drunk scenes, some tender passages of self-sacrifice, and a good deal of cynicism. It was a good beginning, but it was followed by a less promising satiric burlesque, *Mosquitoes* (1927), the story of a cruise on Lake Ponchartrain with a boatload of artists and dowager patrons.

Sherwood Anderson may well have influenced the writing of these two novels, but the attribution to him of major influence in turning Faulkner's interests and talents to his native material appears patently improbable. Before he had finished *Mosquitoes,* Faulkner and Spratling circulated a harsh parody-satire called *Sherwood Anderson and Other Famous Creoles,* an effort which caused an immediate break in the relationship. Only after a trip to France did he return to Mississippi and begin writing *Sartoris* (1929).

With this novel Faulkner initiated what developed into an elaborate quest for human values and meanings through an extended fictional re-creation of his North Mississippi heritage. The large-scale, time-ordered social picture which he finally presents is clear in outline, if often ambiguous in detail. The long sequence of his Yoknapatawpha County novels and short stories focuses consistently on the evil of exploitation and its consequences in mass guilt and violence. Faulkner's favorite word, "outrage," with its variants, expresses his primary sense of the moral perversity of man, and not alone of the Southern white man with whom he primarily deals.

The chronicle, as it pieces itself together in his fiction, begins with the white man's exploitation of the Indian, whom he bullies and cheats—the Ikkemotubi stories—out of his commonly owned heritage of hunting grounds. There follows—again largely in short stories—the exploitation of the land itself through the irresponsible destruction of timber and game, not for need but for private gain. Next, it is the imported black man who is exploited, in the building of a slave

economy and later in complex social and economic systems elaborated
to preserve his inferior status. Following the War Between the States,
the Northern invader exploits both black and beaten white, and finds
a new ally in predatory Southerners who adopt his ruthless principles.
Finally the Snopes clan of the novels, poor whites of a new moral
destitution, move in to exploit the improvidence and remaining patches
of honor to which the old aristocracy clings. Faulkner's most modern
representative figure of the type is the Popeye of *Sanctuary* (1931),
mechanized and impotent, the complete manipulative exploiter who
cannot even perform his own rapes.

Both structurally and texturally Faulkner qualifies as a symbolic
naturalist, but much of his fiction veers far over toward the symbolic
extreme of the classification. His characters, his incidents, even his
conversation and description are never content with an even naturalistic course. Everything has been heightened in Faulkner, as in
Melville, to achieve a supranatural legendary or mythic effect. His
portentous style, built of cumulative sentences with paired and tripled
adjectives and heavy repetitions, suspenseful withholdings, and stepped-
up metaphors, constantly supports the more than human proportions
of his figures. The characters in turn justify the epically violent, wildly
comical, or terribly frustrating incidents in which they become
involved. Only once has Faulkner written a professedly allegorical
novel, *A Fable* (1954), but often his fiction strains in that direction
as he pushes his quest for moral meanings.

Faulkner's most impressive novels and tales belong primarily to the
Depression years. With *The Sound and the Fury* (1929) he announced
a major talent, experimental in technique, clear in perspective, solid
with values, fertile in invention, and original in style. *The Sound and
the Fury,* which has exerted more influence, especially in Europe, than
any other modern American novel with the possible exception of
Hemingway's *The Sun Also Rises,* is organized on a musical analogy,
beginning with a difficult overture, which states all the themes through
the disordered images and memories occurring in the mind of an idiot,
Benjy Compson. Parts Two and Three, seen through the guilty mind
of Benjy's brother, Quentin, just before his suicide, and through the
rank materialistic view of the storekeeper half-brother, Jason, present
the major movements. Each of these parts develops its own peculiar
themes in counterpoint: Quentin's meaningless present time, symbol-

ized in his handless, ticking watch, against the meaning-laden past, guilt against innocence; Jason's single-minded rational greed against his niece's emotional impulse, authority versus revolt. The final section offers both resolution and coda, with the point of view largely objective, but with Negro characters offering the final commentary and contrast.

The Sound and the Fury demonstrates and illustrates one of the major theses in Faulkner's social analysis of the South: the modern degeneracy and final impotence of a caste which had earned its right to hegemony through its basic loyalty to an integrated code of moral behavior. This right and its total orientation, which was based on natural use of the land, it has lost through its own guilty exploitation and compromise with the latest agents of exploitation, the money-grubbers in its own lower ranks—here the marriage of Compsons to Bascombs.

After his masterly tragi-comedy of poor whites, *As I Lay Dying* (1930), Faulkner took up his main theme again in *Sanctuary* (1931), carrying his saga of degeneration into its final phase, with the mechanical man, spectator-sportist Popeye, symbol of the South's—and America's—complete capitulation to an ungrounded, abstract, and therefore impotent finance capitalism. *Sanctuary's* sensationalism, for all its hastily improvised structure, won Faulkner his first popular American hearing, though it added nothing to his final stature as a novelist. However, it was soon followed by a true masterpiece, *Light in August* (1932), in which all his major themes are given full play, in which symbolism is combined with rich realistic immediacy, in which his mature portentous style reaches maturity, and in which the full complexity of his vision of the South's moral problem is given extended relevance to modern man's dilemma.

At the center of this novel, Faulkner has set the utterly ambiguous figure of Joe Christmas, Negro and white, Satan and Christ, martyr and murderer, masochist and sadist. Born "immaculately" on Christmas Day, rejecting pity and welcoming punishment for guilts he cannot fathom, preying on white women and rejecting Negroes, Joe develops into Faulkner's most impressive symbolic creation, a human representative of the recent South's schizophrenic conflicts. Being both black and white, Joe carries a double burden; he is at once the black cross which the white man in his long guilt must bear and face every day of his life, and the enduring victim of white exploitation, suffering

finally spread as on a cross and emasculated for his own guilt and for
the sins of the white race.

Set off against Joe are the equally heightened and symbolic figures
of Hightower, fanatic dweller in the South's irrecoverable past, and
Lena Grove, the simple, patient incarnation of the indestructible earth
itself. Faulkner draws into his novel all the essential elements of his
version of the modern South. The one triumphant element is Lena,
who draws to her protection both the Old South's chivalric remains in
Hightower, and the practical artisan bulwark, Byron Bunch, who
recognizes in her the fundamental verities from which his lonely
city life has isolated him. The calm confidence which Lena inspires,
despite her own "exploitation" by her runaway lover, suggests Faulkner's agrarian answer to the thwarting, the guilt, and consequent
violence that rules his artificial city life.

In his later novels and short stories, Faulkner has greatly extended,
but never essentially altered, the view of man's life and the South's
moral history which *Light in August* presents. In only a handful of
these stories has he rivaled the artistry of his early triumphs. Of the
novels, only *Absalom, Absalom!* (1936) and *The Hamlet* (1940) approach the finished quality of *The Sound and the Fury* and *Light in
August,* though almost all of them contain sections which reveal the
author's inexhaustible creativity and control. The Sutpen story with
which *Absalom, Absalom!* deals contains so many complex problems,
both personal and social, that the narrator, Quentin Compson, who
desperately needs to understand it all, is left baffled, a bafflement in
which the reader must to an extent share since he is provided with no
insights more authoritative.

As the story is exposed through the gradual unwrapping of layer
after layer of obscurity, Col. Sutpen's primal sin of exploitation to
achieve his enormous ambition becomes heavily complicated with a
series of sins, fears, and frustrations which lead him to a humiliating
doom. But the story is primarily, for Quentin, that of Sutpen's sons,
Henry and the blood-tainted Charles Bon. Furthermore, the central
section of the book is occupied with the soliloquy of Rosa Coldfield,
whose closeness to Sutpen as sister-in-law and proposed mistress enables her only to confuse the motivations. From this welter of complications emerges a primary theme of Negro-white relations in terms of
fears, guilt, and, as the inevitable accompaniment, violence.

Sutpen's original ambition had been motivated, at least partially, by a Negro servant's snub to him as a poor white of the back country, and he had proceeded to gather a crew of Haitian Negroes to clear Sutpen's Hundred and erect his mansion. More crucially, he had put aside his wife, in whom he had discovered a trace of Negro blood; and it is his son by that marriage, Charles Bon, who as Henry's friend comes to fall in love with his own half-sister. Bon asks only recognition from his father, for which he will give up both love and friendship. Sutpen's repudiation, followed by Henry's refusal to sanction the marriage, from principles regarding miscegenation, not incest, leads to the violent sequels which wipe out the entire family. Actual miscegenation and the pathological fear of it, then, constitute the prime destructive agents in the world of *Absalom*. Behind these factors, of course, lies the guilt for enslaving the Negro and behind that the greed and false pride which precipitate the Southern man's self-destructive passion.

Faulkner's actual presentation is by no means as single-minded as this simplification would make it appear. Chiefly, *Absalom* is complicated by its narrative filters; in the first place by the pathology of Quentin, who is marked for early suicide, and in the second by Rosa Coldfield's rankling hatred of the man who wished to make a guinea pig of her. The portrait of Sutpen as it comes through these distorted instruments owns few natural features; he acquires, however, all the ambiguous force which Faulkner can lend his semihistorical figures. He represents a whole generation of prewar upstart challengers to the settled old Southern families, the pre-Snopeses, and he is as well the South's self-destructive force which eventually culminates in Quentin himself.

Faulkner's further major works in the Yoknapatawpha series after *Absalom* are the "rise and fortunes of the Snopes family" novels: *The Hamlet, The Town* (1957) and *The Mansion* (1959); *Intruder in the Dust* (1948) and *Requiem for a Nun* (1950). The Snopes cycle (it had already been treated superficially in *Sartoris* and was extended in short stories) has developed with decreasing persuasiveness, though neither of the latter two novels is without its fine Faulkneresque scenes. *The Hamlet* contains, in addition to the fabulous successes of Flem Snopes and his unscrupulous race of poor white exploiters, one of the most hilarious and fantastic episodes in modern fiction, "The

Spotted Horses"; and it introduces one of the most fascinating of Faulkner's creations, the eminently realistic and prophetic sewing machine salesman, Ratliff. Still, *The Hamlet* lacks the unity and organized artistry of Faulkner's earlier masterpieces. The element of the grotesque—and the Snopeses are certainly the most grotesque family in modern literature—overwhelms the occasional strong passages of earthy realism to the extent that *The Hamlet's* final effect is closer to that of the folk tale than to that of the modern novel.

The Town and *The Mansion* fall off from this vein of high fantasy to recount the comparatively prosaic business of Flem Snopes's cynical invasion of the town of Jefferson, his conquest, and eventual, all but willed, fall at the hands of one of his incongruously earth-bound kins- men. In his involvement with the more and more incredible, proliferat- ing Snopeses, Faulkner seems to lose some of his firm grip on even the more realistically conceived characters. Ratliff and Gavin Stevens, despite the latter's romantic involvements, tend to merge into one person, spokesmen in differing accents for the author himself. Flem's wife, a crucial character in *The Town,* remains quite shadowy, seen by a series of observers and taking on for them the seductive potentiali- ties of Helen of Troy. She never becomes humanly alive to any degree. In addition, the episodic structure, already evident in *The Hamlet,* is carried farther in the sequels, where extraneous episodes, some of them worthy of Erskine Caldwell, are introduced evidently to provide diversion.

In *Intruder in the Dust* and *Requiem for a Nun,* Faulkner re- turns to the obsessive Negro theme, directly and forcibly in the former, indirectly and less effectively in the latter. In its plot line, *Intruder* is a detective story, with a young boy seeking out the evidence which will free a Negro from a false murder charge. Thematically, the story con- cerns the moral education of the boy, who grows through aiding a Negro whom he hates for his dignified and stubborn refusal to recognize the white boy's natural superiority. Lucas Beauchamp, des- cendant of the McCaslin Negroes of several short stories and originally of a McCaslin himself, represents a new type in Faulkner's picture of the Southern Negro. Though he had appeared intimately in an earlier story, the Lucas here assumes an independent and newly symbolic life, forcing from the recalcitrant whites a sense of responsibility and even of respect. No longer is the Negro simply the cross which the white race must bear for its sins; he is their conscience itself.

Intruder in the Dust is marred chiefly by the intrusive moralizing of the author through his evident mouthpiece, lawyer Gavin Stevens, and this sort of intrusion continues in *Requiem for a Nun*. But *Requiem* fails basically for other reasons. The opening section, "The Jail," has not even a peripheral relation to this continuation of Temple Drake's story from *Sanctuary,* and the book includes other similarly irrelevant episodes. Centrally, however, it is the major Negro character, Nancy, who fails both as a realistic character and as a symbol. Nancy, a former whore and user of dope, is implausibly hired as a nurse by Temple and ends by killing Temple's illegitimate child, thus sacrificing herself, also most implausibly, for Temple's rehabilitation. Apparently Faulkner wished to create a modern Magdalene, whose new faith embodies the capabilities of the Negro for enduring through suffering. Unfortunately, he failed to endow Nancy with the potentialities to fit her for her final role.

Faulkner's achievements in the short story, particularly in the volume, *Go Down, Moses* (1942), are second to none in his generation, despite the fact that many of the tales fill in gaps which his novel series have left open, and despite the additional fact that a number of his finest short stories have been incorporated in novels. Faulkner is one of the great modern masters of the fabliau (as his final novel, *The Reivers,* proves again) and the symbolic moral tale; indeed, one might venture, a contemporary medievalist beyond compare, as well as our greatest modern novelist.

Of the Fugitive group proper, those whose names appeared on the masthead of *The Fugitive* magazine, Robert Penn Warren was the first to print fiction. However, of those closely associated with the group, priority belongs to Allen Tate's wife, Caroline Gordon, whose short stories date from 1930 and who published the earliest novel, *Penhally,* in 1931. Unlike her associates, Miss Gordon went directly to fiction, without the preliminary apprenticeship to poetry.

Most of Miss Gordon's fiction belongs close to the heart of the new tradition; in fact, she and her husband are responsible for the term, symbolic naturalism, and for its definition. Miss Gordon conspicuously lacks the spontaneity and originality of the more widely read artists in the mode, but she has been one of the most conscientious students of technique and has constantly sought to broaden the range of her subject matter and philosophic understanding. Committed, like her husband, to the conservative agrarian ideal and opposed to modern "progress," she turned immediately to a fictional examination of her heritage, which centers in a rural district on the Kentucky-Tennessee line, adjacent to that of Robert Penn Warren. Only gradually, after an excursion back into Virginia beginnings, did she work her way into the modern era.

Miss Gordon's instinct is for pattern; she works most effectively, therefore, with the historical movement, the family group, the typical, rather than the individual, character. Not until her later novels does she attempt any deep penetration into her protagonists' minds or psychological processes and seldom then does she enter into them with any strongly participative warmth. Her quality as an artist depends upon objective observation and analysis, on a sure control of technique and symbolic extension, rather than upon the arousal of an empathic response to her characters. Perhaps largely for this reason, she has never achieved great popular success, though her work has stood high in critical esteem.

Four of her first five novels explore the past of her region and its families, and all are concerned with the agrarian pattern and its decay. Penhally, a farm estate, stands at the center of her first novel, told by the three successive Llewellyns who care most for it. The family members who wrangle over it and finally lose it at the end of a hundred years assume little importance as individuals, for the author's concern is to portray the shifting attitudes which the estate inspires as the original agrarian ideal loses its hold through the century. For this reason, the life of the novel, with its shifting cast of characters, is rather thin, but it accomplishes its purpose through a completely honest objectivity, unmarred by sentimentality or melodrama.

Love of the land, now concentrated in hunting and fishing, dominates *Aleck Maury, Sportsman* (1934) to the exclusion of all else. Here, the old father, teacher, and devotee of the outdoor life, tells his own life story; yet the feeling of the narrative is perhaps less intimate than that of *Penhally,* for Maury's classic reticence in regard to personal affairs is a fundamental trait. He is representative of a way of life, whose rituals and codes constitute the theme and pattern of the book. He preserves his traditional values by attaching their forms to sport, and never have we been given in a novel such a wealth of knowledge about dog training, fly tying, and such details of hunting and fishing technique.

In her two historical novels, *None Shall Look Back* (1937), a story of General Forrest's campaigns in the Civil War, and *Green Centuries* (1941), the realistic detail and absence of traditional sentimentalities are again notable. On the human and the symbolic levels, however, they are less effective. In the former, Miss Gordon's attempt to relate in a meaningful pattern the men's war to that of the women behind the front and to agrarian values is obscured, rather than illuminated, by narrative sections following three army careers and home family lives in Kentucky and Georgia. The war itself provides the only narrative center, and individual characters remain but thinly realized.

Green Centuries inevitably invites comparison with Elizabeth Maddox Roberts' treatment of the same period and area in *The Great Meadow,* written a full decade earlier. Both these impressive works deal with the historic movement of Tidewater families (from Carolina and Virginia) into the new transmontane Indian country of Kentucky and Tennessee. However, the wide differences in perspective and technique make the comparison an instructive one, not only for characterizing the authors, but for illustrating the development of symbolic naturalism in a decade.

Miss Roberts, for the most part, limits her view to that of her feminine protagonist and similarly restricts her style by adopting the reticences and sometimes stilted artificialities of the eighteenth-century female diary. Within these limitations, she manages to re-create brilliantly minutiae of daily frontier life, the gossip and anxieties of the often unprotected women's community. Her Indians are menacing shadows only, and even the men of her heroine's experience remain incomprehensible, both groups embodiments of the eternal threat to a stable and poetic order which women would establish on a generous earth. In fact, only when she must materialize her Indians and men in direct violent relation with the women does Miss Roberts' novel lose its effectiveness. There are no symbolic extentions beyond those given the Indians and pioneer men as representative of obstacles to feminine security.

Miss Gordon also is concerned about woman's relation to restless

men and to the Indian menace. In contrast, however, she enters the
intimate life of the Indians and elicits sympathy for their plight; she
steps directly into several levels of purely male relationships; and she
handles sexual realities without reticence. At the basis of Miss Gordon's
conception is not an individual eighteenth-century girl with her
personal problems, but a myth which her story reanimates. Rion Out-
law (Orion the hunter), loved by the hardy and once independent
Cassy Dawson (Diana), shares his hardships until he is finally killed
by her brother Frank (Apollo). The mythic parallel extends Miss
Gordon's fiction into a primordial human pattern, but does not commit
our sympathies as Miss Roberts' novel inevitably does. The characters, with the exception of Frank, who remains an abstraction (as
perhaps a god-figure should), are plausible, but the author's wide-
ranging interests and concern for pattern leave us essentially un-
attached to them.

Miss Gordon had inaugurated her second phase before the publication of *Green Centuries* with *The Garden of Adonis* (1937), a novel
modern in its setting and mythic in its pattern of reference. Con-
temporaneously with her husband, whose *The Fathers* was published
in the following year, Miss Gordon adopted the fictional device with
which James Joyce had sought to achieve universal relevance for his
modern story in *Ulysses*—Joyce's masterpiece had won its battle with
United States censors only in 1934. The eighteen episodes of Bloom's
day in *Ulysses* had been demonstrated by critics and scholars to parallel
loosely eighteen episodes in Homer's *Odyssey*. The theoretical justifi-
cation for the extended application of myth to modern literature lies
in Carl Jung's investigations into depth psychology, his insistence on
the retention of racial patterns in the individual's subconscious mind,
ready to be stimulated with powerful effect through literary disguises.
Myths constitute our prime source for the recognition of such racial
patterns of intense experience. As Tate uses the Jason-Medea myth in
The Fathers, Miss Gordon adapts both myths and rituals connected
with Adonis worship in *The Garden of Adonis;* the Orion story, as
already noted, in *Green Centuries,* and, reputedly, the story of
Iphigenia in Aulis in her 1944 novel, *The Women on the Porch.*

The application in *The Garden of Adonis* involves considerable
strain as Miss Gordon attaches it to the agrarian thesis that rootlessness
and displacement from the land breed lust in place of love. Several

unconvincing affairs with women in the Venus role of pursuers, and especially the climactic murder scene, set in a field of rootless hay and deep-rooted clover leave the impression that the author has been dictated to by her mythic and symbolic necessities and has allowed her sense of life to suffer for it.

With no insistence on references and a less complex story line, *The Women on the Porch* exhibits Miss Gordon in full control of her method and at her best as well in evocation of scene and country people. If there is a mythological prototype behind this story of a betrayed wife returning to her Southern homeland and finding it an alien land, perverted from the solid securities she has known, Miss Gordon gives no evidence of it. The three sitting women, Catherine's dreadfully composed relatives, may indeed suggest the Parcae brooding over her fate, but they play no fundamental part in the action. Alienation is the novel's subject: the husband, Jim's, apparently inevitable alienation as a Midwesterner from his native soil for a rootless city life; Catherine's alienation from her homeland because both she and it have lost their proper orientations. The story, presided over by the Nornlike relatives, tends inevitably toward tragedy, and this is prefigured in the graphic scene of a stallion's accidental execution. But Jim's violent reaction when he hears of his wife's infidelity unaccountably comes to nothing, and we are left with an apparent reconciliation. What exigencies required this solution we need not inquire, but it fails, as indeed the characters of the protagonists, and particularly of the vaguely realized Jim, themselves fail to carry the requisite conviction.

The Strange Children (1951) and *The Malefactors* (1956) mark a third stage in Miss Gordon's development as a novelist. Though her method remains that of symbolic naturalism and her concern is still with modern values, she has abandoned mythic reference and substituted religious values for those of the agrarian tradition. Symbolic extension is provided in *The Strange Children* by the mystical romantic novel, *Undine,* which the child point of view character, Lucy, is reading, and by such more natural images as a portrait of Stonewall Jackson and a Holy Roller inscription on a rock by the highway. The blatant "prepare to meet thy God," prefigures for us not only for the revival meeting climax, with its snakebiting antics, but

the final religious meditation by the father (a gross, if necessary, viola-
tion of the established point of view).

"The strange children," who are the adults, are indeed strange in
this novel. Though their intellectual discussions and overt behavior
are brilliantly recorded through Lucy's limited understanding, their
reality as human beings remains extremely questionable. Mrs.
Reardon, an adulteress and wife of a newly devout Catholic, is
belatedly revealed as mad, though her recorded behavior has not hinted
it. The talented and sophisticated poet is deluded into running away
with her. The cynical historian father, having disgustedly rejected the
primitive Holy Roller antics, is led into an incongruous and unpre-
pared religious coda.

Despite its limitations, *The Strange Children* displayed a new talent
for capturing the flavor of modern intellectual and spiritual dilemmas,
both on the surface level of conversational gambits and at a subsurface
level of psychological disturbance. Her 1956 novel, *The Malefactors,*
set in fashionable Bucks County, Pennsylvania, with a similar cast
of poet-critic intellectuals, exhibits a further development of these
powers. Thoroughly Jamesian in its subtleties of technique, even
somewhat ponderously and confusingly Jamesian in the early series
of flashbacks, the book revolves about a natural symbol, a prize bull
being displayed at a large week-end party. Miss Gordon is concerned
to explore the various aspects of modern love: lust, perversions, saint-
liness among others, and to discover her solution in the Catholic faith.

For the informed reader, and it can have little appeal for the un-
informed, *The Malefactors* presents all but insuperable difficulties, the
chief of which is a sense of constant embarrassment. Characters and
events so closely parallel widely known persons and facts that the
book takes on the nature of a public confessional. Hart Crane, Dorothy
Day, and the Tates themselves come constantly to mind, and their
images cannot be erased from their fictional counterparts. Furthermore,
Miss Gordon has not allowed us the remove which the child-narrator
provided in *The Strange Children.* In the minds of husband and wife,
we stand altogether too close, as in an arena theatre. And despite this
closeness, we know the major characters and their motivations only
peripherally. Minor characters appear fully realized, but Miss Gordon's
characteristically oblique presentation of her principals leaves them
only vaguely contoured, in spite of the many sharp details of behavior

and reaction recorded. One is always left in a Gordon novel with admiration for her technique, her ironic revelations, her accuracy in observation, but it is difficult to participate in the lives of her characters and to warm to them.

Miss Gordon has achieved her most complete successes in the short story where her impeccable technique and command of symbol can operate freely with characters sketched in rather than presented in their full complexity. In such finely underplayed stories as "Old Red," "The Brilliant Leaves," and "The Forest of the South," the latter the title piece of her 1945 volume, she employs unobtrusively natural symbols: a deserted house, a fox, and blood-tinted fallen leaves. Each involves, without forcing or melodramatic action, a significant character revelation, and all are written in Miss Gordon's effortlessly polished and evocative style. Others in this volume, like "Her Quaint Honor," are firmly controlled and effective. Only in the slight episodes and sketches, which appear to have been pared from her novels, does this book fall off from Miss Gordon's masterful best.

Fugitives Allen Tate and Robert Penn Warren, as well as honorary Fugitive Andrew Lytle, printed their first fiction in the Thirties after having published volumes of poetry and/or biography. Tate's excursion into fiction lasted only four years, but his two printed short stories and single novel, *The Fathers* (1938), proved his commitment both to reinterpretation of his Southern heritage in agrarian terms and to the methods of symbolic naturalism. The stories, both of 1934, concern ancestor generations of the late eighteenth and postwar nineteenth centuries. "The Migration" details "for the instruction of his posterity" the trek of Virginian Rhodam Elwin to Tennessee, and "The Immortal Woman," centered in Georgetown, brings back from the West an old married Southern woman who personifies the South which is no more, as well as its betrayal from within.

"The Immortal Woman" is an impressive, if not altogether coordinated, story, but its bearings and referential suggestions become clear in *The Fathers,* to which it is a sequel, both chronologically and symbolically. Whatever else one may say of *The Fathers*, it belongs directly at the heart of the new tradition in Southern fiction, with its mythical reference, its exploitation of natural symbols, its detailed naturalistic observation, and its traditional agrarian values. The mythic prototype is the story of Jason and Medea and the more modern instance the earlier period of the War Between the States, as it affected Northern Virginia and Georgetown.

Tate attempts to project ironically in this novel the typical twentieth-century operational man, alienated from sound agrarian-rooted values, the modern Jason who can capture fleeces, abscond with women, throw them over when no longer needed, and proceed to further impressive and essentially meaningless exploits. Tate sets as his narrative point of view character an old man who, characteristically in the modern age, has always idolized the careless, uniformly successful George Posey. The story is the old man's recollection of his attachment in boyhood and youth to this George, who in his aimless "whirling" for lack of a center, brought destruction to his own family and, in his proportion, to the South as well.

Beyond young Lacy's carefully limited view, we sense the values of the Buchan family and their country neighbors in Virginia. They clearly represent a mannered, code-ordered society, thoroughly secure in their somewhat artificial moral and social forms, which the war situation first disturbs and finally destroys. At the center of destruction stands George Posey, married to Lacy Buchan's sister, himself a pinwheel of energy, inevitably making money from North and South alike, and, in his directionless activity, dooming not only the Buchans but his own sister, the "immortal lady" of the earlier story.

Tate builds an exciting, carefully plotted story, in which each sharply defined naturalistic detail carries its freight of significance, and each action its symbolic function in the developing pattern. His picture of the traditional Southern way of life avoids all the cliches of romantic distortion while it projects convincingly its major virtues. Harshness, code-sanctioned injustice, and natural depravity are presented as inescapable adjuncts of a fixed social pattern; yet the stability stemming from an ordered hierarchy of social and moral values, which recognizes the animal facts of life and man's depravity, constitutes Tate's theme.

The technique of selecting as narrator a limited and, from the book's view, wrongheaded child grown old, proves less than adequate in the final scenes, and indeed throughout there is difficulty in the reader's accepting Lacy's worship of a man who he recognizes has destroyed his family. The novel's weaknesses are typically those of the symbolic method. The characters, firmly grasped in their roles as pieces in the pattern, often fail of conviction in their human responses. Lacking Faulkner's extraordinary gift for lifting his people beyond the necessity for realistic behavior, Tate often fails to realize them in their complete humanity.

Andrew Lytle of Murfreesboro, Tennessee, was accorded honorary status as a Fugitive, though his writing career began only after a short detour in New Haven and New York as playwright and actor. Back in the South in 1930, he joined the Agrarian activities of the Fugitives and contributed his essay to *I'll Take My Stand,* the Agrarian manifesto. Furthermore, he emulated Tate and Warren by first producing a Civil War biography, *Bedford Forrest and His Critter Company* (1931). His first short story appeared a year later, and his first novel, *The Long Night,* five years thereafter.

Lytle's true quality as a novelist became evident only in 1957 with the publication of *The Velvet Horn.* Previously he had written two historical novels, *The Long Night* and *At the Moon's Inn* (1941), and a curious story inspired by Henry James, *A Name for Evil* (1947). Both *The Long Night* and *At the Moon's Inn* have decided merits that lift them out of the common run of historical fiction. In the former, a Civil War story, the theme is moral responsibility, brought sharply to focus in Pleasant McIvor's conflict between a family duty of personal revenge and his larger responsibility in the war. The first half of the book develops into a suspenseful adventure story on the model of *The Count of Monte Cristo* as Pleasant tracks down his enemies one by one. With the advent of war, however, what amounts to a new, more serious novel begins. While the war develops to the Battle of Shiloh, which is masterfully handled with an all but Tolstoian breadth, Pleasant's personal battle between private duty and public responsibility is brought to its own climax. Pleasant's story becomes finally symbolic of the war's destruction of the traditional code-sanctioned values of the Old South.

Evidently Lytle, like Faulkner, traces Western man's moral decay back to his original treatment of the Indians in this country. *At the Moon's Inn* goes all the way back to DeSoto to reinterpret this original sin from the points of view of both Spaniards and Indians. Particularly in his re-creation of tribal life which, despite bloodthirstiness and wiliness, is shown grounded in a coherent set of values beyond the comprehension of the single-minded, comparatively uncivilized Spanish adventurers, Lytle admirable succeeds. He is less persuasive with the Spanish, however, DeSoto himself being a simple personification of greed. Lytle is somewhat overobvious, too, and strained in the later sections when he pushes, by means of visions and overt symbols, the analogy of Indian to modern agrarian and Spaniard to unrooted capitalist.

The influence of Henry James grew especially strong among the Fugitive group in the Forties, as evidenced in Caroline Gordon's novels and in Allen Tate's criticism of the period. Lytle's *A Name for Evil* even more clearly reflects James, for both in its ambiguity and in its supernatural atmosphere it suggests "The Turn of the Screw." The realistic autobiographical effect of the early chapters, describing a young couple's difficulties in renovating an old house is shattered by the appearance, to the husband only, of a ghostly visitor, who is at once symbol and the obsessive reality of the past living on into the present. The apparitional Major Brent embodies, however vaporously, the two cardinal sins in Lytle's catalogue, betrayal of the land and of the family continuity on the land. Whether he exists only in the husband's preoccupation with history or in the reality of the original sin, his power is great enough to defeat his modern opponent both in his effort to restore the land and to provide a proper heir. The story can most plausibly be interpreted to exhibit a man driven mad by his obsession with the past and with the land, and readers not so taken up with Agrarian values as the author inevitably so interpret it. There is no doubt, however, if we judge by Lytle's other writings, that the ghost is real and the final crime his.

For his masterpiece, *The Velvet Horn,* Lytle turned to the more congenial influences of Faulkner and Warren. *The Velvet Horn* is highly symbolic, agrarian, and religious in its orientation; cryptic, rhetorical, and poetic in its style. Furthermore, it contains a set of quite real characters driven by pride and lust and need to understand their human roles. Informed by the myths of Eden and the creation of woman from man's rib, the story centers on the Cropleigh family of Tennessee in the '8o's as they struggle with old guilts and human mysteries.

The complex pattern, beginning with the renunciation of a farm heritage in an attempt to recover a pre-Edenic innocence in the natural life of the woods, involves young Lucius Crey's progress from innocence to knowledge through Captain Crey's suicide, the discovery of his own bastardy, and his acceptance of human depravity and error. Lytle's extensive use of religious and sexual symbolism never becomes intrusive because it seems the natural language of the characters who introduce it, particularly of the hard-drinking philosopher mule-raiser and well-witcher, Jack Cropleigh, who, acting as Lucius's mentor, is often the point of view character. A wiser, more epigrammatic and cryptic observer than Faulkner's Ratliff, Uncle Jack also plays a larger, more intimately concerned role, involved at every turn until his involvement brings on his death. An intricately planned novel, *The Velvet Horn* retains a spontaneity and rich feeling of life that mark it as one of the finest products of the new tradition.

The central novelist of the new mode, and the most influential after Faulkner, is Kentuckian Robert Penn Warren. An early Fugitive at Vanderbilt, one of America's finest poets and critics, Warren began to write short stories in 1930, but published his first novel only nine years later. His novels exhibit his experience both as poet and critic, for he organizes them essentially like "metaphysical" poems, and his narrative techniques testify to his critical knowledge of the art form.

A philosophic novelist in the tradition of Conrad, Warren seeks out meaningful patterns in the data of experience and finds symbolic patterns in the flow of images. All of his novels have employed historic events for their factual base. As complements to this realism of the fact, he constructs the imagined stories, tracing out the ideal configuration which man's upstart mind must attempt to impose. Warren's novels always concern man's quest for personal identity—*Band of Angels* opens with Amantha Starr's cry, " 'Oh, who am I?' "—and consequently with his struggle to find a *modus vivendi* which can reconcile the world of indifferent fact and the mind's ideal constructions. The stories tend to be tragedies, for man is seldom capable of the self-knowledge and the integrated responsibility which discovery of his role in the world demands.

The Agrarian novel, *Night Rider* (1939), sets the pattern for all the later novels. Solidly grounded in the 1909 Kentucky tobacco wars between growers and big companies, the story concerns lawyer Percy Munn's doomed efforts to know himself through identification with a cause and with individuals. Warren introduces here, as in later novels, a commentative narrative, in which farmer Willie Proudfit, after westward wanderings, returns fully integrated in knowledge to his agrarian tradition. Here also the typical Warren technique of building recurring images into symbolic patterns is developed. Images of crowd and isolation, of lightness and dark, with concomitants of warmth and coldness, are immediately established. In complex development, they lead to the climactic scene, with the hunted Munn alone in the dark, which is the dark of womb innocence, spraying the night with false light and heat, "the blue frayed flame" of his blindly shooting pistol.

At Heaven's Gate (1943) takes for its historic base the Colonel Luke Lea case in Nashville during the 1920's, as *All the King's Men* (1946) takes that of Senator Huey Long of Louisiana in the 1930's. The former novel is the more complex, as it explores through several points of view the postwar generation's search for pragmatic values apart from their decadent traditions and the traditional moral restraints. A city novel, it exhibits as background the hollow artificiality of a rootless society. The image patterns which reinforce them derive from decay and this artificiality. The book abounds in pictures and metaphors involving filth, deformation, pus, pimples and dung. The false glitter of wealth and prestige is reflected in mirror images, sport, theatre art with its gilts and glints, all essentially unreal. The many voices of this novel—and Warren is a master of voices—are commented upon by the mountain evangelist dialect of Ashby Windham in the peripheral narrative, and by the impersonally cynical city-voice of the concluding sections.

All the King's Men, while it takes its protagonist narrator, Jack Burden, through a succession of modern philosophic positions, primarily opposes the two parts of dissociated modern man in the man of fact, Willie Stark, and the man of idea, Adam Stanton. Inevitably, these men are driven into violence that is fatal to both. Only Jack, whose adoption of surrogate fathers in his search for authority resembles that of Percy Munn, succeeds finally in accepting his sinful heritage and his responsibility toward self and society. Jack's rehabilitation is both projected and reinforced by a series of rebirth images and metaphors, coupled with water images of innocence and womb return. These reach their climax in Jack's return to his mother, whose scream, moaning, and drugged behavior snatching him from sleep herald his difficult return to responsible life.

All the King's Men won Warren a Pulitzer Prize, but it is a less completely satisfying novel than his previous two. Its ideological bones show through too sharply at times, and Burden's excursions into marriage with a sex machine and into various temporary philosophical havens are less than convincing. However, Warren's fertile creative imagination was never more evident; and his ear for voices, from Jack's smart-aleck cynicism and mature reflection to Willy's entourage with their babble of red-neck crudities, and to the grave speculative style of the Cass Mastern commentary narrative, was never keener. The voices themselves provide an echo of the book's dualistic theme.

In *World Enough and Time* (1950), Warren sets romantic idealism, rather than Stark's pragmatism, at the center of his story. Basing his novel on the once celebrated Beauchamp murder case in Frankfort, Kentucky, and on the Old Court versus New Court issues of the 1820's, he focuses the primary interest on Jeremiah Beaumont's tragic attempt to force his romantic ideals on a recalcitrant world represented by Wilkie Barron's practical opportunism, Percival Skrogg's fanaticism, and the Gran Boz's animalism. Again dominant images form patterns to extend the book's atmosphere and its meanings. A key cluster is formed around Kentucky's Indian name, meaning a "dark and bloody ground." Blood imagery from the opening page to the final head-severing permeates the scene. In conjunction, constant stage imagery reflects Jeremiah's conception of himself as a player in a high and noble tragedy.

A more philosophically conceived novel than his earlier ones, *World Enough and Time* employs three levels of insight, Jerry's immediate and reflective, and the author's in possession of the documents in his case. Speculation slows the pace of the story considerably, as Jerry and Warren brood over motive and meaning, but the extra dimension adds philosophic weight in compensation. Only in the commentative Gran Boz narrative, with its excessively depraved "naturalism," does the story's ironic high romance lack conviction.

Band of Angels (1955), concerned with the problem of freedom and centered on Amantha Starr, brought up as a Kentucky heiress only to discover her Negro blood, uses the history of New Orleans during the Civil War as its factual anchor. Less effectively planned than his previous novels, *Band of Angels* peters out beyond its mid-point in colorless episodes of Amantha's Midwestern married life which bring her finally to a lifeless rehabilitation. Up to this point, however, Warren manages with his usual skill and control a moving story of a heroine without the usual perspicacy to probe her dilemmas, for Amantha essentially has no mind to apply to her desperate problems. She develops one only at the expense of the story itself, after the reader has lost the involvement he requires.

Warren's final novel before the '60's, *The Cave* (1959), almost reverses the symbolic pattern of Lytle's *The Velvet Horn,* for where Lytle's major symbol is phallic, Warren's is vaginal. An historic cave exploration and entrapment supply the factual ground for the novel, but Warren has worked the womb aspect of his natural symbol until it palls. So many of these East Tennessee women, young and old, fall flat on their backs at the least male touch, so many illegitimate child-births bring redemptions to old people, and so many failures of the young to complete their affairs lead to frustration that one can only conclude that a freely copulating world is happy. Warren tells this story of a fatal exploration continuously in a cynically informed Jack Burden style, regardless of narrator, with far too many of the qualifications, repetitions, rejections and restatements, which characterized *World Enough and Time,* intruding on the progress of the narrative. Action begins only at page 150, and much thereafter is reaction, with the Greek Nick Papadoulapous's peripheral narrative seeming much less a commentation on the main theme than a perversive diversion. Warren's voice in this novel has lost its flexibility, and his touch with the real life of his area has lost its sensitivity. A 1962 novel, however, *The Wilderness,* suggests that he is seeking to recover the freshness of his early vision.

In the short stories and novelettes of Katherine Anne Porter, the symbolic naturalist tradition reached a new sort of perfection. In contrast to the Fugitive group and Faulkner, Miss Porter was born into a Southern family that, for all its earlier ties with Kentucky's and Louisiana's aristocratic heritages, had already in the new environment of Southeast Texas begun to shake off the traditional sanctities of code and agrarian tradition. Miss Porter had indeed to make her own kind of truce with the past, but her emotional requirements as an artist and woman have led her to a scrupulous examination of her present situation as an American and of her apprehensions for the future of her heritage in an unpredictable world. In one of her earlier autobiographical statements, she reported that "all the conscious and recollected years of my life have been lived to this day under the heavy threat of world catastrophe, and most of the energies of my mind and spirit have been spent in the effort to grasp the meaning of those threats, to trace them to their sources and to understand the logic of this majestic and terrible failure of the life of man in the Western world."

Miss Porter's search for meaningful values in the Western world led her early to Mexico, then to Europe. However, her artistic heritage, largely derived from Henry James, has led always to the individual circumstance, the private history, so that she has never succumbed to the lure of generalization or abstraction. Though she has been publishing stories since 1930, her total production to 1960 amounted to four volumes, including six novelettes and a score or so of short stories. A perfectionist, she writes slowly and will allow nothing but a finished product out of her hands.

Nothing in her technique differentiates Miss Porter from the norm of the new tradition. Her selective scrupulosity in detailing the natural scene and her inconspicuous, subtle manipulation of concrete symbols place her directly in the major Southern pattern. However, she sharply rejects the conservative agrarian ideology which is so often associated with symbolic naturalism. Professedly a liberal thinker, she began by attaching herself to revolutionary movements in Mexico, and her first stories, published under the title, *The Flowering Judas* (1930), dealt with Mexicans and expatriate Americans involved in the civil strife.

"Flowering Judas" itself, the first of her novellas, sets Miss Porter's high standard in a beautifully controlled, highly evocative account of a liberal American girl's relations to revolutionary activity in Mexico City. In her zeal to dedicate herself to a social ideal, Laura finds herself deeply involved with the powerful Braggioni, who is not only repulsive to her personally, but essentially a perversion of the ideals themselves. Wooed romantically also by a young Mexican, Laura finds herself hopelessly confused; her revolutionary sympathies confused with personal attachments and repulsions, her sense of life involved with death, her nights with days. Finally, through a nightmare sequence, she recognizes herself in the image of the flowering judas tree as betrayer both of herself and of the high purposes of the movement.

This story not only fixes Miss Porter's major style; it announces her major theme as well. Throughout her career, she has been primarily concerned with sounding the troubled social and political waters of our time. She has explored particularly the "terrible failure" which has beset every modern effort of men of good will to reform their mismanaged world. There are always cynical self-indulgent Braggionis or confused Lauras or others who betray the ideals and defeat the cause.

Four of Miss Porter's longer stories deal at various levels with man's propensity for defeating himself and his higher aims. The earliest of these, "Hacienda," like "Flowering Judas" set in Mexico and dealing with the political problem, shows the vaguely comprehended destructive force impelling a native to kill his sister. The girl narrator, visiting a hacienda where Russians, with American and Mexican government aides, are making a propaganda film, can only sense the stifling atmosphere of suspicion, censorship, and death which envelops the project. After the tragedy she can only escape.

Close in spirit to "Hacienda" but more explicit and effective in projecting its menaces and symbols is the Berlin story, "The Leaning Tower," title piece of her 1944 collection. This remarkably developed narrative, deceptively simple and natural in its day by day movement, builds its impact through a series of minor crises for an American painter temporarily resident in the German capital as Nazism begins its rise. The animal greediness of the natives, the deliberately infected dueling scar of a student boarder, the malicious nationalism of a celebrating crowd combine with the depressing atmosphere of the city itself to produce in Charles "a most awful premonition of disaster." Particularly in the symbol of the fragile plaster replica of Pisa's campanile, Miss Porter projects the half-understood but concretely menacing evil that is gathering. As in "Hacienda," the protagonist, with "the chill and the knowledge of death in him," is left with no choice but flight.

Escape from the threatening intrusion of a menacing force backed by a society cannot so well be managed by the native himself. In "Noon Wine," from the 1939 volume, *Pale Horse, Pale Rider,* a Texas farmer is brought dramatically face to face with a manifestation of socially sanctioned evil, destroys it, but is himself destroyed by the attendant guilt. An obnoxious representative of "law and order" arrives at Mr. Thompson's farm to earn a reward by turning over to justice as a criminal lunatic the Scandanavian handyman who for nine years has proved the quitely efficient "prop of the family." When the intruder goes after his man with knife and handcuffs, Mr. Thompson, blindly enraged, brains him with an axe. Acquitted, Mr. Thompson is tortured by a discrepancy between his memory of his defensive action and the clear facts which show him in the role of striking the first blow. He is driven to rehearse endlessly before neighbors his guiltlessness until their evident disbelief brings him to suicide. Miss Porter's narrative admits no reference beyond the frame limited by Mr. Thompson's first-person view, but social and political analogies readily suggest themselves.

It was perhaps inevitable that Miss Porter should follow her Southern compeers in fictional reassessment of her heritage, but she does it with a difference. Two long stories, "Old Mortality" and "Pale Horse, Pale Rider," plus six shorter pieces form a series of episodes and character sketches relating the childhood and early womanhood of a Miranda, whose year of birth and general history coincide with those of Katherine Anne Porter. Only the two longer pieces have been fully developed into independent works: the first constituting her most intensive treatment of the relevance of heritage; the second, her most intensive treatment of Miranda herself.

The primary concern in "Old Mortality," as well as in the short sketches, is the assessment of the older generations which embodied the family tradition; in particular the forceful and resourceful grand-mother, and the romantically enshrined great aunt, a tragic belle. When these narratives and portraits are viewed as a piece, Miss Porter's critique of her heritage, traced through Kentucky, Louisiana, and Texas, emerges clearly. Miranda's childish and expanding youthful perspectives gain reinforcement from the grandmother's, those of the family tradition, and from Negro sidelights. The resultant image of the past, with the dust of romance brushed away, reveals itself finally to Miranda as a sordid compound of hypocrisy, weakness and cruelty. Against the injustice of a double standard, the spoiling and preservation of ignorance, the sentimentally justified retreats from life, only the grandmother, reinforced by Negro servant women, stands as the bulwark of the saving reality principle. The pattern of gradual disillusionment which comes with understanding of the societal forces that throttle and falsify the individual's quest for a good life ties this series thematically to the other major section of Miss Porter's work. At the end of "Old Mortality" Miranda takes her stand with the grandmother against the falsities of the past and for a clear-eyed facing of life—but "in her hopefulness, in her ignorance."

"Pale Horse, Pale Rider," the most remarkable of Miss Porter's stories, exhibits particularly Miranda's lingering "ignorance." She has learned to reckon with the palpable hypocrisies and upsets of World War I, but not with the pangs of love or the influenza which accompanies man's grossest inhumanity. Her briefly known Army lover dies of the disease while she traverses illimitable stretches of time and pain in a hospital, to emerge alive only to an excruciating sense of loss. "Now there would be time for everything," Miranda thinks bitterly at the end. There is always time for the meaningless "everythings" in Miss Porter's world, but very little in a greedy, suspicious, and often inhuman society for self-fulfillment. In her long-awaited novel, *Ship of Fools,* published in 1962, she further brilliantly documents her pessimism from the viewpoints of two women who suggest the young Miranda and her older counterpart.

Whatever reservations one may hold about individual books, or even individual authors, the achievements of this first generation in the new tradition must be accounted truly remarkable. Nothing like this creative burst in quality and quantity has occurred in the history of American fiction. No section of the country has so suddenly sprung to literary eminence, and nowhere has artistic maturity been reached so quickly. All of these writers except Miss Glasgow, who experienced her own rebirth, published first novels or books of short stories within a span of ten years, and all of them continued to make careers of their writing. A number of them have become editors, critics, and teachers, as well as creators of fiction; and it has been this fact, together with the influence of their reputations, that has assured the perpetuation of their styles and methods. Particularly in the Fifties, as we shall note, does the effect of their critical and pedagogical activities make itself felt on a new generation of traditionalists. Each year of the past decade has produced a Spencer, a Taylor, a Styron, an O'Connor, a Jones, a Davis, a Sullivan, or a Hebson to carry on the best practice of modern Southern fiction.

4

NEW SOCIAL REALISM

If from the artistic point of view no other group of modern Southern writers closely approaches the level of the New Traditionalists, for sociological interest and significance the most important have been those who have used their fiction for searching criticism of sectional problems. The overwhelming majority of Renaissance novelists have been concerned deeply with the social issues of tradition, prejudice, farm and urban problems peculiar to the South. The more liberal critical spirits, however, have been little affected by the techniques which inspired the New Traditionalists. Realists, they have generally eschewed aesthetic complexities and told their stories straight, though the straightness of their narrative lines is sometimes a slanted one.

The Renaissance in fiction opened with the spate of 1922 novels, all of them problem novels with no relation to New Traditionalism. For these writers and most of their generation, the exemplary authors were Sinclair Lewis, Sherwood Anderson and the Chicago school, Eugene O'Neill and Ring Lardner, all of whom had turned their attention to new interpretations of provincial American life. But in fact models are irrelevant. The Twenties and early Thirties were dominated by sociological explorations and revaluations inspired by the social upsets of the war period. Southerners in particular had been jolted out of their old orientations. The young novelist, disturbed and observant, found the relatively untouched field of Southern provincialism stretching about him, bristling with a new growth of problems. To interpret them, he became amateur sociologist, economist, and psychologist as well.

The rash of 1922 novels from the South included one of the strongest and most poetically written sagas of the soil yet to be produced by an American, Edith Summers Kelley's *Weeds*. Miss Kelley's protagonist, sharecropper daughter and wife in Kentucky's tobacco and cornfields, is the prototype of a long line of cropper heroines, and she remains one of the most sensitively and impressively realized. A high-spirited girl, endowed with natural charm and a pagan love of earth and its animal life, Judy suffers the inevitable disillusionments and erosions contingent on her class position. With rich detail, Miss Kelley recounts the minutiae of daily drudgery in the fields, Judy's compulsive flights to woods and to music for compensation, and finally her problems with child-rearing and marital infidelty. In the end, both spiritually and physically exhausted, asking only peace and an empty security, Judy is left with a faithless husband and his hollow consolation, "We've got each other."

Weeds unfolds its sorry story with the relentless tragic honesty of a *Madame Bovary*. Carefully eschewing any form of overt irony or intrusive author comment, Miss Kelley presents the problem, highly individual in its complications but typical in its outline. Judy's heirs in fiction are legion, particularly during the next decades of depression and readjustment, but none of them has been so effectively realized and solidly presented as this first cropper protagonist.

The two most impressive successors to *Weeds* appeared in the following four years, one by the veteran Virginia novelist, Ellen Glasgow, and the other by the erstwhile poet, Elizabeth Maddox Roberts. A quarter of a century earlier Ellen Glasgow had published novels featuring poor white protagonists, but in none of them had she exhibited the intimate knowledge of rural realities which distinguish Miss Kelley's masterpiece. The major characters of *The Descendant* (1897), *The Voice of the People* (1900), and *The Miller of Old Church* (1911) are all men who, by special favor or ability, are quickly enabled in the fiction to escape their narrow backgrounds into larger lives, in which they become victims of the class prejudices which fascinate their author. However, as if sensitive to the new climate, Miss Glasgow in 1925 chose a poor white heroine for her first Renaissance novel, *Barren Ground*. It must be admitted that a slightly dated, Galsworthian air hovers over this often excellent novel. There is special pleading and a sequence of melodramatic incidents on which the plot creaks; but still in Dorinda Miss Glasgow has created one of the memorable women of modern Southern literature, a disillusioned romantic who carves a career for herself out of her disillusionment.

Elizabeth Maddox Roberts produced in 1926 her first novel, and in many ways her best, *The Time of Man*. The heroine of her low-keyed story is a Kentucky cropper girl who undergoes a series of alternations between happiness and tragedy as she is moved endlessly from farm to farm by her dissatisfied father and angry husband. Miss Roberts' version of the cropper's life has neither the tragic inevitability of Miss Kelley's version nor the opportunistic possibilities of Miss Glasgow's intense feminism; she emphasizes instead a rhythmic process where joy leads to sorrow and sorrow to joy. There is always the next farm, the possibilty of a big break in weather and prices. Despite another eviction, despite the expectation of a repetition in the pattern in sons and daughters, Miss Roberts creates an atmosphere of hope and potential release from the round of failure and dogged struggle which her novel projects.

A very different, polemic treatment of the white tenant problem, one which was to become characteristic of the Thirties and Forties, was inaugurated by a Texan, Dorothy Scarborough, with *In the Land of Cotton* (1924) and *Can't Get a Redbird* (1929). As a plantation daughter herself, Miss Scarborough is considerably more interested in farming problems than in her art. Her protagonist in the earlier novel is an owner's daughter who becomes involved in tenant problems, but large sections of the book are told from the point of view of a young tenant, devoted to the girl and finally killed in an eruption of nightriding. Miss Scarborough endows her cast with implausibly black and white characters, well distributed among privileged and underprivileged classes. What distinction she achieves rests in her clearheaded solutions of the agricultural problems of the time: she forecasts such reforms as crop and price control, extensive use of farm machinery, and government-backed loans, all of which were to be employed in the following decades.

Other novelists exploiting the sharecropper vein in the Twenties succeeded no better in producing literature and proved less adept at prognostication. Ruth Cross of Texas produced only a strained rags-to-riches romance in the *The Golden Cocoon* (1924), and Jack Bethea of Alabama, in *Cotton* (1928), melodramatized his unpalatable high-pressure solution to the farm problem. With the advent of the Depressing Thirties, however, a more realistic form of polemicism appears, particularly in the novels of Harry Kroll and Paul Green.

Kroll, brought up himself as a sharecropper's son in Tennessee and

Mississippi for the most part, brings a hard-bitten immediate knowledge to his *Cabin in the Cotton* (1931). Despite his rigged plot line, which unnecessarily stresses a hopeless poor boy-rich girl affair, Kroll effectively exposes the vicious practices which the tenant system encourages at both levels, of ownership and labor. On the one hand, he exhibits the cynical doctoring of accounts, the excessive interests and carrying charges, the bullying that enables the owners to keep their workers constantly in debt. At the same time, he plays up the thieving, brutish habits of the "peckerwoods," who are bent on cheating each other, as well as the bosses, and whose appetites and habits remain at a primitive level. In an overdone courtroom ending, Kroll proposes replacement of the tenant system by a cooperative farming plan, but the book realizes its impact solely from the harshly realistic presentation of system-bred corruption.

Paul Green, the most important dramatist to emerge from The Carolina Playmakers group, adopted the hill area poor whites as his major subject, not only for plays, but for short stories and two novels, *The Laughing Pioneer* (1932) and *This Body, the Earth* (1935). Green knows his subjects well and knows how to dramatize their often desperate problems. His weakness as an artist stems from the intensity of his sympathy with his subjects. Too often he lapses into sentimentality in his portrayals and special pleading in his denouements. Rural bigotries and inhumanities he exposes with the mordancy of a Sinclair Lewis, and often with Lewis's failure to create living human beings to embody them. In *The Laughing Pioneer,* a study in bigotry, the gay protagonist has early discovered the typical Green solution to the tenant farmer problem, breaking away for a troubador's wandering life. The crippled narrator is eventually enabled to make such a break from the stifling churchy environment when the Klannish pressures become too taxing. Superficially, *This Body, the Earth,* though it has a male protagonist, resembles Miss Kelly's *Weeds.* A solidly realistic story of an ambitious sharecropper son who scorns and defies his shiftless parents to attain ownership himself, Green's novel plays up the landlord-banker combination, plus the lure for women of city social life, to effect the defeat of the independent agrarian ideal. Back in tenant status, the broken Alvin dies before he can effectively aid his promising son, and the story ends its bitter cycle where it had begun, without prospect for the future. *This Body* is Green's most serious and impressive fictional work, but it lacks the poetry, the humanizing moments of warmth that lift a novel like *Weeds* out of the category of bitter chronicle into literature.

Among other first generation novelists, William Faulkner and Erskine Caldwell have devoted novels to Southern poor whites while basically ignoring the tenant farmer problem. Faulkner's exclusive concern with the moral history of his region precludes attention to the economic aspects of his agrarian philosophy. Caldwell's interest in his Ty-Tys and Jeeters is phenomenological and sentimental. Though he betrays strong liberal biases, the situations he sets are contrived largely to reveal the colorful degeneracy of his odd creations.

The major pattern which emerges from the serious cropper novels of the Twenties and early Thirties is a consistent one: the sensitive protagonist grows up in the throttling system, which is realistically analyzed and recorded, then seeks desperately either to escape its frustrations or to force reforms upon it, generally without success. For the system itself, there are no apologists. Quite as effectively as the industrial sweatshop system of the nineteenth century, Southern sharecropping, it would appear, squeezes the lives out of its victims, while it inevitably breeds dishonesty and brutality in owners and workers alike. Yet, the writers who record these conditions in the early Renaissance retain an objectivity which the socially oriented Victorian novelist seldom managed. There are few Fagins and no Oliver Twists in the Southern novels; there is little mounting of rostrums for author orations on the iniquities of the system. All the significant authors have learned to confine their judgments within the characters' viewpoints, thereby increasing both intensity and conviction. There is no radical among the group; the authors generally visualize their roles as those of social historians, without bias or preconception. Evidently, however, in the context of the conservative agrarian policy of the time and the practice of their elders, they appear as a challenging, liberal new generation.

Fiction devoted to the problems of the Negro by white Southern authors has been the most remarkable development of the Renaissance. Since 1920 some eighty-five such volumes written wholly or largely from the Negro's point of view have been published by reputable concerns—and I exclude such "entertainments" as those appearing under the signatures of South Carolina's Octavus Roy Cohen and Kentucky's Irving S. Cobb. Another forty or fifty volumes may be added with the inclusion of novels by Southern Negroes themselves and those by white authors dealing from a white point of view with Negro problems. These writers portray Negroes from all of the Southern states and all of the major occupational groups. They explore the most intimate details of domestic and working life with a realism that has become more and more convincing with each generation.

During slavery days and through the later nineteenth century, a smattering of Negro-centered fiction emanated from the white South, but most often it took the form of testimonials from reputedly happy slaves or loyal employees. Or they were minstrel-like exhibitions of dialectal Negro humor and eccentricity. Until 1920, nothing more significant than the Uncle Remus stories of Joel Chandler Harris, the Creole novels of George W. Cable, and the local color stories of Cable and Thomas Nelson Page had appeared.

The new era was ushered in by a group of sympathetically written short stories and sketches from the pen of the veteran Louisville novelist, George Madden Martin, *Children of the Mist* (1920). But the major irruption came suddenly in 1922 when three white Southerners, natives of Tennessee, Texas, and Alabama, published serious problem novels written wholly or in large part from the point of view of Negro protagonists. From this abrupt beginning, the production of Negro-oriented fiction has swelled with each decade, and quality has more than kept pace with numbers. The most startling feature of this activity has been the increasing part played by women, and particularly young women, in portraying intimate Negro life. In 1921 the young New Orleans magazine, *The Double Dealer,* was protesting against "the treacly sentimentality with which our lady fictioneers regale us." In the Fifties the lady fictioneers are thoroughly at home with Negro husbands and wives, unsentimentally familiar with Negro bars and off-hour crap games. Though more slowly than in traditional forms, Southern Negro-view fiction has matured, and to the point where it can claim half a dozen books of very high literary quality and convincing humanity.

A definite, if uneven, pattern of development can be traced in the history of white-authored Negro-view fiction since 1922. During the Twenties and early Thirties, the emphasis was chiefly sociological and often betrayed a residual sense of white superiority. The local color patterns inherited from turn-of-the-century fiction were in general modified only by a new seriousness of purpose or more thorough study of the subjects. Still, the approach remained largely phenomenalistic. With the Depression of the Thirties and the following recovery years, the emphasis underwent a radical change. The characteristic novel of the Thirties and Forties is decidedly antitraditional. Specific Negro problems on farm and in industry are faced with a new head-on directness. The widespread liberalism of this period penetrates deeply into the South and results in a spate of polemical novels. Finally, in the Fifties, a further shift into what can only be termed humanistic treatment asserts itself. The later Negro-view writers for the most part abandon the case history and the tendentious approach and begin to treat the Negro simply as a human individual.

In the first generation, the unevenness of this historical development is dramatically illustrated at the outset, for the three pioneering novels of 1922 all belong properly in the second, or problem-facing, phase. None of these books is impressive as a work of art, but all have their interesting and informative aspects. Clement Wood's *Nigger* describes in a loose, episodic manner a Negro family's unending search for the "emancipation" promised them by Lincoln's Proclamation. The novel's most notable feature is the singlemindedness with which it exposes the repressive tactics of farmers during Reconstruction and modern Birmingham officials and employers in their determination to prevent any effective realization of the Negroes' dream of freedom. Wood allows no palliatives in his implied condemnation of white injustice, for he never leaves the thwarted family's own view of their efforts and frustrations. The younger generation, city-bred, attempts every means, licit and illicit, to establish the security and independence which the grandfather's dream envisions, but education, work, thievery and whoredom all fail. The dream of emancipation becomes finally only the hallucination of the old man's unhinged mind.

Hubert Shands' *White and Black* presents a picture of white farmers hardly less harsh than that of Wood, but his Negroes exhibit equal natural depravity, together with less intelligence. His plantation owners and tradesmen not only exploit the Negroes' gullibility without compunction, but, because of the scarcity of white women, regularly seduce the tenants' daughters and wives. A particularly "bad

nigger's" rape of a trashy white girl precipitates a lynching and wholesale persecution of the innocent. While Shands' picture of conditions
rings true, his puerile style and naive solutions for his problems heavily
damage the book's effectiveness. The author's spokesman insists that
justice must be done at all costs, while the Negroes recognize their
race as inferior; yet the two groups must be taught to respect one
another. In terms of his story, neither race offers much to be
respected for, and inferiority is rather presumed than actually
presented.

T. S. Stribling's *Birthright* suffers in similar fashion from intrusion
of the author's unjustified conclusions. The novel, clearly under the
influence of *Main Street*, introduces the mulatto, Peter Siner, as the
cultured reforming spirit of Hooker's Bend, Tenn., and he achieves
a failure no less complete than that of Carol Kennicutt in Gopher
Prairie, Minn. Peter's attempts to improve the educational, sanitary,
and moral conditions of the Negro populace meet hypocritical, cynical,
swindling opposition from the white business community, and
ignorance, fear, and brutality from the Negroes. Despite the lurid
melodrama of some of the Negro scenes, *Birthright* reflects, in the
main, honest observation. However, the author often violates his
protagonist's viewpoint in order to insert his own fictionally unjustified
opinions. His racial views attribute Peter's better qualities to his seven-
eights white blood, his moral weaknesses to the Negro residue, though
he does not allow us knowledge of Peter's parents.

After this challenging, if not distinguished, beginning in 1922, the
Negro-view genre in fiction quickly deserted the problem approach for
the more congenial one of sociologically oriented investigation, or
local color. A rash of books, by Edward C. L. Adams of Georgia,
Howard Odum of North Carolina, John B. Sale of Mississippi, Robert
Emmett Kennedy of Louisiana, and Roark Bradford of Tennessee
record the lore, the dialects, the idiosyncrasies of town and country
Negro groups. The authors display considerable insight, not a little
humor, and, at least in the case of Kennedy—*Gretny People* (1927)
and *Red Bean Row* (1929)—story-telling ability. None of these books
is properly a novel, nor yet a sociological study, and in the case of
the popular Roark Bradford particularly, quaintness of language, however unauthentic, and an equal quaintness of hyperbolic action and
belief, cover a multitude of distortions and literary shortcomings.

Bradford's Negro preachers and folk heroes are essentially cariacatures, and their stories a series of repetitious exaggerations calculated to please an undiscriminating public.

On a higher literary plane, but still essentially within the category of local color, are the novels of Dubose Heyward and Julia Peterkin. Heyward's *Porgy* (1925), with the titular addition of *Bess* and Gershwin music, still tours the world, and Miss Peterkin's *Scarlet Sister Mary* won the Pulitzer Prize for fiction in 1929, but neither of these books represents a significant achievement, either as a portrayal of Southern Negro life or as permanent literature. Heyward's genuine interest in Charleston Negro types is evident, but both Porgy's loneliness and Bess's weaknesses are handled sentimentally, and his story finally turns sensational in its search for a climax. Later, in his 1929 novel, *Mamba's Daughters,* Heyward displays a considerably more mature understanding of the various levels of Charleston's Negro society, and his treatment of the Negro sections of the book surpass any previous writing in the genre. Unfortunately, however, the author here introduces semiautobiographical sections of considerable length, and these white-view areas lack both the objectivity and the artistry of the Negro portions.

Miss Peterkin's novels, all of them Negro-bound, display an old Southern weakness, despite their basis in intimate observation; her Negroes are represented as curious phenomena with sensationally odd characters. The fundamental traits she exploits are moral irresponsibility and savage superstition. *Scarlet Sister Mary* gained wide popularity for its lurid mixture of sexual promiscuity, religion, and superstition, with authenticity guaranteed by its author's position as mistress of a large South Carolina plantation. But this novel in particular lacks conviction—*Black April* is perhaps her best. In none of her four books of fiction do basic economic and social problems figure, and white owners appear only as vague beneficent deities.

Miss Peterkin's attitudes appear again in Georgian Nan Bagby Stephens's *Glory* (1932), essentially an expose of Negro gullibility in a suburb, which loses its head over a flamboyant and crooked new minister. Another prize novel, Lily Alexander's *Candy* (1934), winner of a $10,000 Dodd Mead award, exhibits Miss Peterkin's unrealistic conception of owner benevolence, and adds its own author's sentimentality. The book celebrates the loyal, if sexually vagrant Negress,

Candy, while it deplores the ingratitude and shortsightedness of the mass of plantation Negroes who desert the Depression-ridden South Carolina home place for the wicked lure of Harlem.

With the Depression years, economic and social problems of the Negro replace descriptive phenomenology as the major subject for white novelists. No Negro-view novels deal directly with the impact of the Depression on the race, but the new intellectual climate of the Thirties brought socio-economic issues to immediate prominence for Southern novelists as for those from other parts of America. The Negro problem novel takes up in 1930 from the point where Wood, Shands, and Stribling had left it in 1922. Gilmore Millen of Memphis inaugurated the revival on a new level of powerful realism with his *Sweet Man,* a totally Negro-view novel centering on the development of white-hatred. John Henry, a "good nigger," working hard and well to earn a house and land of his own in the Mississippi Delta country, is so continually cheated in crop payments and book-juggling by owners and agents that he deserts a loved and loving wife to take his chances in city life. As a kept "sweet man" of prostitutes in Memphis's early jazz-era Beale Street—described with brilliant intimacy and color—and as a liquor-still worker, John Henry is pushed farther and farther into hatred of the master race. After a jail term for knifing an obnoxious white-trash drunkard, he lives through a prison term and, in a super-fluous anticlimactic ending, murders the rich white woman who has kept him as a "sweet man" in California.

No novelist before Negro Richard Wright has described so boldly and effectively as Millen the molding, through oppression and rank injustice, of a dangerous enemy to the white race. But Millen's vigorous social realism quickly became the typical form for white writers dealing with Negro life. For the second generation of the Renaissance, the social and economic handicaps of the Negro worker on the farm and in the city occupy the center of interest. The particular problem of the mixed-blooded outcast becomes a primary concern with a number of novelists, most notably William Faulkner in *Light in August.* Finally in this period also the scope of the historical novel is expanded by a series of slave-centered stories.

Southern Negroes themselves virtually did not participate in the opening phase of the Renaissance. Not until the mass movement of the Thirties to Harlem and other Northern centers did the Negro begin to develop his own Renaissance, and even then the Southern Negro played a comparatively minor role, Richard Wright standing as the major exception. During the Twenties, the only two notable achievements in fiction by Southern Negroes were Jean Toomer's very uneven but often poetic volume, *Cane* (1923), and Walter Francis White's two fiery novels, *Fire and the Flint* (1924) and *Flight* (1926). Toomer, of Louisiana Creole stock, though born in Washington, D. C., was educated largely in the North and began writing as a poet in association with the early liberal Harlem group. *Cane* was the result of an attempt to reassimilate his Negro heritage through the experience of teaching school in Georgia. The book is a strange formless mixture of sketches, strained poetic passages in prose and verse, brief episodes and semidramatic pieces, all relating to a sensitive Negro in Georgia and Washington practically stifled by the racial and religious attitudes displayed by his own race and the whites. *Cane* throbs throughout with emotion, but it is emotion unmastered and undirected toward any form of resolution.

Walter White, son of an Atlanta postman who died from an unattended injury, was early embittered but unable to leave the South until, at twenty-five he joined the N.A.A.C.P. His two novels are frankly propagandistic and inflammatory, the work of an effective polemicist rather than of a literary artist; their distinction is simply that of pioneering in a fictional area later to be heavily populated.

When the first generation of Renaissance writers turned its attention to the town and city, it was not to discover, as its successors would, the problems of labor and industry, nor yet those of politics. Even the new social situation precipitated by shifts in wealth and status from an established society group to the parvenus did not make itself felt as a prime issue through this period. Personal alienations and clashes between generations, liberal protests against outworn mores and attacks on bigotry were more common than defenses of tradition against social invasion. The novels often developed criticism of the towns' moral climate as devastating as that of Lewis's *Main Street,* but the psychological problems of the young took precedence over public issues.

The more important interpreters of town life in the earlier period came from the more northern tier of states: Kentucky, Tennessee and

Virginia. Uniformly, the locale of their novels is the small town or village, their subject gossip and prejudice. Emanie Sachs published *Talk* in 1924, and it was immediately labeled "a Kentucky *Main Street.*" The novel does pit a girl against a town, which finally breaks her spirit, but social smugness and gossip provide the agency, not parsimony and boorishness, and Delia seeks only to live her own life, not to reform the town's. T. S. Stribling's Agatha Pomeroy, however, as a Northern former actress married to a Tennessee farmer, does attempt to reform the complacently corrupt village to which she comes in *Bright Metal* (1928). Her defeat, despite her damning exposures, is largely a product of stupid prejudices, antifeminism, prying, and again talk. Despite an unsatisfactory ending, Stribling's book contains telling exposures of village hypocrisies in economical, well-paced prose. The same author's *Teeftallow* (1924) has its share of hill town exposures, but its scattershot method and obvious exaggeration rob it of any true effectiveness.

Three very different pictures of Southern town life develop from the varied focuses of Virginians Stanley Hopkins and Murrell Edmunds, and North Carolina and Alabama's Ward Greene. Mrs. Hopkins' slow-paced but solid *The Ladies* (1933) follows the unfulfilled lives of four sheltered daughters of a village institution, a widower who teaches them only excessive modesty and reliance on men. The distinction of this novel, as of her second, lies in the sense of reality and of fatality which the author is able to create in detailing essentially meaningless lives. In *Sixth of June* (1935), a more complex but uncentered work, Mrs. Hopkins assembles a far-flung wealthy Jewish family for a wedding and probes the old ties and animosities as the guests meet again and establish new relationships. As unusual as Mrs. Hopkins' treatment of Jews in the South is Murrell Edmunds' story of German musicians in *The Music Makers* (1927), much the best of Edmunds' numerous books. Later an angry liberal, he offers here a reminiscent little tragedy set in Lynchburg and involving the conflict of musical ambitions with humanitarian idealism and love. Told from a remove and in a minor key, the novel effectively creates the atmosphere of its little cultural island and the tragic tone of frustrated ideals and ambitions.

Ward Greene, though he often skirts dangerously close to the tough school and the detective mystery, knows his Southern town society and presents it with lurid harshness in several of his fast-paced novels. *Cora Potts* (1929) gives a cynical account of the rise of a rebellious country girl from mistress to whorehouse madam, to manufacturer of patent medicines and dentrifices, and finally to marriage into an aristocratic family. A solider novel, *Weep No More* (1932), shifts about among the women of the social drinking set of a Southern city in 1930, exposing a society which has abandoned morals and no longer finds fun in its violations of traditional codes. *Death in the Deep South* (1936), though ostensibly a murder story, is chiefly concerned to expose the parts played by newspapers, politics, and prejudice in the conviction and lynching of a Northern man involved in the killing of a Southern girl student. As always with Greene, the story moves rapidly through taut scenes with sharp revelations, but also with the temptation to overplaying and melodrama not adequately resisted.

A number of other early authors played interesting variations on the social and psychological problems besetting Southern towns and their nonconformist young. From Georgia, Laurence Stallings and Berry Fleming produced novels of considerable substance, Stallings' *Plumes* (1924) a bitterly ironic treatment of a crippled war veteran in postwar years and Fleming's several Thirties' novels accounts of the struggles of sensitive Southerners transplanted to New York and to the Riviera. Welbourn Kelley of Alabama, Harry Hervey and Dorothy Scarborough of Texas, George Looms and Laetitia McDonald of Kentucky, Celeste Lindsay of Northern Georgia, George O'Neal of Alabama, and Jennings Perry of Tennessee wrote uneven novels containing sound social and psychological observation. Probably the best of these, however, are Virginian Roy Flannagan's two satirical novels of the Thirties. *The Whipping* (1930) presents a highly diverting account of moral prejudice applied to a lushly attractive girl, whose tender skin tempers punishment as tolerance and humanity cannot. *County Court* (1937), featuring a fine pagan spirit in the role of behind-the-scenes defender for a girl accused of uxoricide, offers shrewdly accurate, vigorously drawn pictures of small-town characters, together with a sprightly originality of style and incident.

5

NEW APPROACHES:
YOUTH, REGION,
AND HISTORY

An inevitable ingredient of any new literary movement is youth's rebellion against the precedents established or preserved by the parental generation. In the postwar world of "the lost generation," revolt, personal, moral, and artistic, reached epidemic stages among the disillusioned youth of Europe and America. The era of Dadaism, Vorticism, Futurism, of literary magazines like *Blast, Secession, Broom, The Enemy,* and *transition,* was founded primarily on the failure of the elders to provide moral, political, and economic solutions to the century's complex problems. But revolutionary attitudes among the sensitive writers extended beyond these concerns to matters of artistic and literary form as well. At the extremes, hatchets were handed out to visitors at art exhibitions and portions of telephone directories served as poems. More generally, the writer sat down to record his alienation from a world given over to material values and bloody solutions.

Like the rest of the Western world, the South developed its famous rebels, like Maxwell Bodenheim of Mississippi, and its great "lost" spokesman in Thomas Wolfe of North Carolina. Before the appearance of *Look Homeward, Angel* in 1929, a considerable literature involving the sensitive youth's rebellious disaffection had already appeared in the South. Two gifted young women in particular deserve places in the foreground of the new fiction for their treatment of revolt from family tradition and search for meaningful values. Evelyn Scott, a child prodigy from Clarksville, Tennessee, growing up in New Orleans and producing stories which were printed when she was fourteen, initiated the type with her autobiographical *Escapade* in

1923. Already, she had published a volume of poetry and a play, as well as two somewhat premature novels: *The Narrow House* (1921), a rather badly written but sincere attempt to depict marital misery; and *Narcissus* (1922), a considerably more promising study of the self-loving and the self-loathing in a Bohemian set of artistic young people.

The particular "escapade" with which Miss Scott's third story deals is her flight to Brazil at twenty with a married biologist. With both families and the societies which they represent opposing them, and with Brazil itself inhospitable in climate as well as in native attitudes, the couple's story is one of desperate struggles against every sort of affliction and oppression. Miss Scott describes with acute sensitivity the place and the people, capturing with unforgettable sharpness the degradation of lives lived in poverty, filth, illness, and the mental anguish of the persecuted. *Escapade* is, as the subtitle calls it, *A Fragment of an Autobiography,* but its success, as literature, depends in no way on the verity of its fact.

Unlike many of her contemporaries who proved unable to escape the restrictions of the autobiographical pattern, Miss Scott went on to produce distinguished novels in a variety of more objective genres, including a Tolstoian religious tragedy set in New England, *The Golden Door* (1925); an unusual kaleidoscopic treatment of the Civil War, *The Wave* (1929); an intellectual study of ideals and sexual relations in *Eva Gay* (1933); and a nonconformist experiment, *Bread and a Sword* (1937). Similarly, a second precocious Tennessee girl, Carmen Barnes, who published her first novel, *School Girl* (1929), when she was sixteen and reached the best-seller list with it, went on to produce three other popular novels, then reached fictional maturity with a complex, interestingly constructed story, *Time Lay Asleep,* (1946), about a young woman's attempt through sharp and sensitive re-creations of her childhood and family histories to discover directions and meanings for herself.

In many ways the most brilliant of these women, Frances Newman of Atlanta, published her first novel of sensitive youth only after she had reached the maturity of thirty-eight, but it proved one of the most stimulating and controversial books of its era. *The Hard-Boiled Virgin* (1926) exhibits one of the rarest of virtues in Southern fiction, true originality both in conception and style. Sensitive as well as highly intelligent, Miss Newman turned sharply away from her Southern belle training to search for new emotional and literary values in New

York and Paris. Her suicide in 1928, precipitated by blindness and pneumonia, was her final rebellious act following publication of her second fine novel, *Dead Lovers Are Faithful Lovers.*

In the presentation of her semiautobiographic story, *The Hard-Boiled Virgin,* Miss Newman adopts a quiet, unobtrusively ironic tone, omits dialogue entirely, and, in firmly chiseled and often aphoristic declarative sentences, details the painful processes by which a brightly intelligent and self-conscious girl attempts to prepare herself for woman's proper end, a "good marriage." Fearful as a child of being unable to muster the proper appeals for the proper man, Katherine Faraday gradually develops an elaborate technique, carefully memorizing the interests of prospective husbands. She succeeds so well in interesting them that she is forced to retreat into a protective virginal complex. The author, despite her clear sympathy with Katherine's emotional problems, holds rigidly and lucidly to her amused, ironic view of the heroine, as well as to those of her less than satisfactory suitors.

Dead Lovers, written in the same cleanly objective and witty style, is little less successful as a novel, though the author conveys less sense of identification with her two women protagonists and less warmth in her treatment of them. The opening section presents, from the point of view of a fashionable young bride in Atlanta and Richmond, an ironically devastating portrait of high Southern society. The view shifts in the second part to that of the highly perceptive mistress of the bride's husband in New York. The reversion to the wife in the final section exhibits her safely and happily widowed, bearing back from New York the corpse, whose infidelity she need no longer suspect and fear. Both pitiful and pitiless in its witty picture of the nice girl's dilemma, the novel takes no moral position and allows no sentimental lapses.

The youthful idealist in conflict with his immediate heritage and that of his society dominates a number of semiautobiographic novels of the Twenties, including those of Maryland's Fulton Oursler, later to achieve tremendous popularity as a rediscoverer of the West's Christian heritage in terms of simplified retellings of New Testament stories. Oursler's four early novels, all dealing with frustrated young married men aspiring beyond their prosaic circumstances, possess, at least initially, a zest and a satiric flair. His brush company clerk-artist in *Behold This Dreamer* (1924), his sensitive piano salesman in *Sandalwood* (1925), his poet-advertising man in *Stepchild of the Moon* (1926), and his experimental girl and would-be writer in *Poor Little Fool* (1928) have in common dissatisfied spirits and young aspirations toward the artistically oriented life. But Oursler's enthusiasm and his ironic integrity fail him increasingly. He falls back on easy romantic solutions, then gives up serious work to become a prolific hack writer, chiefly of biographical romances.

Two young Tennesseans with a light touch contributed brightly told tales of the Twenties to his genre. Jennings Perry's *Windy Hill* (1926), though thin in its characterizations of the romantic young hero and the cool hometown siren, has the virtues of sharp observation and amusing commentary. Ridley Wills, one of the early Fugitive group, produced two early novels distinguished by their amused ironic tone in describing the aberrancies of sensitive youth: *Hoax* (1922) and *Harvey Landrum* (1924). In *Ethan Quest, His Saga* (1925), Harry Hervey of Texas, author of three exotic romances, presents a married idealist who deserts family and security for a disillusioning life of vagabondage in the Far East. Less adventurous, Lella Warren's girl protagonist in *A Touch of Earth* (1926) proceeds from illicit affairs to a settled role as wife, mother, and author. Texans Frank Elser and Donald Joseph project overidealistic protagonists, Elser's ambitious newsman in *The Keen Desire* (1926) being unable to find true satisfactions outside of his imaginative life, and Joseph's college youth, in *October's Child* (1929), discovering betrayals in the mother and the roommate whom he had naively worshipped. Georgian John Fort in his first book, *Light in the Window* (1928), offers an incredibly innocent son of a Southern colonel led on to catastrophe by a Northern girl; while Edith Taylor Pope's *Not Magnolias* (1928), another first novel, gives us a more believable sensitive college girl in a not quite credible series of emotional complications.

All of these minor novels betray in varying aspects and degrees the faults of excess to which the sensitive romantic, and particularly the young romantic, is liable. Unlike Miss Newman, in particular, they fail to attain the novelist's proper objectivity and balance. The result is often an embarassing excess of self-concern or an unconvincing excess of apparent self-satire, equally embarrassing for the reader. These faults, together with the formlessness which almost invariably accompanies them, we must recognize as the limitations of Thomas Wolfe's genius. It is instructive to view them in all but pathological exaggeration in the novels of Wolfe's contemporary, Howell Vines of Alabama. Gifted like Wolfe with an exuberant talent, Vines carries every virtue to the limits of romantic excess. Not at all a rebel, Vines seems to dwell constantly in a paradisal world of his own manufacture, though its location is not far from the hellish smelter fires of Bessemer and Birmingham. *A River Goes With Heaven* (1930) details with never-flagging ecstasy and prolixity a summer-long love affair of the young protagonist with nature on the Warrior River and with Halma, a "lavender-skinned" and obviously soulful beauty who worships him to distraction. Everyone in the cast of this novel, in fact, including five lovely brown-eyed girls who love him and Halma equally, tells him that he is clearly a genius. Though nothing is adduced in the book itself to justify the epithet, young Hal Lister does not dispute their insight. It is true, certainly, if we may identify author and protagonist, as we seem clearly meant to do, that he displays real ability at poetic description of nature, animated by what is evidently a deeply felt pantheism. Even these virtues, however, undergo a species of cancerous development in his second novel, *A Green Thicket World* (1934), proliferating into a fantastic mystic symbolism, involving the apostrophized trees, river, red birds, sexual matings at every level, violent deaths, and metamorphoses.

There can be no question of Thomas Wolfe's stature as the giant among American writers of sensitive youth fiction. Everything about him suggests the gargantuan: his energy, his appetites, his talents, his Whitmanesque love of self, of earth, and of humanity. Whatever may be said, and a great deal must be said of his lack of discipline, literary and personal, and of his debt to his perceptive editor, Maxwell Perkins, *Look Homeward, Angel* (1929) remains the most poetically impressive first novel produced in the renascent South.

Look Homeward, Angel qualifies no better than Wolfe's other three major novels as an artistic masterpiece, for Wolfe's genius is essentially discursive and self-indulgent. He writes rather in the manner of the intimate diarist than that of the creator of a work of art. His talent is for recording, with rare insight and command of language, the whole flux of experience, not for seeking and working out the patterns of significance in the record. Everything that occurs to the highly sensitive man, Wolfe, is immediately grist for his mill; the sound of a river's name as relevant as a father's death or the feel of a train cushion or a first experience with sex. His appetite for experience is immense, but he lacks an organ for transforming the raw stuff into digestible form. Perhaps because he is so voracious of values, he cannot integrate them into any hierarchical order. His is a democracy of taste carried to the limits of anarchy. The brilliance of poetic evocation and language, therefore, with which he presents Eugene Gant's North Carolina childhood, adolescent loves and losses in *Look Homeward, Angel,* and the insatiable adult quests of his other alter egos in *Of Time and the River* (1935), *The Web and the Rock* (1939), and *You Can't Go Home Again* (1940), succeeds in producing not four novels but the single extraordinarily detailed life history of a romantic sensibility.

The novel offers an appealing but treacherous form for a man of Wolfe's sensitive capacities and his intoxication with language, for its amplitude, both quantitative and qualitative, constitutes a continuous temptation to overindulgence. The incautious and underdisciplined tend to throw into its maw all the scraps of poetry, essay, and fantasy that come piping hot out of their sensibilities. Wolfe, an inchoate poet and dramatist, required all the discipline which those stricter forms tend to enforce. Yet, as his experience in drama at the University of North Carolina and Harvard demonstrate, he felt frustrated at the restrictions which demands of the theatre forced upon his expressive urges.

Look Homeward, Angel exemplifies all of Wolfe's very real virtues, in addition to a freshness, a Thoreauvian dawn sense, that the later volumes increasingly lack. Like most romantics of his type, he deals most effectively with childhood and adolescence, for in those years of legitimate self-absorption the egocentrist finds his most congenial terrain. On the less compliant ground of the adult world and responsibility, he tends to slip over into self-pity or unfocused bitterness. Wolfe's reiterated "O lost! Lost!" is the perennial cry of the disoriented adult yearning back to the child's self-centered undemanding universe. The re-creation of this universe, in his best short stories as well as in *Look Homeward, Angel,* constitutes Wolfe's major achievement. Peopling it with the hugely dominant figure of old Gant and many another drawn more than life-sized in their passions, their obsessions, and their eccentricities, heightening the emotions and even nature itself, he creates a legitimate child-perspective, eminently proper to the personality of young Eugene.

However, when essentially the same perspective is applied to the teacher and student of *Of Time and the River*, the reader can but feel embarrassingly the lack of emotional maturity in the point of view. In place of the objective picture of the frustrated romantic, as we have it in *Madame Bovary*, we get only Tom Wolfe, perpetual adolescent blundering and bleeding in an indifferent universe to which he cannot accommodate himself. Still, Wolfe, and particularly the young Wolfe, will continue to be read, and not only because the sensitive romantic is always with us. Such brilliant characterizations as those of the elder Gants are not common in our literature, and such scenes as those of Ben's death are rare enough in any fiction. And in excerpts at least Wolfe's work will continue to haunt anthologists, for he remains one of America's finest poets in prose.

Of Wolfe's immediate successors in the first generation, only two are noteworthy, though Zelda Fitzgerald's frantic and incoherent bid to rival husband F. Scott's fame, *Save Me the Waltz* (1932), provides an instructive lesson in misguided ambition. Green Peyton of the notable Virginia family of Wertenbakers wrote two serious novels in which sensitive young protagonists face problems of heritage, land attachment, and sexual attractions. *Black Cabin* (1933) has youthful faults of excessive analysis and flimsy structure, but its emotions ring with authenticity. More mature and in every way better written, *Rain on the Mountain* (1934) centers on a young man's attempt to return to a heritage and haunting past. The perspectives which the story develops out of complex personal relationships, the pretenses and violences bred of a decadent code, and the hectic times lead to recognition of change and to a final desertion of the South. Poet John Peale Bishop's second venture in fiction, *Act of Darkness* (1935), is a badly organized novel, with the first-person story of an adolescent's sexual development invaded by a more lurid account of his uncle's moral lapse and subsequent trial. Bishop's book exhibits true sensitivity and considerable psychological penetration; its structural weakness serves once again to illustrate the besetting weakness of the youth genre.

The two literary genres in which the pre-Renaissance South had been most prolific, if we exclude sentimental verse, were local color fiction and the historical novel. The distinction between local color and regionalist fiction, like that between the true historical novel and historical romance is not always easy to draw. To define local color writing as that which chiefly emphasizes "individualities of background, dialect, and custom" is to fail to provide a sharp enough tool for critical differentiation. If the crucial area of demarcation can be isolated, it must be found to lie in the author's point of view toward his material. If he regards his subjects as phenomena whose peculiarities excite interest, rather than as human beings whose problems in part stem from their peculiar backgrounds, he can surely be labeled a local colorist. Thus George Washington Cable, Kate Chopin, and Grace King of the earlier period most often demonstrate their colorism by their finger-pointing phenomenalistic approach to their Louisiana Creole characters. So in the Renaissance proper such highly popular writers as Erskine Caldwell and Jesse Stuart for the most part produce such exhibitions as Ty Ty and the Tussie family. It matters not at all apparently that the author be himself a native, subject to all the special influence of environment and tradition; the colorist still writes like the wide-eyed foreign observer or investigator.

One on the major areas of local color interest in the South during the late nineteenth and early twentieth centuries had been the relatively inaccessible mountain regions of Kentucky, Virginia, North Carolina, and Tennessee. A tradition of melodramatic and sentimental fiction, heavily overlaid with color, had been firmly established in popularity by such novelists as Charles Neville Buck, Mary Murphree, and John Fox, Jr. The transition into the Renaissance era is certainly less abrupt in this Blue Ridge-Cumberland area than in any other, but even here the new authors of the Twenties and Thirties take their region more seriously than as a colorful setting for lurid feud tales, romances of "Lonesome Pine" girls, and religious tracts.

As was the case with the treatment of the Negro, the mountaineer appeals to the early Renaissance novelist as a subject for sociological, linguistic, and economic study. For Maristan Chapman (pseudonym for a Tennessee wife, British husband team) the fascination seems largely linguistic as they rediscover the lingering Elizabethan tang in the speech of isolated highland communities. In otherwise undistinguished, and often sentimental novels, which recognize local problems but commonly solve them on an unrealistic level, they are at pains to reproduce the colorful poetic qualities lingering in the dialects. Beginning with *Happy Mountain* (1928), told entirely in their carefully curried version of native speech, they produce romantic novels only a few cuts above the pre-1920 standard.

A long series of novels which treat mountain life with serious attention to economic and attitudinal problems and with regionalist elements stressed only as they contribute directly to character and narrative was initiated by an all but forgotten resident of Bryson City, North Carolina—Stanley Olmsted. Late in life, after he had written several turn-of-the-century romances, he shifted in *At Top of Tobin* (1926) to a serious, probably autobiographical, re-creation of a family and a small mountain community. The book is slow, all but plotless, often overwritten in nineteenth-century fashion, but it builds solid characters in a fully explored environment. Told from the point of view of an overly sensitive six-year-old boy and that of his dissatisfied ambitious mother, the story exploits graveyard imagery, symbolic of the passing of old traditions, and the natural joy in nature's prodigality, which fails to satisfy the newer generations.

Something of the same appreciation for the mountain country and regret for its insufficient appeal for the young inform Anne Armstrong's *This Day and Time* (1930), but Miss Armstrong's sordid picture of the meanness, jealousy, and violence among the city-infected youth adds a new realistic dimension to mountain fiction. Harry Kroll's *Mountainy Singer* (1928), largely a vehicle for displaying the author's collection of songs and legends, suffers as much from intrusive polemics against formal education for unspoiled mountain youth as from a luridly contrived story. Similarly, Grace Lumpkin's *To Make My Bread* (1932) overweights its story polemically, this time in a Marxist direction. An unallieviated picture of a mountain family's miseries, the book won a Gorky Award and a wide audience as a play, *Let Freedom Ring*.

The first masterpiece of the mountain genre was the work of a Louisiana native, Fiswoode Tarleton, who founded and edited *The Modern Review* and published two volumes of fiction before his early death in Bryson City. *Bloody Ground* (1929), a series of connected episodes in the lives of two ridge communities, offers a grimly authentic portrait of coldly proud, feuding families who preserve their hard-won dignity at the expense of all tender emotions. Individual episodes

are skillfully built from initial suspense to stark drama, but the cumulative effect, for all the plethora of violence, produces a full sense of
understanding, even of sympathy. Tarleton is a master of the tense,
taut scene, and if the units of his work are sometimes less than
short stories, they remain at least the most powerful set of episodes
yet written about the Appalachian people.

Tarleton's subsequent novel, *Some Trust in Chariots* (1930) proves
less effective, largely because he has a tractarian point to prove. Bringing a group of missionary-minded Northern educators into an
illiterate mountain area in order to educate them, rather than their
would-be pupils, into knowledge of real life supplies a precarious
theme for serious fiction. However, Tarleton handles it with typically
rigorous sincerity and dramatic force. He never lapses into satire or
special pleading to make his point, and his sure, economical handling
of the local color elements reinforces the drama without disturbing the
perspective.

None of the other early mountain novels carries the impact,
together with the authenticity, of Tarleton's work. Dubose Heyward,
after the success of *Porgy,* moved into the North Carolina mountain
area and produced *Angel* (1926). While his somber, passionate story
of a girl's revolt against the heavy restrictions imposed by a preacher-
father possesses moving scenes and exhibits a sensitive control, its
characters lack the feel of authenticity. Emmett Gowan, on the other
hand, a native of La Vergne, Tennessee, succeeds in creating a most
convincing atmosphere with solid characters in his *Dark Moon of
March* (1933), but at the expense of drama. His exuberant dialectal
version of a Romeo-Juliet romance in *Mountain Born* (1932) shows
more flair for incident than for character, while *Old Hell* (1937)
exaggerates in a Caldwellian vein of comic invention a mountaineer's
wild search for oil on his improverished land.

Most of the out-of-the-way places and peoples of the South have
been explored fictionally in the last forty years by local color writers,
native or transplanted. It remained, however, for a small area in the
northeastern part of Florida to produce three of the most distinguished
regional novelists of the early period—Edwin Granberry, Edith Taylor
Pope, and Marjorie Kinnan Rawlings. Except for *Colcorton,* a Negro-
centered story, Miss Pope's novels cannot be classified as regionalist,
despite her beautiful evocations of the St. Augustine country in sev-

eral other books. On the other hand, Granberry and Miss Rawlings, neither of them born in the area, heavily emphasize the regional scene and atmosphere in all their work. Granberry, a Mississippi native, spent an early five years in the Oklahoma Territory before arriving at ten in the Peninsular State, while Miss Rawlings settled in Cross Creek, Florida, only in her thirty-second year, after a childhood in Washington, D. C., and a news career.

Granberry's first novel, *The Ancient Hunger* (1927), set in the Oklahoma Territory, depends on its regional setting not only for its bleak atmosphere but for its peculiar juxtaposition of Puritan reticence with Slavic mating hunger. Snakes and stallions, dry heat and windy cold supply a starkly poetic background for the New England-bred girl's tragic struggle with herself and the strange codes of the immigrant colony. The poetry of place which distinguished this novel carries over to the Florida settings which become the exclusive locale of his later novels and short stories. Strangely enough, Granberry published fiction for only four years, then settled down at Rollins College as one of the first of the many creative writing professors produced by the Southern Renaissance.

When he turned to the Florida scene, Granberry proved himself a deep-seated romanticist, but that rarest of romanticists, a disciplined stylist and technician. *Strangers and Lovers* (1928) mixes its romantic story of an innocent woods-filly with sordidly realistic detail, and finally with melodrama. Particularly in the early sections, which develop the wild, shy love affair between the ignorant cracker girl and an equally innocent orphan boy, Granberry controls a lyric harmony of place, character and tone through a series of brief, economically written scenes. At the same time, he uses realistic native dialect and the crudities of scrub country life to establish a base of verisimilitude. As the story becomes involved, however, with a predatory rich woman and the mob violence of the bigoted community, it loses its special flavor and falls off into melodrama.

The Erl King (1930) avoids the pitfall of melodrama by the simple expedient of stripping away the elements of realism and social implication. The result is pure Brontean surreal romance. The characters in this novel are no more and no less real than Jane Eyre or Heathcliffe, and the atmosphere of heightened superrealistic romanticism lifts this book above the necessities of naturalistic representation. The story, set in the St. Augustine area about the turn of the century, is focused on young John Littlepage, who, having lost his mother at his birth, and feeling alienated from his grieving, taciturn father, finds a brooding satisfaction in woods, sea, and legendary stories of a Ponce de Leon ship wrecked on the offshore coral reefs. Following his dream life, John consorts with gypsies and finally takes the girl who loves him through a series of tense, ultimately tragic episodes, as she insists on following his unpredictable explorations and retreats. Strange as it appears in outline, *The Erl King* is saved by its moodal intensity, its beautifully sustained atmosphere, and its lyric language.

Miss Rawlings had written verse as well as news copy before she bought her Florida orange grove and settled to re-create in fictional terms the country of her adoption. Her second novel, after many failures with short stories, was a Book-of-the-Month Club selection, and her third won her a Pulitzer Prize. From the beginning a sensitive writer with a lyric feeling for the scrub country and particularly for its animal life, Miss Rawlings lacks Granberry's intensity as well as his romantic preoccupation. A realist, she prefers the leisurely saga-like treatment of her subjects to the tersely dramatic. Her quality depends considerably more on pure local color than on tone and mood. Local flora and fauna, local dialect and custom, dominate her work, but she is most successful in her treatment of the nature-oriented child. Less an artist than Granberry, she offers constant variety and interest, but seldom can she unify her observations and reactions in terms of a developing theme. Philosophically she is consistent, for all her books exhibit her sense of the evanescence of human life, its rigors and tragic disappointments, and her mature understanding of nature's inherent cruelties. Always, however, she retains her full appreciation of the natural world, and always she records its moods in sensitive prose. She is a Thoreau matured and reconciled to fact.

Her first novel, *Jacob's Ladder* (1931), a relatively slight story of a young Florida cracker couple moving from job to job as hostile nature, corrupt law, their own prejudices, and aspirations for independence drive them, sets the tone for her later work. Young Florry's sensitive feelings for the natural world, reflecting her author's, suffer the same disillusionment which her husband's confidence suffers in the world of men. *South Moon Under* (1933) offers her basic philosophic

attitudes in the life saga of a scrub country woman battling the land
and her law-defying neighbors, raising a woods-loving son who must
battle the law itself to survive in the stilling activities to which he has
been driven by economic necessity. The hard-bitten story indicates
that, though evil abounds in natural man and in nature's own
workings, civilization inevitably corrupts and only the earth can offer
true emotional solace. Miss Rawlings' later novels continue to develop
an increasingly pessimistic view of man's nature and condition. *Golden
Apples* (1944) is a bleak and finally melodramatic story of two
children growing up in the hammock and orange grove country.
The Sojourners (1953), set in New York State at the turn of the
century and published in the year of the author's death, chronicles a
long series of tragedies in the life of a farmer, alone in his rich appreciation of agrarian values and of the products of the earth.

Only in *The Yearling* (1938), her Pulitzer Prize novel, does Miss
Rawlings manage to unify and compress her material into an artistic
whole. The risk she takes is considerable, for the basic story, that of a
boy's attachment to a pet fawn, is fraught with every sentimental
hazard. She succeeds only by a consistent and careful underplaying of
the emotional possibilities, by balancing joys and fears, loyalties against
loyalties. The father's indulgence constantly runs athwart the mother's
intense practical sense, and Jody's innocence must finally succumb to
the harsh realities. When his mother, too pressed by the deprivations
of the yearling deer, must shoot it, Jody runs away, but finally must
return to the world of fact, himself now a yearling. The epigraph
from Miss Rawlings' final book reads, from *Ecclesiastes,* "For we are
strangers before thee, and sojourners... our days on the earth are
as a shadow...." Miss Rawlings' own sojourn was evidently light-
ened only by her deep love for the earth she walked, but she left
behind a patch of true color that is more than shadow.

Of all the early Southern local colorists, the most widely read both
here and in foreign countries has been Erskine Caldwell. Though he
can reasonably be classified as a militant liberal or as a popular sensa-
tionalist, Caldwell's primary method is that of the colorist, his
interest that of portraying men and women rather as fascinating
objects than as human individuals. Even when his subject is a Swede
in Maine, he does not desert his phenomenalistic approach. When he
attempts, as in *Trouble in July* (1940), an evidently serious treatment

of racial injustice, he produces only a group of stock characters, led by a grotesque figure of a sheriff, and a highly sentimentalized Negro boy victim, characterized chiefly by his love for rabbits.

For the most part, and altogether in his most popular books— *Tobacco Road* (1932), *God's Little Acre* (1933), and *Journeyman* (1935)—Caldwell treats the poor white of Georgia according to an unvarying colorist formula. Characters are first reduced to a primal animal innocence, then endowed with a single fanatic obsession or eccentricity. They never come across the printed page as people, but only as absurdly amusing or grotesquely fascinating examples of a new subhuman species. Superficially his characters resemble the most exaggerated of Faulkner's poor whites, but Faulkner always lifts such figures to the level of symbol; with Caldwell they are allowed simply to wallow. Furthermore, Caldwell's flat style, his insensitivity to subtleties of fictional presentation, allow him no means to redeem the crude vulgarities he delights in recording.

The historical novel has long held a particular fascination for the South. Before the War Between the States, the cult of Sir Walter Scott and his chivalric romances had so permeated the codes and manners of the aristocracy that historians have seen in it not only the patterns of Southern feudalistic standards of chivalry and *noblesse oblige* but a major cause of the war itself and of defeat. After Appomattox, the South nursed, along with its wounds, its memories. In the form of memoirs, verse, and finally novels, the heritage of Scott was preserved and expanded with an increment of legend. Cultivated amid mementoes and scrapbooks, old lace, and battered flags, the nostalgia for ante-bellum days found its way into fiction modeled on that of Scott himself. Seldom indeed in the flurry of late nineteenth-century historical novels does a sordid reality enter to muddy up the crinolines or to abrade the polish of a gallant in gray. The authors tend to be female and the books high romance.

The Renaissance of 1920 did not stem the flow of historical romance; indeed it continues unabated today, for the legend of a Golden Age never dies in an imperfect world. But the newer writers of the South, bent on realistic reassessment of their heritage, scorned the popular stream and began to mark out new channels in their exploration and re-creation of history. They developed most importantly the symbolic naturalistic method, by which the pattern of history, with its evident relevance to present problems, emerged through the screen of realistic fact and detail. The technique for dealing with the past developed by Tate, Gordon, E. M. Roberts, Warren, Faulkner, and the others has produced the most significant body of historical fiction of our era.

A second type which sprang up during the early Renaissance period in opposition to the historical romance was one popularized elsewhere by the anthropological studies and style revivals of the nineteenth century, the attempt at literal re-creation of the past in fictional terms, the deglamorized historical novel. For many an honest, talented, and literarily less sophisticated Southerner pondering his family heritage in a period of rapid change, the painstaking reconstruction of the past, stripped of the legend, became almost a duty. There was a constant temptation, naturally, to accept the more generally appealing elements of the legend as fact and to produce, therefore, a *Gone with the Wind,* which could seduce a Pulitzer Prize committee by its air of authenticity, while it lost none of its best-seller appeal to the devotees of swashbuckling romance. Still, a formidable list of uncompromisingly serious Southern authors have re-examined heritages from thirteenth-century England to the turn of the twentieth century here and in the homelands of immigrant families.

Before Margaret Mitchell won her fame in 1936, two other Southerners had been awarded Pulitzer Prizes for their historical fiction: T. S. Stribling in 1932 for his Alabama trilogy and Caroline Miller in 1934 for her piney woods Georgia saga, *Lamb in his Bosom.* Stribling, after helping to initiate the Renaissance with mulatto-centered *Birthright,* had produced four Caribbean adventure stories, two further social novels set in his native Tennessee hill country, and one on an Arkansas plantation. The ambitious project of tracing in detail the fortunes of the Vaiden family from ante-bellum days through the 1920's began auspiciously with *The Forge* (1931), and proceeded with diminishing effectiveness through *The Store* (1932) and *The Unfinished Cathedral* (1934).

The trilogy as a whole was evidently conceived as a Faulkneresque —or anti-Faulkner—moral history of the South, predominantly ironic; but Stribling has neither the philosophic grasp nor the structural ability of Faulkner. *The Forge,* detailing the rise of solid James Vaiden from blacksmith to planter, and his fall during war and carpetbag eras back to the smithy, is notable for its impartial treatment of war issues and Negro-white relationships, as well as for its dramatization of character conflicts. *The Store,* in which son Miltiades Vaiden allies himself with the "New South" forces and the town, carries us through a series of ups and downs, with reliance on coincidences, sudden revelations, misunderstandings and belated efforts at compensation, to a realization on the part of Miltiades that his half-Negro son, for whose lynching he is responsible, has alone preserved the stubborn integrity of the Vaiden heritage. In *The Unfinished Cathedral,* a modern story involving chiefly Miltiades' young wife and her former lover, now a preacher, Stribling reduces his history to a series of chances, always ironic but essentially meaningless, and his characters to dupes of fate rather than responsible actors. It is difficult to say what Stribling finally meant to convey in the symbol of the destroyed incomplete cathedral, in the ironic confusion of values, and in the romantic nostalgia of this book, other than an apocalyptic version of the Depression as the timely Destroyer of a decadent tradition.

Caroline Miller, like too many of her twentieth-century compatriots, failed to follow up her initial success with *Lamb in His Bosom;* she produced only one other novel, *Lebanon,* and that only after a lapse of ten years. *Lebanon,* in fact, repeats to a large extent the character types and scenes of the earlier novel, with some reversals of sex. Miss Miller's quality recalls more than a little that of Elizabeth Maddox Roberts. She offers an unhappy, harshly poetic version of early nineteenth-century frontier life with a feeling for the land, for the minutiae of responsible housewifery, and for the pangs and joys of a girl's growth into the burdens of womanhood and motherhood. *Lamb in His Bosom* develops no unifying theme, though it is well and honestly told. The long series of birth and death scenes, broken only by brief intervals of gaiety and hope, grows monotonous, especially as the setting remains substantially unchanged. Miss Miller conveys a wide understanding for human weakness, as well as for the strength to combat natural tragedies, and she displays some sharpness in her treatment of religious superstition and prejudice. If not a major writer, Miss Miller, in her rather limited way, indicates the high level

of competence which the South's untutored novelists have been able
to achieve.

Other realists of the first generation made distinctive contributions
to the historical novel, notably John Fort, Evelyn Scott, Edith Taylor
Pope, John Stuart Montgomery, Berry Fleming, and James Boyd.
In the cases of Montgomery and Fleming, realism takes the comic
form of exaggeration and satire, a relatively rare Southern approach.
Montgomery's *Tall Men,* a Literary Guild selection for 1927, sets an
amusing spy and counterspy extravaganza on the high seas during the
days of the War Between the States. His *The Virtue of This Jest,* a
Book League of America choice two years later, offers an eighteenth-
century English rogue story, complete with loose picaresque structure
and a stock of bawdy songs and episodes. Fleming, a Georgian like
Montgomery, sets his early story of comic roguery, *The Conqueror's
Stone* (1927), in the Carolinas of pre-Revolutionary times. He spins
a skillful and colorful yarn about a cynical former pirate, who returns
unpunished to his father's plantation only to be entranced out of his
cynicism by a compassionate woman.

John Fort's *God in a Straw Pen* (1931) exhibits less interest in
history and even its protagonist, assistant to a hell-fire evangelist, than
in the poor hill people. Fort produces in a series of swift vignettes
glimpses into the lives of the emotionally starved families, for whom
the revival is entertainment, orgiastic release, sexual stimulant, and
sexual substitute. An earlier novel, *Stone Daugherty* (1929), the story
of a strong, harsh Tennessee trader with the Indians, is insistently
called "not a historical novel" by the author in his Preface. It is not
historical in the sense that Fort intends his strongly written narrative
to demonstrate still very current primitive passions and prejudices.
With minimum attention to setting and custom, Fort concentrates
his considerable talents on the tragedy of lives bound by fear and
hatred.

Evelyn Scott's chief contribution to the historical novel is a remarkable attempt to reassess the whole of the War Between the States
through a sequential series of episodes concentrating entirely on
human responses to the events which were reshaping their lives. Miss
Scott chooses her characters at moments of crisis, from Lincoln, Lee,
Davis and Grant down to the commonest soldier and commonest
whore, and almost always succeeds in conveying a moving human

reality. If the long book is not altogether a success, the fault lies not in the execution but in the plan. The reader is forced to make constant readjustments as characters and setting change, and the result is memorable scenes rather than the total view which was intended. Extended over too long a period of time with too large a cast of characters, *The Wave* remains a remarkable *tour de force,* but not a unified work of art.

Edith Taylor Pope not only achieves artistic unity in her first historical novel, *Old Lady Esteroy* (1934), but she combines a delicate sense of history and place with penetrating psychological portraiture. Primarily, the novel, set in 1935 and 1875 near St. Augustine, Florida, offers a graphic portrait of the boldly rebellious wife of an old general, jilted by her lover, and become finally a shrewd, selfish matriarch, doddering at eighty, clutching to hold her slipping grip of the family she has long dominated. Miss Pope creates a rich atmosphere of semitropical lushness and luxury, of sun and storm, to set off the old lady and to reinforce the rebellious passions of her granddaughter and the daughter of her old lover. The success of this novel and of her later *Colcorton,* a story of miscegenation, contributes to a sense of disappointment in her return to the 1830's with an honest, well-authenticated, but comparatively undistinguished account of the establishment of orange groves and the unenlightened treatment of Seminole Indians by the new Florida settlers, *River in the Wind* (1954).

James Boyd makes a less distinctive contribution to the realistic historical novel than others of his group. On the other hand, his example and his encouragement did more, perhaps, to establish the popular genre than the efforts of all the others. Of an old North Carolina family, forced by health to retire early from a newspaper and publishing career, he came back to Southern Pines, took up fiction largely as a diversion, but soon, with Struthers Burt, had established a literary center to which aspiring authors migrated. His first novel, *Drums* (1926), set in Revolutionary Carolina, established him as a sound, realistic chronicler, with an ability to project character and action without resort to cliches and yet with popular appeal. *Marching On* (1927), his Civil War novel, and *Long Hunt* (1930), a frontier story, consolidated his reputation, without adding materially to his literary stature.

Among the other serious historical novelists of the early Renaissance period, none combines the necessary creative and historical abilities with marked success. Frances Fox's *Ridgeways* (1934) builds a solid five-generation Kentucky story, reminiscent of Caroline Gordon's *Penhally*, but without her predecessor's stylistic distinction. Gerald White Johnson's *By Reason of Strength* (1930) is essentially the biography of a pioneer Scotch woman in North Carolina. Virginian H. J. Eckenrode's *Bottom Rail on Top* (1935) proves better political and social history than novel. Evelyn Pierce's Texas story of a girl's attempt to break through small-town restrictions, *Hilltop* (1931), does not seem to require its early setting, while Pendleton Hogan in *The Dark Comes Early* (1934) pursues his dramatic story of the same era in Texas rather alongside his historical research than integrated with it.

The multicolored and diversely textured strands of first-generation Renaissance fiction cannot be woven into any consistent pattern. The body of this work, no matter what its literary antecedents, suggests primarily reaction to war-born dislocations and disorientations, to traditional attitudes now seen from new perspectives, to moral and social issues brought into new focus. If any of the reactions may be singled out as most representative, they are those of a Thomas Wolfe and a William Faulkner. Wolfe's spirit is rebellious, groping, voracious of experience but incapable of mastering it. In Faulkner, critically and morally concerned, the quest for understanding typically leads backward into history. As Warren's Jack Burden finds that "You can't have a future without a past," so Faulkner's characters discover that virtue cannot exist without its roots in the soil from which it sprang. These attitudes, both springing from felt and observed change, are antipathetic, but between them lies the whole range of modern Southern attitudes as the fiction exhibits it. The succeeding generations of writers do little to extend this range; they do a great deal, however, to enrich and intensify it.

6

THE LATER
TRADITIONALISTS

The new Southern tradition in fiction, in the form of symbolic naturalism, had already established its critical standing by the time the second generation of the Renaissance began to publish. Largely through the efforts of the Fugitive critics, particularly Tate, Warren, and Cleanth Brooks, writing in literary quarterlies, the prestige of the earlier novelists in the tradition had been widely recognized by 1940. Young writers of the late Thirties and Forties, however, show little influence of their predecessors. For the most part, they exhibit more concern for the pressing problems of their unstable times than for refinement of technique. Eudora Welty learned, certainly, from her chief sponsor, Katherine Anne Porter, and Edward Kimbrough evidently from Faulkner and Warren, but direct influence appears with surprising rarity. Only in the third generation, that of the Fifties, when writing courses blossom out in the colleges and universities, often under the direction of Southern authors and critics themselves, when textbooks and anthologies produce their effect on the young, does the New Tradition proliferate into a kind of second renaissance.

The second generation, therefore, offers only a handful of new traditionalists: Eudora Welty, Carson McCullers, Robert Ramsey, Edward Kimbrough, and Jane Morton, all of the center; Anne Winslow and Bowen Ingram of the periphery. Of these, Kimbrough, the most clearly derivative, and Ramsey studied at the University of Alabama, the first Southern school to stress a creative writing program. Two others studied Music and Art before discovering their chief talents. Miss Welty, on the advice of Katherine Anne Porter, stayed clear of the writing schools.

Like her sponsor, Miss Welty of Jackson, Mississippi, has won her major place in Southern letters largely through her mastery of the short story. She has published three novels, none of them important achievements to stand by her shorter fiction. The first, *The Robber Bridegroom* (1942), half legend, half fairy tale, is a sort of parable of pioneer innocence corrupted by greed for land and money—a slight treatment of a major New Traditional theme. *The Ponder Heart* (1954), even slighter, extends too far the type of ironic caricature of small town women so neatly done in her short story, "Why I Live at the P. O." *Delta Wedding* (1946), a solider achievement if not quite a novel, presents a multifaceted view of a large, well-to-do planter family assembled on the occasion of a daughter's wedding to her parents' overseer. In the absence of anything resembling a plot—in addition to the marriage, a parted couple reunites—Miss Welty sustains interest by constantly shifting her focuses, introducing recalls from the past with a few minor crises, as the central preparations for the event proceed.

As a group portrait, both intimate and objective, *Delta Wedding* succeeds admirably. From several perspectives within the family proper, we realize fully the strength of the unit, bound by love and an absolute loyalty. From a remove, particularly through a young lower-class wife, we see smugness, spoiling, feminine domination, envied but not approved. The self-sufficiency of the Fairchilds absorbs into its gently omniverous maw all the foreign elements which enter their sphere of control. Their confidence is never more than mildly disturbed and their essential way of life never threatened.

The major value of this novel for the student of Miss Welty's fiction lies in its definition of her thematic concerns. The Fairchilds would seem to represent a survival of those saving qualities for lack of which most of the characters in her short stories suffer, a communion of people to love and to guarantee spiritual protection. In general, her people, those of the city and those of the small town, live isolated lives, seeking love, recognition, a meaningful unit of society to which to adhere and from whom to draw sustenance. Miss Welty appears indifferent to the larger social and political problems of her region. Her subject is people, in all levels and in all conditions save those in high places; their foibles, their assertions of dignity, their mistaken impulses, their graces and animalities, their faiths and their yearnings. The largest social unit she deals with is the family or the church group, neither of which, as a result of modern dislocations, is truly a unit. Even her symbols are usually local, reticently handled features of the local scene.

Her first volume, *A Curtain of Green* (1941), contains many of Miss Welty's finest stories, most of them concerned with the poor, the ignorant, or the maimed. Versatile as she is, she treats them with irony, with pity, but always with a sufficiently objective understanding. From the overt and pitiful episode of righteous but frightfully misguided women trying to deal with a half-witted, love-struck girl in "Lily Daw and the Three Ladies" to the delicately subtle "A Piece of News," where an ignorant backwoods wife discovers through a chance bit in a newspaper a new perspective on herself and life, the stories display a wide variety of personal experience. The beauty parlor gossip piece, "Petrified Man," handled entirely in conversation, and the self-justificatory monologue of "Why I Live at the P. O." illustrate her diversified approach to ironic character revelation. In the strong story, "Powerhouse," and in the controlled pathos of "A Worn Path," she deals symbolically and directly with Negro character.

Miss Welty's major themes emerge more importantly in the next two books of short stories, *The Wide Net* (1943) and *The Golden Apples* (1949), both volumes loosely unified by setting. All the stories in *The Wide Net* take place in the vicinity of the old Natchez Trace, but their time spans, their methods, and their tones range widely. The highly symbolic "First Love" involves Aaron Burr's plot and its disillusioning effect on a young admirer, and the equally symbolic, beautifully told "A Still Moment" centers on naturalist Audubon. But the volume also includes such diverse modern stories as the brutal "At the Landing" and the ironic title piece. In *The Golden Apples* we are confined to the village of Morgana, Mississippi and a set of families pictured in interrelations over a two-generation span. Here, as in *The Wide Net,* themes of isolation, loss of innocence, or a more general modern disorientation come to dominate the narratives.

The adroitly managed "June Recital," which concentrates her most important thematic concerns, may stand as Miss Welty's key story. An innocent young boy in his isolation from the family spies on mysterious happenings in a deserted house next door while his pre-occupied older sister, finally drawn into the mystery, discovers the secret of lonely desperation. Both thwarted low-caste Virgie Rainey and the madly lonely old piano teacher, Miss Eckhardt, have been driven to their desperate compensations by the world's rejection, and they end by "roaming on the face of the earth . . . like lost beasts." Innocence and disillusioning knowledge, disorientation and separateness, with depravity and madness as symptoms, all appear crucially in the resolution of the story. Nowhere else has Miss Welty combined so effectively her larger themes.

For the first time in her 1955 volume, *The Bride of Innisfallen,* Miss Welty ventures outside her regional boundaries to include travel pieces and even a retelling of the Circe myth. Only one of these stories, however, reaches the high level of her work with native subjects, an ironic revelation of Italian moral values as glimpsed through the awakening understanding of a young girl on shipboard, "Going to Naples." Several rather typical Southern stories and a fantastic historical one round out this volume, but none stands with the earlier group already mentioned, or with "The Death of a Traveling Salesman," "Moon Lake," "A Memory," and "The Key." This is not to say that Miss Welty is beginning to suffer from that commonest of failings in American letters, that of being written out early. In fact, she is cautiously expanding her horizons, and it is not inconceivable that she may produce a very different sort of masterpiece in the future, as Miss Porter has done.

Carson McCullers of Georgia, if she is not a Porter or a Welty in mastery of short forms and as a stylist, combines some of Miss Porter's liberal breadth with Warren and Faulkner's skill in weaving together large patterns of experience into meaningful designs. Like Faulkner, she exhibits a partiality for grotesques, but her concern for the lonely and loveless, with failures of communication and self-betrayal ally her more firmly with her feminine compatriots. Her world, whether it is the Southern town or the metropolis, is peopled with the heart-hungry "lonely hunters," for whom she can find no spiritual food and no haven.

In her first novel, written when she was 22, Miss McCullers not only defines and gives concrete life to her major theme but she displays an extraordinary grasp of diverse character problems. One of the first of a growing number of young Southern women, she deals directly and effectively with a Negro family. In addition, her cast includes a thwarted labor organizer, an impotent restaurant owner, an obese Greek mute, and a fatherless tomboy. However, it is another mute named Singer who provides the center about which the others cluster in their need for understanding. Though Singer is deeply immersed in his own obsession with the Greek, he must play the role of father confessor to the four disturbed principals. He can act only as sounding board, of course, echoing back the needs and plaints, while he suffers his own desperate loss. Clearly symbolic, the ironically named Singer seems to sum up all the finally unsatisfactory recourses of modern man in his heart's loneliness: religion, psychiatry, political or social expedients.

All of the major characters in *The Heart is a Lonely Hunter* (1940), are presented realistically and sympathetically with the exception of the mutes, who exist chiefly in a symbolic dimension. Almost the reverse is true of *Reflections in a Golden Eye* (1941), where the major characters, almost all to some extent perverted, lead symbolic rather than convincingly realistic lives. In place of Singer as symbolic center, Miss McCullers offers a complex of natural images, particularly the autumn sun and animal or bird eyes which reflect back the self who seeks meaning in them. The people of the Army base, from the simple-minded Private Williams to the complexly disturbed homosexual Captain Penderton, are uniformly obsessed. Since love and true communication are blocked off by obsessive self-concern, and even the God's eye of the sun can only blind, tragedies of unfulfillment and misunderstanding inevitably result. If *Reflections in a Golden Eye* is a less humanly persuasive book than its predecessor, it is none the less an impressive achievement in the New Tradition.

Miss McCullers comes down solidly to earth and the intimate everyday life in *The Member of the Wedding* (1946), a story which seems to have grown out of tomboy Mick Kelley's in *The Heart is a Lonely Hunter*. Limiting her view to that of a motherless girl, the author takes her through three phases of adolescence, in which she progresses from tomboy Frankie, through exotic F. Jasmine, to feminine Frances. She lives a typical alien and lonely life with only monumentally solid Negro cook Berenice as limited confidante until she attempts desperately to identify herself with her brother's wedding. The excruciating collapse of her dream of romantic communion leaves her shattered but still able to begin building a new dream with a girl who shares at least a part of her needs. Despite the apparent simplicity of Miss McCullers's telling, she has performed a subtle and delicate feat in handling the gentle irony inherent in Frankie's limited view and in her long, devious conversations with tolerantly disapproving Berenice.

Miss McCullers' shorter pieces, published in *The Ballad of the Sad Cafe* (1951) often betray a rather thin New Yorkerish quality. Only "A Tree. A Rock. A Cloud." where a young boy listens uncomprehendingly to an old transient's account of the ambiguous ways of love, rises to her highest standards. The title novelette, however, a return to her symbolic, or perhaps better parabolic, manner, stands comparison with *Reflections in a Golden Eye*. The characters again are extremes, the action somewhat fantastic, particularly in the climactic stomp-and-gouge match between the female protagonist and her ex-criminal husband, but, like Faulkner, Miss McCullers here manages to heighten the language and atmosphere of her story to the point where it acquires a sort of legendary credence. The obsessions are exclusively those of love and its counterpart, hate, and all the characters exhibit the fatal tendency to learn hatred for those who would envelop them in love, and love for those without love or merit. The central action is neatly framed by the haunting lonely songs of a chain gang and emphasized by repeated descriptions of the "dreary" mill town, offering lifetimes of boredom.

With this story Miss McCullers' pessimism seems to reach its own climax. Whatever possible remedies for man's loneliness and obsessive self-concern seemed to have been hinted in her earlier books, the prime need was for love. She never suggests the agape of universal brotherhood—Blount the labor organizer and the idealistic Negro doctor Copeland in *The Heart is a Lonely Hunter* implicitly deny such a possibility since they fight each other on being left alone without Singer. Now eros, too, is shown to be uniformly and terribly defective, as, indeed, it is more directly in the short stories. There is left only the withdrawal of Biff Brannon, the artist's withdrawal, a suspension "between the two worlds" of love and terror.

The burden of carrying the New Tradition's development through the Forties was not left entirely on the shoulders of Miss Welty and

Miss McCullers, as Southern critics and anthologists usually imply. Most significantly, Robert Ramsey of Memphis employs the ironic limited view technique and achieves a new dimension in his mastery of tone. His first novel, *Fire in Summer* (1942), presents an extended portrait of a ubiquitous tenant farmer type, most closely resembling the early Ab Snopes of "Barn Burning." A stubborn, harsh, constantly frustrated bigot, he is rendered convincing through the matter-of-fact, fatalistic account of his family's Depression summer by the ten-year-old son, who accepts him as a familiar natural catastrophe.

The carefully maintained tone of simple, naive acceptance, tinged with hope, as the boy recounts the fantastic and tragic violence of the man, keeps the reader's teeth set. From the first moment when Spence Lovell stops his wagon to watch a house burn and righteously curses those who would have him help to save it, Ramsey allows the reader no interval of relief. Violently independent, Lovell pursues his rigid ascetic code, hating Negroes as the ultimate cause of all his frustrations, driving his defiant daughter into pregnancy and flight, viciously beating out any sparks of revolts in sons and wife, destroying car, garden, privy, and finally himself. Through all the destructions, the wild tragic-comic pursuits, and the madly mistaken accusations, Spence is seen as an honest God-fearing man. The reader, constantly seeing through and beyond young Blue's simple account, is forced simultaneously to extremes of hate and pity.

Ramsey produced another triumph of tone before his less successful Mexican novel, *Fiesta* (1955). In *The Mocking Bird* (1951), again a story is told from the limited understanding of a young boy, but the tone and atmosphere suggest a different author. The ever-immediate sense of danger and destruction which Ramsey projected in *Fire in Summer* through images of snakes, fires, and guns, is replaced here by a hazy feeling of surrounding evil and impending doom, generated by the warning voice of a mockingbird at night, a painted owl, a dead cock, and a graveyard. The atmosphere of dream, finally of nightmare merging into reality, sustains the mood and colors young David's view of events with a ghostly moonlighted sheen. The widowed father's love affair, frustrated by the family's opposition and particularly by the adolescent sister's desperate intransigence, must be pieced together from allusions, evasive answers and significant emotional responses, all beyond David's understanding. Yet the essential pattern is transmitted, the characters are sharply felt, if not clearly comprehended, and the essential tragedy fully grasped.

Ramsey has no developed philosophy to offer, but his books are complete artistic wholes. With Edward Kimbrough of Mississippi much the opposite is true. Kimbrough tries to say a great deal about the central conflict in the New South, that between traditional attitudes and those of the business and social interests which challenge them, but he is not completely successful in integrating his conceptions to form unified works of art. After an early political novel, *From Hell to Breakfast* (1941), the account of a cynical Mississippi demagogue's campaign for re-election, Kimbrough evidently discovered Faulkner and Warren. *Night Fire* (1946) and *The Secret Pilgrim* (1949) clearly owe a stylistic debt to the masters of the New Tradition, while the plots in their scenes of melodramatic violence often out-Faulkner Faulkner.

Kimbrough's novelty lies in his adaptation of the New Traditional methods to strongly liberal ends. *Night Fire* employs the obvious symbols of its title to suggest the dark web of Negro-white relationships, woven of fear, rivalry, and false pride, which require the illumination of human intelligence. But it is essentially the story of maturation to responsibility on the part of a resigned, easy-living man of good family who, by risking his own and others' lives to save an innocent Negro from a politically inspired lynch plot, is able to reassert the highest values of the old tradition. On the other hand, *The Secret Pilgrim* is built on a mythic base, like Tate's *The Fathers,* introduces a wildly Faulknerian riot scene in an old soldier's asylum, and features a Warren-like search for a father relationship. This story, too, gives a liberal cast to its conflict between materialism and humane values, between Calvinistic concepts and sexual need.

Kimbrough never quite manages to integrate his themes into the mythic structure of Jason's quest, but his more radical difficulty lies in his character portrayal. Like many liberals, he tends to simplify his characters, a reduction which allows them to be placed neatly in categories of good and bad. The fault is disguised to a degree by the portentousness, sometimes pretentiousness, of the style. The violent movement, the time shifts, the withholding for suspense, the feeling of outrage, all the Faulkner characteristics are there. Only the larger aspects of conception and character portrayal are missing.

Jane Morton's single novel, *Blackbirds on the Lawn* (1944), is a much more modest undertaking, exhibiting no direct influences and propounding no distinctive philosophy. Her subject is a recurrent evil, symbolized by the blackbirds, and the battle against it by two aging members of long-warring families. Handled quietly and tastefully, the drama brings together the retired editor and the rival matron in the interests of justice and an old love. With sensitivity and perception Mrs. Morton probes her characters and evokes the rural Kentucky scene, enriching her fabric with unobtrusive natural symbols and authenticating it with cleanly caught detail. Though she cannot, on the basis of this one short novel be regarded as a major figure, she clearly belongs with the developers of the New Tradition.

Two Tennessee women, Anne Goodwin Winslow and Bowen Ingram, earn their credentials as New Traditionalists largely through their sophisticated use of a Jamesian irony. Mrs. Winslow, who was over sixty when she published her first fiction in *A Winter in Geneva* (1945), enjoyed a brief but fruitful period of literary activity, completing four novels in four years. In her short stories she often suggests an American Katherine Mansfield working more directly in the shadow of Henry James. Her revelations of character and motive are eminently Jamesian, if the irony is usually gentler. All woman-centered, the stories expose with charm and wit the foibles and sometimes all but tragic follies of widows, wives, and callow girls. Her novels bring her closer to the later Ellen Glasgow as she explores turn-of-the-century emotional problems. A nostalgic sentiment pervades all these delightfully reticent stories, but they are saved by an unfailing intelligence and her characteristic sense of the ironic. *Cloudy Trophies* (1946), *A Quiet Neighborhood* (1947), *It Was Like This* (1949), and *The Springs* (1949) have in common an avoidance of action and the big scene in favor of sophisticated conversation and shrewd analysis. The conflicts, usually involving the romantic and the practical, Southern attitudes versus Northern, or male versus female, are projected through animated discussions and concluded often with Jamesian renunciations. Literary references and quotations abound in speech and thought, and often these supply mythic or legendary prototypes for the surface situations. Mrs. Winslow's indirection and her penchant for reference give her stories a flavor of dated artificiality, but in her first three novels the characters are so thoroughly understood and intelligently presented, both subjectively and objectively, with controlled technique that a warm sense of life pervades them.

Bowen Ingram's irony is less intellectual, eminently human and modern. Her first novel, *If Passion Flies* (1945), hardly a Traditionist book, tells a sophisticated and often witty story of a wife's attempt to understand herself, her husband, and the other man against a background of social upheaval brought on by the Army's invasion of her conservative small Tennessee town. *Light as the Morning* (1954), however, is all irony, as a priggish adolescent boy recounts his social troubles with a city country club set. The story in which young Les McCoin unconsciously reveals himself has a sort of *Catcher in the Rye* brightness in the telling. The boy's pretensions, his inability to understand his family's blindness to what a club and car can do for a budding career, are handled with sharp wit but with understanding and sympathy. In the final sequences where Les begins to discover solid values in the old family home, Miss Ingram reveals essentially liberal attitudes. Her quality lies, however, in her deft treatment of the petty vanities and snobberies of a pushing social set.

As a group, this middle generation of writers in the New Tradition can scarcely bear comparison with their illustrious predecessors. The thinness of their ranks would seem to relate directly to the movement of ideas, and that in turn to the economic concerns, of their period. The national interest in social movements, in collectivist solutions to the world's problems challenged young intellectuals everywhere. Problems of personal identity and heritage, even problems of literary technique, tended to give way in the minds of young authors before the more pressing issues of labor and industry, politics and economics, race and creed. The Renaissance chorus continues to swell, but the major areas of enrichment occur in liberally slanted fiction, including Negro and poor white view, urban and rural problems, political and religious analyses and exposures. Not until World War II brings about a new disillusion with collective action does the emphasis swing back to the personal. The symbolic naturalist methods, which have become entrenched in the curricula of the schools, enjoy an astonishing proliferation in the fiction of the Fifties.

Some forty talented Southern writers who published their first fiction in the 1950's must be considered as direct or peripheral inheritors of the New Tradition. Some of them were trained at Vanderbilt, Kenyon, Florida, Iowa, and other schools of creative writing by Fugitive teachers or their critic followers. Others certainly must have absorbed their techniques early through Brooks and Warren's textbooks, Davidson's rhetorics, or the New Critical articles in reviews. The disillusion with collectivisms and social action following the Nazi defeat and Hiroshima led novelists to turn back to the personal problems of sin and guilt, of family and heritage, which had preoccupied many of the early Renaissance generation. The aftermath of the Second World War, like that of the first, brought challenges to values for the returned soldier and the disoriented civilian. The result was something of a new Renaissance. But established techniques were available now, and few of the young Southerners burned with a fever for innovation.

Of the central group of eighteen writers of fiction, Elizabeth Spencer, Leroy Leatherman, Madison Jones and Walter Sullivan all studied at Vanderbilt; Peter Taylor and Wesley Ford Davis worked at Kenyon where Fugitive John Crowe Ransom led the critical school and edited the *Review*. Two others attended Princeton—George Garrett and Walter Clemons; two Duke—William Styron and Ovid Williams Pierce; one, Iowa's creative center—Flannery O'Connor. All of the others were college graduates, and more than half of the group have become creative writing teachers. It is clear that we are dealing here with a critically trained and artistically sophisticated generation.

The conservative agrarian preoccupation which characterized the first generation of the New Traditionalists appears much less prominently in the Fifties group. In fact, the majority of the young are city born, and a number of them liberal minded or completely divorced in their fiction from theory. Only the nucleus trained at Vanderbilt, the old Fugitive center, continues to emphasize the agrarian pattern. All of them are concerned to some extent with recent Southern problems, but the bond which unites them is primarily that of technique. Furthermore, their concern with the problems of innocence and guilt, with family and heritage, mark them off from the legion of other talented Southern authors of the period.

Elizabeth Spencer of Mississippi and Peter Taylor of Tennessee, two of the oldest of the new group, both publishing first in 1948, have established the firmest reputations among the latest New Traditional-

ists. Miss Spencer's three novels in the late Forties and Fifties, with
the addition of her 1960 *The Light in the Piazza,* have assured her
position in the direct line of descent from Faulkner, Warren, and
Eudora Welty. Taylor's two volumes of short stories, again with the
addition of another in 1960, and his one novel, *A Woman of Means*
(1950), have set him equally as high in critical esteem.

Miss Spencer's first novel, *Fire in the Morning* (1948), owes more
than a little to Faulkner's example. Much of her mentor's turgidity
of style, his preshadowing and probing of motives, his portentousness
and slowly developing revelations, reappear here in new contexts. A
Mississippi Snopes family with a difference, the Gerrards, sophisticated
and loosely attractive in the second generation, attract the Northern
wife of solidly agrarian Kinlock Armstrong and complicate, through
her, Kinlock's crusade to exact retribution for the Gerrards' legal steal
of family land. Though it costs Kinlock his father in the end, and his
uninitiated but thoroughly decent wife months of anguish, the Gerrards are ultimately routed and agrarian integrity re-established.

The subsequent, *This Crooked Way* (1952), develops considerably
more complications of theme and motives without essentially depart-
ing from Faulknerian techniques and concerns. Amos Dudley, a
Mississippi hill country boy, having felt God's hand on him, identifies
himself with the Biblical Jacob in his recognition of his sins and in
his confidence of worldly success. Clinging to his secret pact, he wins
the rich Delta land and the rich Delta heiress he had set his heart
on, but loses almost everything else in the process, including his hope
of seeing the ladder of angels. The opening first-person narrative by
Amos is followed by sections of his moral indictment related by his
friend, his niece, and his wife, all of whom find him basically loveless
and ruthless in his single-minded pursuit. Amos returns in the final
section to recount his defeat and to reaccept his family and their
religion.

In all but the hasty and inconclusive ending, Miss Spencer creates
her situations and characters with artistry and insight. The various
speech patterns of her narrators distinguish and define them while
they add authentic color. The more violent, and sometimes melodramatic, incidents are moved off-stage, or muted, while their implications, morally and emotionally, activate the compelling foreground
drama. After the wife's climactic reassertion of her will, however, the

book's power is spent. What with government dams, big winds, baptisms, throwing of money into the river, the mass movements of Dudleys into Amos' place, and even a subnarrator, the final twenty-five pages come perilously close to a travesty on Faulkner.

Miss Spencer's third novel, *The Voice at the Back Door* (1956), attacks boldly and directly the major problems of the modern South: the racial issue, corrupt politics, intolerance and resistance to change. Previously Negroes had appeared in her novels only as superstitious, garrulous appurtenances; here she goes so far as to adopt a dedicated worker for racial justice as one of her point of view characters and to turn her story on the injustice done him. There is considerable of Warren's *All the King's Men* and Faulkner's *Intruder in the Dust* to be noted in Miss Spencer's plot and themes, but she handles them in her own quiet, sensitive manner and with broad sympathy. With a minimum of symbolic extension, she touches intimate details of all her characters' lives with a sure hand and brings them into revealing emotional and ideological clashes.

Idealist crusader Duncan Harper, cynical realist, bootleg liquor operator, Jimmy Tallant, compromising politician Willard Follansbee, Negro Beck Dozer, and the women, Duncan's wife and his former girl, the rebellious Marcia, project their clashing points of view until all are caught in the swiftly developing climax. Only Tallant is changed in the process—into a militant supporter of equal rights—but the town's injustice and intolerance are manifest. The story, though it rigidly adheres to its points of view, clearly indicts the red necks and the upper levels of society for their bigoted and inflexible inhumanity. Still, Miss Spencer's careful objectivity, in contrast to the too obviously weighted bias of so many liberal novelists of her generation, preserves a rare artistic integrity.

The Light in the Piazza (1960), set in Italy and involving a feeble-minded American heiress, is a slighter, more popular work, though it reflects no abandonment of Miss Spencer's high stylistic standards. The story turns on a moral issue and a difference in cultural standards. It lacks the complexity of character, the broader philosophic and moral involvement of her earlier work. Still it suggests that she, like Eudora Welty, is seeking to extend her range beyond the specifically Southern problems with which she had been exclusively concerned.

Peter Taylor's brilliance exhibits another facet of the New Tradition's later mastery of form and feeling. His command of the short story medium can be compared only with that of Katherine Anne Porter and Eudora Welty in our time, but he eschews both the social issues of the former and the overt irony and occasional violence of the latter. His stories do not involve the major issues which have disturbed the modern South, except peripherially to private human dilemmas, nor do they relate to the so-called Gothic school of Southern writing. All of Taylor's stories are marked by restraint and by an absolute mastery of his medium. Though his subject matter in *A Long Fourth* (1948), *The Widows of Thornton* (1954) and *Happy Families Are All Alike* (1960) is most distinctively Southern, he is the least chauvinistic of regional writers. His concerns are primarily adolescent awareness of adult emotional complications, revelations of self and of family past. His key is uniformly low to the point that at times it falls almost flatly on the ear. But there is always substance and always the final "epiphany" which Joyce achieved in his *Dubliners* stories.

Taylor's one novel, *A Woman of Means* (1950), concerns the effect of city life and money on family relations in a St. Louis setting. The story is told from the point of view of a thirteen-year-old boy who has been divorced from the security of a farm background and thrust into the uncentered and individualistic pursuit of the worldly success which his father has failed to achieve. The rich stepmother's parallel failure, in not achieving a pregnancy, a symbolic projection of the sterility of city life, leads to her madness and finally to the complete divisive disintegration of the family. Taylor's novel reveals him, as his short stories seldom do, as basically in sympathy with the agrarian tradition, conscious of his heritage, both as a Southerner and as an artist.

Leroy Leatherman, William Styron, and Flannery O'Connor, all born in the Twenties, seem to initiate a new generation in the modern Renaissance. All published their first books before they were thirty, and they have continued to produce novels and short stories which place them among the most talented writers of their generation.

Leatherman, of Alexandria, Louisiana, a student at both Vanderbilt and Kenyon, is undoubtedly the most traditionally orthodox of the three. His two novels, *The Caged Birds* (1950) and *The Other Side of the Tree* (1954), reveal a complete and thoroughly understood commitment to the practices and themes of symbolic naturalism. Both of his novels are projected primarily through the eyes of Jim Daigre, eight years old in *The Caged Birds* and seventeen in the later novel. Both books rely heavily on their symbolic patterns and on the thematic concerns with innocence and guilt. Like many of the talented products of Fugitive training, Leatherman creates a finely woven texture of language and imagery to lend naturalistic body to his philosophically and symbolically conceived narratives. Behind his fictions lies the whole body of achievements of the New Tradition.

The Caged Birds is rich, even lush, in symbolism. Love, particularly possessive love, provides the main theme of a story told from Jim's, his mother's, and their next door neighbor's viewpoints. The attempts of all the major characters to fulfill themselves through another, husband, wife, or child, lead to frustration and death. The lovebirds of the title, the mother's gift rather to herself than to her son on his birthday, enact a similar pattern of incestuous love and death. A chess set, towers in various embodiments, and mythological references contribute to the symbolic extension of the modern story. New oil wealth in the Louisiana town contributes to the tragic developments, but Leatherman's preoccupation is with the personal emotional problems, not with social upheavals.

Jim Daigre has grown to a confused late adolescence in *The Other Side of the Tree*, one of the more impressive novels of the New Tradition's later phase. Framed between sections of Jim's story of modern impotence and lost direction, Leatherman introduces an involved Faulkneresque narrative, set at the turn of the century, involving Jim's ancestors and clearly setting the pattern which leads to his predicament. Young Jim is told the story after his frustrating romantic approaches to a girl who wants more than he is capable of offering her. The great old tree under which Jim is told the story by an old swamp-haunting storekeeper becomes for him the tree of knowledge under which he discards his feeble romanticism, symbolized in a treasured Tennyson poem. Though he has learned to understand both his heritage and himself, he remains essentially impotent, inescapably a member of his generation.

The framed story out of the past rubs off the glamor from Jim's conventionally romantic conceptions, particularly of the legendary Ida Fields, symbol of all that man seeks to attain. Worshipped at a distance by innocent poetic Jacob Sidney, she is raped away by one of the boldly materialistic Wainwrights, and quickly converted to the joys of the flesh. As Leatherman depicts it, the South has always suffered and continues to suffer from the incompatibility of its animal passions and its cult of the spiritual ideal. Jim realizes the necessity for integration but he is powerless to achieve it.

William Styron of Virginia, whose brilliantly written and forcefully characterized first novel, *Lie Down in Darkness* (1951) has been followed by a graphic short novel, *The Long March* (1956), and the powerful but undisciplined *Set This House on Fire* (1960), represents best the new semiexistentialist leaning of the World War II generation. Styron bursts with talent, often reminding the reader of a more controlled Thomas Wolfe in his lyric passages, but his concerns are more nearly akin to those of F. Scott Fitzgerald. He observes with striking penetration a new "lost generation," not only one bankrupt morally and living feverishly, but one whose major problem has become suicide or the willful seeking of death. Her father's all but incestuous love for Peyton Loftis in *Lie Down in Darkness*, her failure to replace him in marriage, her consequent "lost" irresponsibility, lead to actual suicide, even as she dotes on her beautiful naked body. Cass Kinsolving of *Set This House on Fire* constantly harbors suicidal impulses and indulges in long, frequently desperate meditations on death, but it is the rich playboy exploiter, Mason, who actually forces his own death.

Despite its brilliant picture of American artists and dilettantes in Italy, despite some probing and sensitive character portrayals and effective use of symbols, *Set This House on Fire* never coheres into a unified work of art. Styron presents too much material which cannot be absorbed within the novel's thematic and structural framework. The book sprawls as the author indulges himself in philosophy, in rhetoric and richly presented but extraneous episodes.

Lie Down in Darkness is similarly rich, in Negro revival scenes, fraternity parties, a ghastly wreck of a wedding party, and a football game orgy. But here Styron keeps solid control of his desperately disoriented cast and of his diction, despite its tremendous versatility. The pattern of failures in self-indulgent and overpossessive love, clung to in the absence of permanent and selfless values, is manifested in a variety of relationships, all set symbolically against the colorful religious orgy of the Negroes. Styron's Virginia setting in this novel adds considerably to its atmosphere, but he is not fundamentally concerned with the South's characteristic problems. His problem is simply that of existence for a generation which can longer find meaning for it.

Flannery O'Connor of Georgia represents most effectively the new Catholic wing of the Tradition, and she introduces what may be called a new mode of "fantastic naturalism." The characters in her two novels, *Wise Blood* (1952) and *The Violent Bear It Away* (1960), are almost invariably fanatics, and they are all dominated by the religious obsessions of the most fanatic. In both cases, young protagonists rebel violently against almost exclusively religious training but remain obsessed with a perverted missionary zeal. In *Wise Blood,* Hazel Motes' fanatic missionary antireligion crusade results in disillusionment and his preacher father's death. Driven to sin against every item of his father's code and to preaching madly against it from a car top on downtown streets, he becomes involved with two other fanatics, particularly a youth whose "wise blood" determines all his degenerate activities. Fourteen-year-old Frank Tarwater's revolt in *The Violent Bear It Away* against the teachings of his bootlegger preacher greatuncle leads him to burn the house in order to cremate the dead old man, drown his idiot cousin, and finally burn the whole woods before he goes off to imitate the old man in itinerant preaching.

Miss O'Connor evidently visualizes her stories as extended parables illustrative of the destructive violence brought about by modern man's individualistic attempt to take the solution of problems into his own hands. The Catholic church is never mentioned, but it looms as the traditional answer for those ignorant and for all who are driven mad by the excessive responsibility which lack of an accepted code and authority thrusts upon them. "Wise blood" is a substitute leading only to animal depravity, and those who are driven violent bear away the kingdom of heaven.

For all her accent on the fantastic and on strange symbols of perverted religion, Miss O'Connor demonstrates in numerous scenes from her novels, as well as in her fine collection of short stories, *A Good Man Is Hard to Find* (1955), a mastery of the telling little naturalistic incident, and a sharp eye for the graphic detail of the environment. Her clean, neatly wrought prose succeeds in putting a convincing footing of realism under her often grotesque and frequently unpleasant inventions.

Three talented writers, all of them older than the group just discussed, and all of them in training essentially outside the direct influence of the Tradition, discovered their own ways into it during the early Fifties. John Bell Clayton of Virginia, born in 1906 and dead in 1955, belongs chronologically to the first generation, but, after a successful newspaper career, he published his first short story, winning the first O. Henry Prize, in 1947, and produced a first novel, *Six Angels at My Back*, in 1952. In the two following years two further novels appeared, *Wait, Son, October Is Near* and *Walk Toward the Rainbow*. Then, following his early death, a volume of short stories, *The Strangers Were There* (1957), completed his literary production. Of these books, surprisingly varied in quality, only a handful of short stories and *Wait, Son, October Is Near* qualify Clayton as a New Traditionalist.

No major fault mars the fast-paced *Six Angels*, but it is no more than a well written thriller with good Florida color. *Walk Toward the Rainbow*, at the opposite extreme, proves itself a formless, often incoherent, sometimes—it would seem—embarrassingly autobiographic, account of a man's escape from a bad marriage, which has been haunted by his incestuous memories of a sometime dead sister. Much of the book is simply bad Thomas Wolfe and especially the author's final paean to America, a reversal of the protagonist's book-long indictment.

Wait, Son, October Is Near places Clayton in the front rank of those sensitive portrayers of childhood's awakening to the world of realities. From James and Joyce, through Southern figures like Caroline Gordon and Robert Ramsey, this limited point of view technique has produced some of the most effective fiction of our era. Like his predecessors, Clayton understands the importance of symbolic images for his ten-year-old protagonist and is able to project them beyond the boy's comprehension. Though Tucker English's inner conversations are realistically illogical and he grasps only vaguely his father's sin and retributive death, his violent reaction to tragedy, stemming from the heroic images with which he has been brought up, are thoroughly logical from his view.

Clayton's deft handling of point of view, his sensitive evocation of farm life, of old people, of young reactions are evident also in such fine short stories as "The Silence of the Mountains," "A Warm Day in November," "Incident at Chapman's Switch," "Sunday Ice Cream," and several sketches from *The Strangers Were There*. At his best, Clayton belongs with the more sensitive writers in the later Tradition, but he is also the most uneven.

Ovid Williams Pierce, who, between summers at his childhood home at Weldon, North Carolina, teaches in Southern institutions, has produced two quietly effective novels defining a past and passing way of life in a secluded plantation area of the South. *The Plantation* (1953), the more modern in setting, describes the effect on faithful Negroes and predatory white relatives of the death of a highly respected owner of the old-plantation school. *On a Lonesome Porch* (1960) harks back to post-Civil War times to picture women and Negroes returning to cope with rehabilitation problems in the absence of war-lost owners and managers.

Pierce owes very little to his predecessors in the New Tradition, but he manages his craftsmanship, through limited views, including those of Negroes, with consummate skill. No violence, none of the obsessive guilts which haunt so many of the South's more accomplished authors appear in Pierce. His is a beautifully restrained nostalgia for an eminently satisfactory farm life which suffered all but fatal reverses in the War Between the States and again is threatened by greedy lower castes of the New South. Despite the lack of variety and excitement, *The Plantation* in particular exhibits a widely sensitive talent, discreetly employing natural images with symbolic effect, to re-create a way of life centered on personal sacrifice to a humane order.

Byron Herbert Reece, a native of the Georgia hills, a farmer and a teacher, was for his first eight years of creative life solely a poet. After his first novel, *Better a Dinner of Herbs* (1950) and even after his second, *The Hawk and the Sun* (1955), he remained a prolific and interesting poet. The earlier book, an experimentally conceived and poetic treatment of a tragic situation, is hardly a finished novel, but it displays a diverse talent and particularly a sensitivity to complex guilt patterns. The first section consists of a series of interior monologues by a young boy, his uncle, a bereaved wife, an idiot and others as they wake on the morning of the dead preacher's funeral day. These are presented with great sensitivity and variety, dreams mingling with them to aid in the establishment of guilt patterns. Part II takes us back to trace the history of the guilt patterns, particularly with the uncle Enid and boy Danny, until the culminating tragedy and its aftermath. For all its fine metaphorical diction and its copious and effective use of symbols, this book never quite organizes itself into a complete unity. The dream images which control the early behavior of Enid and Danny are lost as Danny fades from the center of action and Enid's vengeance swallows all else.

The multiple-view approach of *Better a Dinner of Herbs* is managed with considerably greater force and effect in the second novel, *Hawk in the Sun*. Reece concentrates this story of racial violence on an August day and, by following the doomed odd-job man, Dandelion, about town and shuttling the point of view from him to those he meets and gradually out to others in the town, he builds an ever-mounting suspense. The story gains breadth as it gains momentum, involving finally all the elements of the town and taking on perspective with a history teacher's long view, merging into the Egyptian myth of Osirus, butchered and reincarnated as the hawk, Horus. The rich metaphorical style is rigidly contained in simple sentences so that the almost Biblical effect lends powerful support to the implied condemnation of primitive, pagan savagery. *The Hawk and the Sun* combines the best practices of symbolic naturalism with vigorous social protest as effectively as any other novel of the Renaissance.

The latest central group of New Traditionalists are among the most vigorous and artistically sophisticated of modern American novelists. Madison Jones and Walter Sullivan, both of Nashville and products of Vanderbilt, write in close knowledge of the tradition's styles and themes. Wesley Ford Davis, a Florida native and product of Rollins College, Arkansas, Kenyon, and Stanford, is now a teacher of writing techniques. Only Ann Hebson, a native of Montgomery, Alabama, but from early life a resident of Louisville, Ky., and Vurrell Yentzen, part Cajun and part Danish Texan, break the student-teacher pattern. Miss Hebson, a graduate of Grinnell College, trained on newspaper work; and Yentzen, though he attended Texas A. and M., appears to have arrived at his technical proficiency virtually without expert guidance.

Madison Jones and Walter Sullivan, despite their similar influences, stand fictionally at almost opposite poles in their attitudes toward the Old and the New South. Jones absorbs heavily and pessimistically the agrarian preoccupations and concerns with original sin of the earlier Nashville group, while Sullivan assimilates much of the spirit of modern Southern liberalism.

Madison Jones's 1957 novel, *The Innocent*, stands out as one of the most disturbingly painful works of its era, but it is also one of the best written and soundly constructed of recent Southern novels. Bringing back to a Tennessee farm community a newsman long in the Northeast and profoundly dissatisfied with the materialistic values he has found there, the story develops his "innocent" agrarian ideals in the new world of the South until they become, in their frustration, identified with animal brutality. Immediately on his return, Duncan Welsh blunders into a wrestling match in which an "innocent" farm boy is killed challenging a professional at a fair. This death prefigures Duncan's own as he challenges the new elements, and allies himself with animal force in his desperate attempt to restore inherited values, long since discarded, for the material values from which he has fled.

This book, both in its animal symbolism and in its pitting of the darkness of primal innocence against the blazing light of knowledge, recalls the patterns which Robert Penn Warren made viable as figurations of the South's decay in *Night Rider* and *Brother to Dragons*. Jones's exploitation of these themes and images, however, is entirely his own, and he invests them with a frightening compulsion and all but nauseous reality that is unique. In his 1960 novel, set in the early 1800's and called *The Forest of the Night*, Jones goes even farther in his depiction of basic human corruption and guilt. A gruesome sort of *Pilgrim's Progress* through animalistic sloughs and bogs of human depravity, the book develops a horrible picture of frontier life, but again a realization of primal guilt on the part of the innocently ideal crusader in the forests of man's moral pretensions. Again, too, Jones's linguistic power and ability to evoke the concrete image of living reality raises his allegory far above the common run of historically based fiction.

Walter Sullivan, in his *Sojourn of a Stranger* (1957) and *The Long, Long Love* (1959), chiefly recalls Robert Penn Warren, though the resemblance in style is slight and occasional, and in theme only peripheral. The problem, at least, in *Sojourn of a Stranger* is that which has occupied Warren and many other Southerners in recent years, that of Negro rights and what in America has been called "freedom." Sullivan sets his story in pre- and post-Civil War Tennessee, but it has obvious and eminently sane implications for the disturbed South of today. When 1/16 Negro Allen Hendrick, blue-eyed blond son of a reformist father who married an intelligent Creole Negress on principle, inherits an estate with a hundred Negro slaves, he runs directly athwart every sort of Southern prejudice. He pushes against injustice and prejudice too soon, too hard, and too far, goaded by his reciprocated love for the daughter of a captain who had fought under his grandfather. Rejected by the girl's father and beaten by her brother, he fights in the war out of hate and revenge. Returned from the Confederate Army as a captain, he discovers his image in a former slave, who, out of a misapplied hatred, waits to kill him after having burned down the plantation house. Recognizing his destructive error from Ben's, he attempts to win back Kate, but it is too early for her to accept his new understanding of himself. Although the application of Allen's story to the desegregation problem becomes clear on reflection, Sullivan's unhurried, thoughtful telling in a lucid, evocative prose never forces the parallel.

Sullivan's 1959 novel, *The Long, Long Love*, is, by the standards of symbolic naturalism, a simple book. Lucidly, through two basic points of view, we are offered the life history of a man dedicated to the past. Horatio Adams, of an old Tennessee family, deeply concerned with death and unable to share his daughter's religious faith, can believe only in the persistence of memory, and is therefore dedicated to the cult of his General grandfather's martyrdom. After his first wife's suicide, his too young second's tragical flight leads Horatio to understand his basic retreat from life. This rather un-Traditionalist theme is skillfully carried through an alternation of Horatio's "Life and Times" and his daughter Anne's "Recollections," with only a single deviation by the eventual son-in-law, a historian who uncovers the sad truth about the revered general. The tomb and monument of the old hero, violated by Halloweeners and by Horatio himself finally, provide both direct motivation and symbol. Deftly worked, with clear self-revelations of character, *The Long, Long Love* indicates that Sullivan has fully understood and adopted the techniques of the New Tradition, and that he has understood and re-evaluated its heavy concern with the past.

Wesley Ford Davis, Vurrell Yentzen, and Ann Hebson have centered their first novels on adolescent sex problems, complicated by the older generation's sins and fumblings. They illuminate their stories with rich patterns of image and symbol imbedded in sensitively, concretely realized surfaces. There are some echoes of McCullers in Miss Hebson's *A Fine and Private Place* (1958) and a few of Faulkner in Davis's *The Time of the Panther* (1958), but all of these authors have written essentially original and compelling works of art.

Davis sets his complex story in a Florida logging camp where the adolescent narrator, Tom, is staying with aunt and uncle and two brothers in a boarding house. Beset by sexually hungry mature women and lured by little girls, the handsome Tom pursues his way through sordid and elevating experiences against a rich natural background, until he can slough off his innocence for matured knowledge of the world. The book constantly juxtaposes earthy sexual episodes and high poetry, wood-, as well as human, peckers and the ivory bill, bobcats and mermaids, outhouse scrawls and Keats. From this lush welter of images and experiences, Tom, after his first complete sexual experience, emerges "aiming at the highest conceivable star," but attached firmly to earth in recognition and acceptance of his animal nature. Davis's remarkable novel is marred only by a too-Faulknerian interlude and occasional overly mature reflections by his fifteen-year old protagonist. But his story teems with full natural life and with beautifully handled, always relevant, imagery.

Miss Hebson's *A Fine and Private Place* also details a progress from innocence to knowledge on the part of an adolescent, here a girl, Travis, who gradually discovers the sexual lapses of her elders and is frustrated in her own first love by them. Travis, however, does not, like Tom, reach a satisfying integration. When she discovers that Peter, with whom she has found herself and a kind of love, is almost certainly her father's bastard, she arrives only at disillusionment and the necessity for escape to assert her personal freedom. Miss Hebson exhibits a fine sympathetic grasp of diverse characters as she exposes them in small sections governed by their various points of view: the belle-type ineffectual mother, the intellectual but guilty father, the Negro servant, Peter's mother and her rich upstart husband. But her triumph is largely in the delicate presentation of Travis and the success of her symbolic images of spider and minotaur which haunt her view of the parent world.

Vurrell Yentzen's strongly written first novel of a Cajun family in Louisiana, *A Feast for the Forgiven* (1954), has received little of the attention it deserves, perhaps because it was originally misclassified as a local color story. Yentzen brings to his extraordinary tale of childhood's awakening to sex and sin an intimate and convincing sense of people, manners, and speech. His delicate handling of the girl Clotillia's point of view and his sure control of rich Catholic imagery and blood symbolism mark him as a fine new talent in the patterns of the Tradition. Set on the Bayou Sang, his story of young Clotillia's introduction to death and sex, coupled in her mind with evil through shocking blood images, concludes with a remarkable child's interior monologue. Here the obsessive visions of violence, blood, and swamp scum lead the girl to an essential knowledge of sin and the harsh conclusion, reinforced by her own body's awakening, that pleasure itself is necessarily evil. *A Feast for the Forgiven* is a remarkably sustained, richly symbolic, and thoroughly unpleasant novel, one of the finest certainly to emanate from a relatively untutored talent in the American Fifties.

Two other recent writers, George Garrett from Florida and Walter Clemons from Texas, both graduates of Princeton, have indicated in first volumes of short stories that they belong among the more accomplished followers of the New Tradition in Southern fiction. Garrett's *King of the Mountain* (1957) contains highly sensitive stories of childhood and youth, sketches of life in Europe and in the Army, all of them characterized by acute observation, insight into emotional complexities, and an eye for the revealing image. In his first novel, however, *The Finished Man* (1959), Garrett writes a rather disappointing political story, well written but lacking the force, complexity, and symbolic power of *All The King's Men*. Clemons' *The Poison Tree* (1959) demonstrates a highly developed talent for probing idiosyncrasies of disturbed children and slow-minded adults. All of these stories of the Gulf Coast are keenly perceptive revelations of the mind and emotions working in unexpected ways, and all of them reveal a sensitive feel for the effects of language.

Three equally talented women writers, who published volumes of short stories in this period belong also with this central group. Shirley Ann Grau of New Orleans produced a remarkable volume, *The Black Prince,* in 1955. For a young Southern girl, she shows an astonishing knowledge of Negro life and insight into their emotional difficulties. In addition, her mastery of different types of narrative—violent realism, heightened symbolic legend, adolescent love episodes, parables of modern corruption and irresponsibility—indicates a highly flexible and original talent. Miss Grau's 1958 novel, *The Hard Blue Sky,* further illustrates her ability to project the individual scene, the uncommon character and the natural background. However, this episodic story of Gulf islanders never coalesces into a unified novel. Her 1962 novel, *The House on Coliseum Street* indicates that she has returned to tighter structure and intimate realism.

Betsy Lochridge's *Blue River* (1956) avoids the problem of unification by casting her novelistic material in the form of a series of short stories. An Atlanta woman, for years a newspaper columnist, Miss Lochridge knows her Southern town thoroughly and very sensitively lifts the veil on its disturbed and thwarted inhabitants. Like Miss Grau, she deals often and perceptively with Negroes, though she never enters their point of view as Miss Grau so successfully does. Miss Lochridge excels in the small revealing incident, often reinforced by unobtrusive natural symbols. Both in method and in themes, often involving guilt, Miss Lochridge is close to the center of the Tradition.

Doris Betts' 1954 volume of short stories, *The Gentle Insurrection,* written when she was only twenty-one, established her immediately as one of North Carolina's most promising young writers. With a rare command of form and a mature perceptiveness in human relationships and emotion, she concentrates in this book on failures of understanding and difficulties of communication. Adept at irony and whimsy, as well as tragic effects, she seems chiefly preoccupied with memory and the revelations which death or imminent death bring. So too in her fine novel, *Tall Houses in Winter* (1957), which centers on a cancer-stricken professor's return to his small home town and to the memory of his love affair with the woman his brother married. With many incidental insights into the town's life as the ironic Ryan reviews it, Miss Betts carries her story forward and backward through memory until understanding and compassion lead Ryan to a new desire to live. The house, with its cramped and crooked room, and the throat cancer itself provide integral and enriching symbols to strengthen theme and fiction.

A considerable number of talented and artistically sophisticated younger Southern writers have absorbed the techniques and styles of their illustrious predecessors, but have failed thus far, and for various reasons, to produce works of enduring substance. An overstress on Faulknerian mannerisms, an overpreciousness of style, an overconcentration on symbol at the expense of substance, a weakness in human understanding partially vitiates the effectiveness of an otherwise impressive book. Almost always these writers display a genuine sensitiveness, almost always they exhibit a real understanding of structural form, and always they can write compellingly.

The most gifted and original of these is Truman Capote of Louisiana, whose special sensitivity to the moods and imaginative flights of children and innocent childlike adults enables him to cast spells of grotesque enchantment. Capote concentrates on the so-called "Gothic" elements so often noted in Faulkner, but he presents them with a preciousness and whimsy all his own. It is true that the result suggests rather the filigree work and unfunctional gargoyles of the Gothic style rather than the precariously balanced but soundly based structures themselves. For Capote builds essentially flimsy stories, decorated with lavish and often decadent symbols, and his characters exists less as solid human beings than as projections of a feverishly active imagination. Extraordinarily fecund in imagery and master of the sensuous power of words, he creates a highly individual and poetic style. His three novels—*Other Voices, Other Rooms* (1948), *The Grass Harp* (1951), and *Breakfast at Tiffany's* (1958)—all conspicuously lack substance, but have his characteristic heady surfaces. Many of the individual episodes, especially in *Other Voices,* and several of the short stories in *A Tree of Night* (1949) where he deals with his precocious innocents exhibit a true and original, if always a precious, talent.

Already, it seems evident, Capote has inspired a follower in Robert Bell of Alabama, whose *The Butterfly Tree* (1959), centering on loss of innocence, contains many of the poetic and symbolic excesses of Capote but carries less human conviction. It is the sensational element in Faulkner, however, that most often leads the later male novelists astray. James Aswell, David Westheimer, and Philip Stone are conspicuous illustrations. Aswell of Louisiana, a newspaper columnist, has all of the New Traditionalist manners in his three novels: *Midsummer Fires* (1948), *There's One in Every Town* (1951), and *The Birds and the Bees* (1952). However, all of his fast-paced books, featuring improbable, off-beat characters, run to sensationalism, as if the author were keeping an eye cocked at the popular market. Texan-born Westheimer damages both his Negro-view novel, *Summer on the Water,* and his promising novella, *The Magic Fallacy* (1950), by improbably contrived sensational elements. The latter story, excellently told from an adolescent view, fails to make convincing a stepmother's seduction and careless dropping of the sensitive boy. Westheimer has also produced a highly diverting account of a TV junket to London in *Watching Out for Dulie* (1960). Young Philip Stone, "godson of William Faulkner," and son of his lifelong friend, is guilty of numerous Faulkneresque excesses in *No Place to Run* (1959). He writes with knowledge and tension, but his cast of crooked, sick, and vicious principals and his lurid political plot suggest the work of a rabid anti-Southern crusader.

Of the many other younger men who clearly comprehend and employ major aspects of the Traditionalist pattern, Thomas Hal Phillips of Mississippi, one of Strode's students at Alabama; Edwin Huddleston, a Tennessee newsman; William Humphrey, a writing teacher from Texas; Harris Downey, also a teacher from Louisiana; and Leon Odell Griffith, demonstrate impressive potentialities. Humphrey, author of a volume of short stories, *The Last Husband* (1953), and a novel, *Home from the Hill* (1958), has obviously done more than leaf through Faulkner's works. Though some of his short stories, like the artist colony piece, "The Fauve," strike poignant original notes, for the most part he sounds tones and echoes themes long familiar. He can write, and particularly he can convey the feel of the woods, the excitement of the chase. There are, however, too many bastards peopling *Home from the Hill,* too many ironic misunderstandings, particularly of parenthood, and too many killings of the wrong people or the right people for the wrong reasons.

Huddleston's *The Claybrooks* (1951) is written with all the sharp evocation of scene and mood, the tautness, and the sure grasp of character which characterizes the best of Southern fiction. Only some plot manipulations which strain credulity and a lack of density limit the effectiveness of this fine first novel. Downey's novel, also a first one called *Thunder in the Room* (1956), lacks chiefly direction and a final significance. One of the most poetic of later stylists, brilliant in metaphor, and controlling an effective irony, Downey adroitly handles four points of view as they reflect on an execution and the political corruption which led up to it. With more congenial subject matter and theme, Downey could well achieve major status.

Leon Griffith, a student under Andrew Lytle, like Downey concentrates on a single day's crises, as they appear from several points of view, and displays the same central weakness of conception. *A Long Time Since Morning* (1954) witnesses that Griffith, too, is a born writer, though Lytle's influence is manifest in his heavy use of symbol and philosophic overtone, and there is included a strained Faulknerian episode as an old maid strives vainly to lose her virginity before committing suicide. There are tense, sharply done episodes throughout the book, but the story falters to a lame conclusion as the idealist protagonist simply shakes hands with the corruption he has uncovered in the Florida town. Mississippian Thomas Hal Phillips, who has four Fifties novels to his credit, and who handles his complexly symbolic structures in the best Southern tradition, is limited only by his most inadequate treatment of women. Though his themes are varied, the usually tragic stories consistently turn on male to male attachments: a latently homosexual friendship in *The Bitterweed Path* (1950), both a father-son and a Negro-white relationship in *The Golden Lie* (1951), a son's feud with father and brothers in *Search for a Hero* (1952), and a complex set of emotional ties among a cropper's son, an owner, his son, and a sawmill worker in *The Loved and the Unloved* (1955). No woman appears importantly in Phillips' work except for the fanatically religious, deeply repressed mother in *The Golden Lie*. Girls are shadowy, worshipped, lost; the only heterosexual affair is a grotesque perversion of love. The novels, despite the sense of incompleteness which the misogynous bias leaves, remain among the most effective of later liberal works in the Tradition.

A scattering of women novelists, none of them of major status but all of considerable artistic sophistication, wrote single novels during the later period reflecting familiarity with symbolic naturalist techniques. All family stories set in rural areas or small towns, they focus complex relationships about central symbols. In Barbara Giles' Louisiana bayou country story, *The Gentle Bush* (1947), the swamps which breed fear and harbor decay supply the primary images to reflect a liberal editor's disgust with traditions gone corrupt and menacing. Caroline Ivey, with Faulkneresque language and a grandfather clock as symbolic center in *The Family* (1952), an Alabama story, introduces a rootless Northern husband into a tightly knit, landbased family, tied to rituals and traditional patterns, with tragic consequences. In her Texas story, marred by touches of sentiment and caricature, Alma Stone makes the old plum tree of her title, *The Harvard Tree,* the physical, as well as symbolic, focus as she develops a ten-year-old girl's loss of innocence against a background of the elders' futile search for the illusion of an irrecoverable past. Somewhat similarly, the Texas-set *The House in the Mulbery Tree* (1959) by Zena Garrett involves the symbolic tree, which serves as a girl's observation post—and tree of knowledge—from which she learns of evil. But no touch of sentiment, rather a plethora of filth and decay, fills this richly poetic account of Elizabeth's first menstrual summer.

Operating as it were on the fringes of symbolic naturalism, or in some cases beyond it in new sophisticated techniques, one older and three younger writers of considerable originality can be considered best with this group of artistically sensitive novelists.

James Agee, first a poet, then a militant Christian liberal, and finally a cinema expert, wrote his first novel in 1951, *The Morning Watch,* a remarkably intense and disturbing story of a Good Friday vigil by three preadolescent boys. Agee's amazing association of high church and vaginal imagery, which he had already developed in his unique book on sharecroppers, *Let Us Now Praise Famous Men,* is extended here with phallic concern and a snake symbol. Though this book, like so much of Agee's writing, is done with such a feverish intensity that the effect is truly agonizing, it testifies to a rare, if tortured, sincerity.

A Death in the Family (1957), published in the year of Agee's untimely death, and later made into a prize play on Broadway, established the author as one of the major figures of the Renaissance. This poetic, deeply moving novel about the effect of a Knoxville man's sudden death on his six-year-old son and the rest of the family achieves its poignancy by the sensitive restraint with which it treats harrowing emotions. Agee's intense poetic fervor is held firmly in check throughout this story so that the effect is that of throttled power, never carelessly expending itself. The point of view shifts constantly about among various members of the family, including the child, Rufus, and each is portrayed by himself and others with rare penetration and sensitive honesty. Enriched by sharp evocations of sound, smell and natural images, the unpretentious story is carried largely through the delicate handling of strong emotion and nuances of feeling.

William Goyen of Southern Texas, another highly poetic talent, provides almost no solid substance for his novels, tales and stories; instead, he spins a delicate web of memories, fantasies and dreams. He succeeds less well, therefore, at novel length than in his briefer pieces, collected in *Ghost and Flesh* (1952). Most of these latter evolve through concrete images and symbols to preoccupations with death and ghostly presences, hallucinations and solitary self-pursuit. Goyen writes beautifully and with extreme sensitivity, but he allows the real world to enter only as a harsh intrusion into the life of the mind. The major concern of these stories is the eager, yearning search for self, or the ghost of the self, and the past. Especially in the strange, highly sensitive "A Shape of Light," he seeks with complex symbolism to express the inexpressible.

Of Goyen's two novels, the second, *In a Farther Country* (1955), called "A Romance," but actually a confused symbolic dream fantasy, fails at every level. *The House of Breath* (1950) succeeds rather as a long fragmented poem of *The Waste Land* type than as a novel. A multifaceted stream of recollections as they come to haunt a young man on his return to the decayed family home, *The House of Breath* defines the places, the characters, and particularly the compulsion of the young to escape a town gone over to oil greed. Sometimes overly poetic, emphasizing death, decay, and human wastage, the book richly illustrates Goyen's fragile talent while it demonstrates the unsuitability of the novel medium to his gifts.

The rarest of phenomena in the prolific Renaissance is an existentialist novelist, and John Barth, once a musician and now a college teacher, can only be termed an existentialist. Barth's first two novels demonstrate not only his knowledge of symbolic naturalism but his rejection of it in favor of an ironic philosophical method of revelation based on introspection and objective reporting. These two novels, *The Floating Opera* (1956) and *The End of the Road* (1958), project protagonists basically without personality or character, men of a generation wholly indeterminate in values or responsibility. The problem in *The Floating Opera* is simply that of suicide, as the logical response to a meaningless life, but logic plus paternity lead the protagonist to the realization that values, no matter how relative, are values that can allow living quite as readily as nonliving.

The End of the Road projects the "twin serpents" of "Knowledge and Imagination" as the stranglers of Laocoön in the statue young Jake Horner keeps as an emotional barometer on his mantel while he involves himself with the wife of an incomprehensibly oriented, utterly logical fellow teacher. Clearly, both of these unpleasant ironic novels offer portraits of America's newest cynically valueless generation. Though the background in both books is Barth's native Eastern Shore of Maryland, the implications are general and extremely relevant to modern man's dilemma. Barth has added in his 1960 historical novel, *The Sot-Weed Factor,* the most lusty, colorful account of seventeenth-century innocence in a corrupt world that has come from a Western pen since Voltaire's *Candide.* But in his realistic detail and his brilliant reproduction of period style, Barth goes far beyond Voltaire's allegory to produce a masterpiece of irony with modern existential relevances.

Pati Hill, who has been a Powers' model in the States and in Paris and a contributor to the *Paris Review,* produced her first experimental novel, *The Nine Mile Circle,* in 1957, and followed it with a thoroughly French story, *Prosper,* in 1960. Her first novel, hearkening back to a childhood in Virginia—though she was born in Ashland, Kentucky—offers a fragmented account of a summer's experience in the lives of two adolescent girls. What emerges from the girls' play and the flash backs, managed in short glimpses from various viewpoints, is a vivid sense of unreality, of mirror images reflected ad infinitum. An underlying tragedy informs the book, but the basic children's view never allows the reader more than a surface penetration into its essence. Miss Hill's sophisticated technique allows us only glimpses into the reality of adult experience while the foreground is occupied with the basic unrealities of preadolescent life.

Prosper, Miss Hill's story of a provincial French widow and a young opportunist, has been compared with the better novels of Stendhal and de Maupassant. Though the praise is excessive, at least in the first instance, a thoroughly Gallic flavor and economy pervade the simple narrative. Miss Hill offers first a warm, sympathetic picture of Mme. Bonhomme's grief, recovery through passionate love, joy and final despair at the discovery of her pregnancy. With his mistress' suicide and the consequent complications for him, the carefree Prosper turns practical French peasant, marries sensibly, works hard, and achieves a contented success. Miss Hill may well be writing a parable of the French way of life, or of youth and age in modern society, but her strictly confined story allows itself no pretensions. What appears is a simple earthy story, completely French in atmosphere and in detail.

The renewed vitality of the symbolic naturalist tradition in Southern fiction as it manifests itself in the distinguished novels and short stories of the past decade suggest that it will continue to dominate our writing until some major disruption of intellectual patterns shifts Southern concerns into new, less personal or introspective, channels. The techniques have proved flexible enough to carry highly liberal, as well as conservative, attitudes; highly feminine, as well as paternalistic, approaches. But the themes which have been most effectively carried by the Traditional methods are those of innocence and guilt and the individual's relation to his heritage. The most commonly satisfying pattern sets a young boy or girl at the crucial period of his discovery about evil, sex, or family deviation. Here the severely limited view, the sharply recalled natural detail, the extension to symbol, are all most logical and most telling. Novels of return to the changed but deeply remembered heritage succeed almost as naturally in the established techniques.

But these themes may not continue to absorb the novelist and his audience. Already in the novels of John Barth (and more lately in Walker Percy's prize-winning *The Moviegoer* of 1961) we may sense the beginnings of a movement which has already become established in France as the *anti-roman* and with Britons like Alan Sillitoe. If guilt be transferred to deity and the past become irrelevant, the techniques of symbolic naturalism can no longer serve. But the South as a whole, caught up in new social upheavals precipitated by desegregation and reapportionment laws, is perhaps not yet ready to contemplate its existential soul.

7

THE NEGRO AND THE
NEW SOUTH

The spirit of exploration and criticism which characterized Southern fiction of the Twenties and early Thirties had already begun to produce a clear division between the embattled defenders of custom and tradition, particularly of the agrarian way of life, and the liberal proponents of change, who saw about them bigotry, intolerance, and injustice. The Depression, when it made its influence felt on farm and mill, widened and deepened the gap. The literary spokesmen of the right drew up their early manifesto in 1930, published as *I'll Take My Stand: The South and the Agrarian Tradition, By Twelve Southerners,* and followed six years later with *Who Owns America?* Southern liberal writers issued no credos. They ranged from mild supporters of Roosevelt's New Deal to such at least temporary radicals as Myra Page, Grace Lumpkin, Leane Zugsmith, Olive Dargan, Murrell Edmunds, and Erskine Caldwell. If liberalism had a center, it was located in and about the University of North Carolina, where Frank Graham as president had gathered a group of progressive sociologists and literary men. Vanderbilt University, where most of the Fugitives and others had taken their stand, despite some progressiveness in the upper echelons of the school, remained the agrarian stronghold.

The most striking, and perhaps the most significant, manifestation of Southern liberalism occurred in the area of the Negro-centered novel. Local color treatment of the Negro continued as a minor genre through the Thirties in such stories as E. K. Means' combination of wild chase, depravity, and humor, *Black Fortune* (1931); Richard Coleman's predominantly violent and highly colored account of

Charleston's Negro district, *Don't You Weep—Don't You Moan* (1935); and Lyle Saxon's serious study of relations between mulattos and pure Negroes on an isolated Louisiana plantation, *Children of Strangers* (1937). Traditional attitudes continued to appear from time to time, as in such saccharine faithful servant stories as Harriet Castlin's *That Was a Time* (1937) and Elizabeth Kytle's *Willie Mae* (1958); or in brutal exposes, like C. S. Murray's Sea Island story, *Here Comes Joe Mungin* (1942).

The bulk of the Negro-view novels of the Thirties and Forties, however, came directly to grips with the economic and social problems which afflict the Negro in a white-dominated world. Following Gilmore Millen's ground-breaking *Sweet Man,* a series of white novelists took up realistically the Negro's plight as tenant and sharecropper, factory worker, and city odd-job man. The treatments are uniformly sympathetic and, for the most part, markedly liberal. For example, two Mississippi novels, Robert Rylee's partially Negro-view *Deep Dark River* (1935) and William Russell's all-Negro *A Wind Is Rising* (1946), illustrate vicious injustice practiced by plantation owners and their families. In Rylee's story, the owner himself is senile, but his sons and overseer conspire to frame a murder charge against serious, patient, freedom-seeking Moses, who is aided only by a conscientious woman lawyer. Though Rylee's expressed philosophy is at best mildly liberal, his story proves a stinging indictment of the white community. Again in *A Wind Is Rising,* a vicious son of the owner precipitates the crisis, again framing a murder charge. The major story of this novel, however, concerns the education of the victim's brother as he tries unsuccessfully to enlist national liberal organizations in his pursuit of justice. Even strong Southern liberals like Russell have no faith in organizations. An equally harsh exposure of white corruption in dealings with Negro tenants, Alabaman Welbourn Kelley's *Inchin' Along* (1932), develops into an ironic success story, as plodding, undiscouraged—and lucky—Dink Britt arrives at his goal of independence despite all that the white man and nature can do to him and his light-toned wife. Again a too attractive wife figures, along with nature, this time to frustrate an East Texas tenant, in John W. Wilson's *High John the Conqueror* (1948). Wilson achieves an unusual effectiveness in the polemical novel by presenting his lustful owner in a not altogether unsympathetic light and by exhibiting his Negro, Cleveland, taking out his frustrations all too humanly on his guiltless but available family.

Several white authors concern themselves with the plight of the Negro who escapes the agrarian conspiracy for the lures of city pleasures and factory wages. The factory itself as ogre figures only in Julian Meade's sensitive *The Back Door* (1938), in which the Virginia Negro tobacco worker slowly dies of tuberculosis while the philanthropic whites argue with selfish real estate groups over the feasibility of a Negro sanitarium. Life in the slums and tough joints of the Negro quarters of Southern cities receives graphic treatment, however, in novels emanating from Texas, Alabama, and Georgia. Elizabeth Wheaton's *Mr. George's Joint* (1941) details in brutal terms the efforts of Gulf Coast Negroes to wrest a precarious living from gambling and liquor while the white law harries them. In Lonnie Coleman's *Escape the Thunder* (1944), the total indifference of white-administered justice to his race's problems forces a wronged man and his wife to accomplish their own revenge on the quarter's tough boss. It is Edwin Peeple's *Swing Low* (1945), however, which, in its vividly described Atlanta slum, with its filth and smells, cheap whiskey and cheap life, predatory whites and corrupted Negroes, brings to the reader as well as to the country boy protagonist the full sense of urban degradation as it is forced on the black population.

A very different, but little less effective view of the Negro's plight in a white-ruled South appears in James Saxon Childers' ponderously titled *A Novel about a White Man and a Black Man in the Deep South* (1936). In this uneven but always interesting half Negro-view novel, a highly talented and well educated Negro and his white college friend are denied normal human intercourse with the result that "red-neck" political prejudice and pressure succeed finally in destroying a love affair and a life.

While such primary novelists as Faulkner, William March, Eudora Welty, and Carson McCullers, not to mention Erskine Caldwell, were attracted to Negro-view writing in the Thirties and Forties, the liberal trend developed two new thematic resources: the white mulatto and the slave of ante-bellum days. The serious treatment of the too white, too attractive mulatto girl in a deep-South environment, once a favorite subject for dime-novel writers, was revived, somewhat inauspiciously, in Marie Stanley's *Gulf Stream* (1930), and achieved its height of popularity in Lillian Smith's *Strange Fruit* fourteen years later. On the evidence of the novels to date, this theme naturally lends itself to sensationalism or to popular sentimentalization. Even Miss Smith's best seller, angrily liberal in its point of view, centering a sharp attack on the poor white element who made Negroes their scapegoats for economic reasons, fails to carry conviction on a human level, since the author presents as protagonists only naive babes in a bristling wood.

In the same year Edith Pope, a more accomplished novelist, published *Colcorton,* an unobtrusively liberal-minded study of a Florida quadroon's attempt to bring up her son as white. Highly effective in its evocation of an unusual setting and in its sensitive portrayal of its central character, *Colcorton* falls into the trap of sensationalism in the unnecessary sequences which follow on the boy's discovery of his Negro blood. Similarly, David Westheimer, a stylist and master of setting, succumbs to the lurid in the final episodes of his *Summer on the Water* (1948), where a pale colored maid, after an affair with a white lover, commits suicide. Again, Barbara Anderson's *Southbound,* a loose but perceptive account of a talented white Negress's attempt to establish herself in the white worlds of Ohio, New York, and Paris, resorts to shocking coincidences in its final pages to produce a *volte face* for her heroine.

The renewed popularity of this theme led to its exploitation, first in Cid Ricketts Sumner's highly sentimental *Quality* (1946), made into a movie under the title, *Pinky,* and two weak novels about light Negroes passing in the North by Georgian John Hewlett, *Wild Grape* (1946) and *Harlem Story* (1947). On a considerably higher plane than these is a solid Virginia novel by Roy Flannagan, *Amber Satyr* (1932), in which the typical pale Negress-white man affair is reversed. Here the Indian-featured part-Negro protagonist is male and heavily pursued by his white woman employer until her trashy white brothers discover her unanswered love letters and viciously punish the guiltless man. The soundest novel on this theme with a modern setting is a product of the Fifties, Helen Upshaw's *Day of Harvest,* published in 1953 when the author was twenty-five years old. Eschewing polemics, Miss Upshaw holds to an admirable objectivity as she shifts about a Louisiana town through many levels of Negro and white society during a fateful night and day precipitated by her pale Negro protagonist's affair with a desperately faithful white man.

The liberal attitudes which govern these treatments of the race issue extend as well to the revival of the slave-centered historical novel. Frances Gaither reopened this vein with an Alabama plantation story, *Follow the Drinking Gourd* (1940), and followed it with an account of a Mississippi slave revolt, *The Red Cock Crows* (1944). Again, however, no notable novel of this type appears until the Fifties, when Elizabeth Coker's *Daughter of Strangers* (1950), and Robert Penn Warren's *Band of Angels* offer stories of light half-breed girls brought up as white, then relegated to slave status. Miss Coker's is an impressively solid book, lacking only the distinction of style and philosophical depth which Warren controls.

The remarkable literary development of the Fifties in the South is nowhere so evident as in the Negro-view novel. Intellectually and emotionally, the white Southern writer has grown to a fully responsible maturity in his treatment of Negro subjects. So convincing has the identification become that in book after book competent Negro readers have been persuaded that the author is a Negro. Furthermore, a number of these writers have developed the artistic means to create lasting literature out of their new understanding and sympathy.

A new high standard, both of authenticity and of artistic quality, was established by Jefferson Young's unpretentious little masterpiece, *A Good Man* (1952), the simple story of a Mississippi cropper's ambitious attempt to paint his weathered cabin. Prince Albert's mutedly tender family life, his dignified but determined attitudes against white opposition to his "uppitiness," are portrayed without a touch of sentimentality or of special pleading. Even in defeat, brought about by his wife's fear of reprisals, Albert loses no stature. The richly built sense of his unity with family and the soil he cultivates survives the catastrophe. Young's fine structural and verbal economy and his feeling for the meaningful detail brilliantly support his convincing human portraits.

The quiet sensitiveness of Young's writing also characterizes another first novel, Peter Feibleman's *A Place Without Twilight* (1958), set in and about the author's native New Orleans. Though considerably broader in scope, dealing with a large family and its social relationships, Feibleman's novel concentrates as completely on character and relationships as does *A Good Man*. The major theme, a "different" Negro girl's attempt to find herself in relation to past and future and in terms of her potentialities, is reminiscent of Warren. So also is the extensive use of symbols. But Feibleman's chief distinction is his ability to create an authentic Negro atmosphere and believable Negro characters in moving situations.

Byron Reece's *The Hawk and the Sun* (1955) and Ovid Williams Pierce's *The Plantation* (1953) project only half their stories from Negro viewpoints, but these sections carry the same human conviction as Young's and Feibleman's novels. Other young writers of impressive ability and originality have produced completely Negro-bound novels exhibiting surprising insight and knowledge. Twenty-one-year-old Lucy Daniels, daughter of Jonathan Daniels, seems intimately familiar with city Negro life on several levels in her *Caleb, My Son* (1956), a liberal-minded tragedy involving the impact of the desegregation decision on a Carolina family. Walter Lowry's *Watch Night* (1953) tells its story through the thoughts of a cultured Louisiana Negro as he awaits execution for a rape of which he is guilty only in his own mind. An uneven book, often too reminiscent of Faulkner, *Watch Night* attempts a difficult intimate character revelation with moderate success. Alfred Maund of Louisiana in *The Big Box Car* (1957) offers an unusual sort of modern Negro Canterbury hegira, lurid tales told by runaway Negroes on their way North. Maund's stories of experience with whites are brutal, fantastically comic, or simply grotesque, but they show flashes of true insight. The book culminates in a frantic—and bawdy—Chaucerian escape from railroad police and a sudden resolve to work for Negro betterment.

Mississippi poet and novelist Hubert Creekmore has written the most ambitious of the pure Negro-view novels, *The Chain in the Heart* (1953). His long, loosely knit book, centered on a Negro laborer and the bastard son of his wife, seduced by a white organizer, becomes practically a history of the Negro in the twentieth century. He explores in detail sex relationships of Negroes and Negroes and whites, unions in the South, Communist inroads, the effect of World War I and migrations to the North, with evident knowledge in the large and in detail and with conviction of the white man's long guilt.

Two other all-Negro novels, *All the Kingdoms of the Earth* (1956) and *Move Over, Mountain* (1957), by North Carolinians Hoke Norris and John Ehle, display real understanding of Negro problems and character in country and city, but little artistic distinction. Norris's back country story lacks a fictional center as it moves through two generations of several families to a community climax which rouses, and finally stills, racial animosities. Ehle's tighter city narrative pits a strong but "touchous" boy against his slick Northern-trained brother, but oversimplification and sentimentality distort this attempt to demonstrate the "almost" readiness of the Negro to assume full social responsibility.

Four books at least half from Negro viewpoints, two of them by young women, add further depth and lustre to the production of the Fifties. In particular, Shirley Ann Grau's volume of short stories, *The Black Prince,* displays remarkable narrative ability and understanding. Charlotte Payne Johnson's tragic Louisiana novel, *Watching at the Window* (1955), contains an unusual portrait of a Negro boy obsessed by dreams of whiteness and fatally attracted to a white prostitute. Miss Johnson builds strongly and surely, with effective use of symbols, to the climactic convergence of the two lives. Brainard Cheney's third novel, *This is Adam* (1958), is distinguished chiefly by its sensitive and deeply sympathetic picture of a responsible, loyal Negro overseer, who aids his helpless widow employer in a land-ownership battle with unscrupulous bankers and predators. Finally, one of the two novellas in North Carolinian Paxton Davis' volume, *Two Soldiers* (1956), develops the portrait of a simple, misunderstood Negro private who kills his captain, but nurses and wins the respect of his captor.

Novels dealing directly with the racial problem from a white view proliferate from the mid-Forties and are given new impetus in the late Fifties by the desegregation order. For the most part, these are violent stories seen by an observer rather than a direct participant. A number of the authors are, in fact, newspaper men, who report vividly but seldom with distinguished artistry. The exceptions are Worth Tuttle Heddon's quite liberal story of a Virginia girl's education through teaching in all-Negro Willard College, *The Other Room* (1948), and Lonnie Coleman's *Clara* (1952), a story of a cook and mistress told by the cold wife, who eventually realizes her inadequacies.

The basic pattern of these novels is established in *The Winds of Fear* (1944) by Hodding Carter, born in Louisiana, but a Pulitzer Prize winner as a Mississippi newsman. An involved story of racial fear and intolerance, Carter's tense story involves the whole town, as well as the editor-protagonist, before major catastrophe is averted and the conclusion reached: "If you stood against the thing, people would eventually listen." Donald Joseph's 1946 novel, *Straw in the South Wind*, brings a similar liberal view to bear on the case of a Texas Negro seamstress and mistress who is falsely accused of murder. Another Louisiana native brought up in Mississippi, Clark Porteous, offers a strong, intelligently liberal reporter's view of a lynching in *The South Wind Blows* (1948), and Victor Johnson in *The Horncasters* (1947) produces a sound, leanly written, and unweighted story of radical jealousy and violence in the oyster and crab industry of Southern Maryland.

A magazine editor, Georgian Arthur Gordon, continues the lynch motif in a sharply written novel based on an actual case, *Reprisal* (1950). The story centers on Negro and liberal counterviolence and offers no solution to the circular problem. The later Fifties produce four novels involving the segregation issue, from Georgia, Arkansas, Kentucky and North Carolina. Douglas Kiker's *The Southerner* (1957) has the virtue of a bright, witty style in its reporter view of a liberal's dilemma in battling prejudice when a Negro friend insists on enrolling his child in an all-white school. Francis Gwaltney's badly organized *The Number of Our Days* (1959) succeeds only in the final episodes as a liberal newly wealthy businessman galvanizes an Arkansas Board of Education into routing a violent, prejudiced mob. *The White Band* (1959) by still another veteran newsman, Louisville's Carter Brooke Jones, offers a broad spectrum of the white types who produce segregation violence, but his characters remain merely types.

Only Lettie Rogers' *Birthright* (1957), the story of a girl's year of teaching in a North Carolina town, achieves real distinction among the desegration novels. Young Martha Lyerly, too liberally intelligent, too attractive, and too uncompromising for her job in a community governed by a family, a tradition, and a bigoted fear of innovation, is eventually driven out for her support of integration, but not before she has planted the seeds of change. With wit and irony, as well as warmth, compassion, and psychological penetration, Miss Rogers depicts an entire town without sacrificing her sharp focus on disturbed individual characters.

Southern-born Negroes have not as yet produced a Renaissance of their own, though a handful have contributed to the general American awakening of Negro literary talent. Richard Wright of Mississippi in particular brought to an early climax the movement originated by Carl Van Vechten and his associates in Harlem. Despite his undeniable power, Wright is not an accomplished novelist like Midwesterner Ralph Ellison. He is too obsessed with racial injustice for proper objectivity, and too prone to employ melodrama for bodying forth his indignation. Still, his violent *Native Son* (1940), together with his earlier group of long stories, *Uncle Tom's Children* (1936), and the autobiographical *Black Boy* (1945), prove him one of the most forceful and stimulating of modern American writers. All of Wright's books, whether or not they take the form of fiction, are highly charged polemics. His intense seriousness does not extend to form or style, and his people run to extremes of good and evil, his plots of luridness. He has but one theme, yet the emotional drive with which he expresses it compels attention and holds it.

The great migration of the Thirties which brought thousands of Negroes from Southern fields to Harlem and other Northern centers made available for the first time to many the possibilities of cultural development. With the Negro renaissance under way, a receptive liberal audience prepared, and publishers interested, the opportunity was there for new Southern-born talent. But few had sufficient background to take proper advantage of the situation.

Judged by the standards of Southern white-authored fiction, the Negro novels appear undistinguished in artistry and thin in substance. To compare, for example, Mississippi Negro George W. Lee's *River George* (1937) with the strikingly similar Gilmore Millen's *Sweet Man* is to discover that Millen portrays, not only his Beale Street life, but his black protagonist more graphically and more convincingly. George Henderson's story of a rural Alabama Negro community, *Ollie Miss* (1935), conveys a lusty feel for life and the simple satisfactions of the farm, and its sequel, *Jule* (1946), is equally successful in the early country scenes, less effective when it moves to Harlem.

Perhaps the most interesting of Southern Negro novelists is Zora Neale Hurston, a folklore specialist from the all-Negro town of Eatonville, Florida. Miss Hurston has a special flair for dialect and for communicating a rich joy in living, something which few white novelists have been able to capture so convincingly. Particularly in *Jonah's Gourd Vine* (1934) and *Their Eyes Were Watching God* (1937), she creates a unique atmosphere, much of it through hyperbole. These novels of the all-Negro community, however heightened, have a ring of authenticity in voice and atmosphere, a quality whose lack makes her ambitious study of a poor white marriage, *Seraph of the Suwanee* (1948), a comparative failure. The only Negro novelist to concentrate on white point of view writing is Frank Yerby of Augusta, Georgia. He has been phenomenally successful, turning out best sellers every year, all of them sea adventures and historical romances featuring casts of white pasteboard characters. The only solid historical novel by a Southern Negro, it should be noted, is *Black Thunder* (1936) by Louisiana-born Creole Arna Bontemps, who is one of the most important Negro critics as well.

Of Negro novels featuring racial violence, the strongest, excepting Wright's, is that of another Mississippi native, William Attaway. Attaway, too, contributed a white-view novel, *Let Me Breathe Thunder* (1939), a mildly effective Steinbeckian hobo story. For his second novel, Attaway turned to labor strife in the Pennsylvania steel mills. *Blood on the Forge* (1941) complicates the race issue with union-scab conflicts for its three Kentucky farm Negroes, and involves them heavily in the murderous melee which eventually results. Less successfully, Waters Turpin of Maryland, after building a sound family chronicle, ends *These Low Grounds* (1937) with a football game murder and a lynching resulting from the displacement of Negro factory workers. Turpin's second novel, *O Canaan* (1939), again a family story which takes a Mississippi household to Chicago, is valuable chiefly for its picture of race riots and other Depression problems as they afflict a highly conscientious Negro group.

Only one important Negro novelist of Southern extraction has appeared in the Fifties, Julian Mayfield, a native of South Carolina. John O. Killens of Georgia shows some promise in his loose and heavily propagandistic story of hotel bellboys in a battle to organize a mixed union in *Youngblood* (1954), but he shows little grasp of the novelist's art. Mayfield is a different matter. With *The Hit* (1957), he exhibited an intimate knowledge of Harlem and a thorough insight into the frustrations and compensating dreams which lead unfulfilled Negroes to gamble on the numbers game. His second novel, *The Long Night* (1958), a poignant and economically told account of a ten-year-old boy's attempt to bring back home the $27 his mother has won on the numbers, does an impressive job of creating the atmosphere of a Harlem Saturday night and of building the desperation of the beset boy.

The sloughing off in recent years of Southern Negro creativity is perhaps a reflection of the slowed migration to the North. More than likely, however, as the very active and aware young Negroes, who have launched new campaigns in the South for equality, mature, a new wave of racist novels approaches. Social change is perhaps the greatest single stimulus to the creative mind.

Whatever the Negro himself accomplishes in fiction there can be no question but that a rapidly growing number of white Southern writers have not only recognized his problems in their full complexity, but have built through the years a sympathetic and finally an empathic understanding. It is certainly too early to predict on the basis of literary developments a final rapprochement, but history suggests that the attitudes and ideas first developed in literature end in social action.

8

NEW ASSESSMENTS: TOWN AND FARM

Relatively few of the white-centered farm novels of the Depression era reflect the radicalism which characterized the intellectual currents of the times. Radical ideas, born of disillusionment with finance capitalism, spread widely through the country, but only rarely and in dilution to rural areas. In the South, two novels by Grace Lumpkin, *To Make My Bread* (1932) and *A Sign for Cain* (1935), are the lone representatives of Marxist fiction, farm style, and the Marxist tendency to transform real economic problems into black-and-white patterns for propagandist purposes. Miss Lumpkin, though she lived in many sections of the South, was neither cropper nor tenant, and her personal radicalism hardly reflects basic attitudes in the traditionally conservative, however disgruntled, rural communities of the area. Charlie May Simon, wife of Arkansas poet John Gould Fletcher, in her novel, *The Sharecropper* (1937), better represents the liberal attitudes developed by depressed farm conditions. In simple, artless style, she details the croppers' hardships as hard-pressed owners resort to desperate, dishonest tactics to keep them in debt and to prevent their forming a union for self-perservation.

Miss Simon's book, however, has little of the power that makes of Charles Curtis Munz's *Land Without Moses* (1938) the strongest liberal indictment of white sharecropping practices. From its initial sequence, in which a continually frustrated cropper kicks his son's pregnant bitch to death, this brutal treatment of East Texas plantation operations builds the most hopeless of pictures, where landlords cheat on New Deal quotas, always at the expense of their sharers, use their women at will, and manage always to hold them in financial bondage.

Munz's novel does pile on its rapes and other violences, but it retains a fundamental integrity and rigidly excludes propagandistic author intrusions.

Most of the later white cropper novels eschew the broader political and economic issues for more immediate social problems. Edward Cochran's five Mississippi novels, for example, chiefly concern caste and local agricultural difficulties, as he traces his cropper's rise to *Boss Man;* and Annette Heard's *Return Not Again* (1937) tells an earthy story of a wife's ambitions and frustrations as she attempts to break out of the Mississippi "peckerwood" class to which she was born. Texas's gift to the Steinbeck tradition, George Sessions Perry, after producing a Brazos River hobo story, *Walls Rise Up* (1939), mixing humor, sex, and sentiment, describes in *Hold Autumn in Your Hand* (1941) a tenant's difficult life finally brought to equilibrium through his capture of a huge catfish long sought by his mean neighbor.

W. W. Chamberlain's solid story of tobacco culture, *Leaf Gold* (1941), reverses the normal Depression pattern by bringing his tenant to success both as a farmer and as a family man, married to a waitress with ambition and taste. By contrast to the conscientious Bert, his shiftless fellow tenants are condemned, but Bert and his wife make their way as much through the favor of the generous old owner couple as through their own efforts. Chamberlain is certainly no radical in his view of tenant problems, but only John Faulkner, brother of the more famous William, stands up as fictional spokesman for the Southern conservative element in this era. His *Men Working* (1941) is surely the most slanted, if also one of the most amusing, satires to be directed toward the W.P.A. program. His devastating picture of cropper families migrating hopefully into town in order to stand in queues and wreck property as they apply their ignorant, filthy, and gullible backwoods standards in an unfamiliar environment, is matched only by his heavily weighted account of governmental blundering and bungling. *Dollar Cotton* (1942) does better by its natively honest but economically naive cropper grown rich on high-priced war cotton and poor on deflation, and fixes its indictment directly on his irresponsibly spendthrift wife and children, indirectly on a poorly managed national economy.

Through the later Forties and Fifties, Southern poor whites appear less often in novels centered on farm economy than in stories of city life, particularly those involving politics. When they do figure in country settings, they play other roles and illustrate other themes. In Hubert Creekmore's *The Fingers of the Night* (1946), a fanatic father personifies religious bigotry against the rebellious sex instincts of his daughter. This tense Mississippi variation on Stephen Crane's *Maggie,* skillfully alternating its narrative views, presents tragedy with moving directness, so that the final indictment rests wholly within the event. In a less concentrated novel, considerably thinner in character analysis, May Mellinger, daughter of a shingle worker in several Southern states, brings a new occupational group to fiction with her *Splint Road* (1952). Detailing the harsh life of mill camps in swamp country, she stresses a family's struggle to maintain decent standards in cleanliness, morals, and education in a life where such conceptions are rare deviations. Still further afield is Carlyle Tillery's *Red Bone Woman* (1950), introducing a new subject of local prejudice, the Spanish white, or so-called "Indian white" of Louisiana. An integration story, crudely but forcibly written, Tillery's novel fundamentally concerns the racial education of an old-family farmer, who in his loneliness and sexual deprivation, has married an at first dirty "red bone" woman. When the issue becomes educational equality for the Spanish whites and violent racialist mobs oppose it, the book becomes the precursor of late Fifties segregationist fiction.

The latest novelist to deal originally with the back-country poor white is Borden Deal, another Mississippi native and another product of the University of Alabama's writing classes. In *Walk Through the Valley* (1956) he deals rather conventionally, but liberally, with a hill farmer's obsession for rich valley land. *Dunbar's Cove* (1957), a story of T.V.A.'s destructive effect on a farm and a tradition, further illuminates Deal's progressive orientation as well as his real attachment to the land. As a novelist, however, Deal discovers his true talent in a modernized folk tale, *The Insolent Breed* (1959), a continuously lively saga of the musical Motley family in their often wild, finally successful, battles with religious bigotry through backwoods communities of Alabama and Tennessee. Deal, who once worked with a circus and a showboat, constitutes his Motley clan as champions of a liberal zeal for art and sensuous living, challenging emotionally and even physically traditional Southern Puritanism. The picaresque story, peopled with Dickensian characters and told with Dickensian verve, combines an earthy humor with an air of the fabulous, while through it blows the liberal antidote to the New Tradition's heavy insistence on original sin and guilt.

While the liberal critique of the new South's problems and the traditionists' concern with fading agrarian values constitute the two most significant aspects of back-country fiction from the Thirties through the Fifties, they are by no means the exclusive preoccupations of farm and plantation novelists. Family rather than crop, social rather than economic difficulties chiefly attract the writers who deal with the owner class. Only a few serious works, like Charles Barnette Wood's deeply pessimistic story of North Carolina tobacco culture, *First, the Fields* (1941), and Louise Crump's liberally oriented Mississippi plantation novel, *Helen Templeton's Daughter* (1952), treat the agricultural economy as primary.

Preservation of the farm family and the estate in the face of declining income and the beckoning opportunities of city life becomes a major problem during the Depression years and remains one of the younger generation. Most of the novels exploiting this theme involve a strong-willed woman—though a man occasionally serves—a matriarch or tough offshoot of pure or hybrid stock who stands staunchly, if not always four-square, against threatened disintegration. There are a few instances, such as Harlan Hatcher's *Patterns of Wolfpen* (1934) and Christine Govan's *Jennifer's House* (1945), where the primary lesson learned is an acceptance of the demonstrated fact that one cannot "restore a way of life." The dominant woman who does "restore" or manage to hold on to "a way of life" generally comes off less likable than admirable, after the manner of Ellen Glasgow's Dorinda in *Barren Ground,* or the grandmother in Katherine Anne Porter's family stories. Vivienne in Emily Godchaux's Louisiana story, *Stubborn Roots* (1936), a girl, like Dorinda, without her own heritage, turns into a similarly loveless and much less attractive proud woman, whom the author exposes with merciless irony. Harriet Hassell's protagonist in *Rachel's Children* (1938), also hard and stubborn, despite her overpowering attachment to the land and dedication to continuity, almost destroys her own plans through an unwholesome jealousy of her son's able wife.

Another thoroughly unpleasant woman in Alabaman Helen Norris's *Something More than Earth* (1940) displays an unyielding possessiveness rather than a love for the soil itself, but she bargains on a young stranger's fascination with the rich plantation to make a loveless marriage. A strangely effective, starkly Gothic tale of unrealistic, heightened emotions, reminiscent at times of the Brontes, results. Alice Walworth Graham's ruthless young female in *Natchez Woman* (1950), ironically treated, manages everything but her own married life; restores a mansion, organizes the "Natchez Pilgrimage," and generally exploits both old and new South elements to realize her ambitious plans.

The most unusual novel featuring a cold, hard country woman is Vinnie Williams' *Walk Egypt* (1960). In a style bristling with native Georgia aphorisms, folk metaphors, and rhyme phrases, this flavorful story describes Toy Crawford's lone battle to preserve her inheritance of farm and mill. She loses to nature's destructive whims and to her own inconsistency, but manages finally through emotional participation in a Negro religious service to break her inner ice-block. The weak woman, a comparative rarity in Southern fiction, has her day in Foxhall Daingerfield's Kentucky tragedy, *Mrs. Haney* (1933). The much abused protagonist in a story understood through intermittent glimpses by a higher class neighbor struggles feebly to hold up her head on its twisted body against the force of an incurably trashy family. With effective blood imagery heightening the climax, the poor woman finds strength to deliver the decisive blow for her children's future.

The strong man as preserver dominates Barbara Averitt's Maryland story, *Hear the Cock Crow* (1949), and Shelby Foote's Mississippi tragedy, *Tournament,* of the same year. Miss Averitt pits a modern mountain-born wife against a decaying household, held together only by the will and work of her uncompromising brother-in-law. This well-planned, if overtly undramatic, story develops in identification with young Edwina's progressive cosmopolitanism, which succeeds until her husband defects to his brother's will and the old agrarian attraction. Foote's strong man builds back a Mississippi plantation which has been destroyed during Reconstruction days only to discover that his children lack the vigor and ambition to pursue his lifelong dream.

Farm life involves basic human drives, as well as problems of succession and control. As Vinnie Williams plagued her heroine in *Walk*

Egypt, so are men troubled and tortured by sex problems in several of the more intense novels of country life. William March's turgid *The Tallons* (1936), not his most successful novel, carries a psychological sex rivalry between brothers to a violent and ironic conclusion. In 1947 Peirson Ricks published a solid North Carolina story, *The Hunter's Horn,* revolving about a young farm boy's sense of guilt for a sexual defiance of his father's stern religious code. An uncle's tolerant understanding of guilt's complexities and attempt at mediation serves to precipitate tragedy, but finally also to free the boy from his mental anguish. Another well-sustained novel, told in the form of a last will and impenitent confession, *Harbin's Ridge* (1951) by Henry Giles of Kentucky, catches something of the Warren ring in its recounting of family killings for sexual offenses.

The Depression conditions which brought about such a large-scale exodus of Negro farm workers to the North, forced many white farmers as well to desert agriculture for life in the cities. But Southern cities, like their Northern and Western counterparts, had little but factory shutdowns or strike conditions, breadlines, and W.P.A. projects to offer. These were quite novel phenomena in the South, which had so often in recent years promoted itself to Northern investors as an area of not only cheap but docile, conservative labor. When wage-cutting and layoffs came to mill and factory, when the patient former farmer became impatient or promised prosperity, when organizers appeared to promote the impatience and stiffen resistance, the educated public divided sharply in its response. Industrialism and its promoters, native or "foreign," had been accepted with qualms, then with hostility by many of the older families, who recognized a threat to their less bustling way of life, as well as their traditional control of social and political institutions. Their humanitarian heritage often tended to align them, however gingerly, with the workers as against the "progressive" business interests of the community.

It should not be altogether surprising, therefore, that the Southern novelists, often of good families, who concerned themselves with the Depression problems of town and city, show primarily liberal, and sometimes radical, leanings. Businessmen seldom produce imaginative literature, and their sons and daughters do so only when they have broken with parental patterns. Scions of disaffected old families, as well as the precocious children of disaffected workers and the sensitive disinvolved, become the authors. So it happens that no Southern apologist for industry, and only a rare conservative, appears as a novelist in the later Thirties or thereafter, while the critics of industrial capitalism are many.

The three most radical of the economic novelists are all women: Myra Page of Virginia, Leane Zugsmith and Olive Dargan of Kentucky. Miss Page, as a matter of fact, is frankly Communist in *Gathering Storm* (1932), a mill story involving both black and white workers, and in *Moscow Yankee* (1935). She is merely liberal in her life story of a miner's daughter, *With Sun in Our Blood* (1950). New York supplies the setting for most of Miss Zugsmith's realistic labor-oriented novels. Of her six serious books, only one is Southern in setting, and that, *The Summer Soldier* (1938), reflects the point of view of a Northern liberal. At her best, despite strong helpings of propaganda, Miss Zugsmith can write a warmly human and convincing story, as in *A Time to Remember* (1936), about a New York department store strike. Too often, however, as in most tendentious fiction, character depth is sacrificed to propagandistic requirements. Writing as Fielding Burke, Miss Dargan stresses Marxist ideas in her fiction almost as insistently as Miss Page, but she tells sounder, more apparently authentic stories of union organizing, strikes, and riots in the North Carolina mills.

These novels are, of course, symptomatically rather than artistically important. Most of the liberal-minded authors of fiction managed to get across their views more subtly, without missionary intrusions. Willie Snow Ethridge from Georgia in her *Mingled Yarn* (1938), for example, achieves an impartial effect by focusing on a mill owner's loyally prejudiced daughter and opposing her untenable positions to those of her husband, a conscientious editor. An intelligent treatment of Depression textile problems, Miss Ethridge's book is clearly liberal in final import, though never overtly weighted.

Still more effective in its objectivity is Eugene Armfield's total view of a mill and factory town, *Where the Weak Grow Strong* (1936), presented in a series of vignettes and episodes. Tuttle, North Carolina, is the protagonist of this novel, but the reader learns gradually to know and judge it from a liberal viewpoint subtly suggested by the characters' own behavior as Armfield draws them together for a local celebration. A very different approach, humorous fantasy, is that of Charles Givens of Tennessee, in *The Devil Takes a Hill Town* (1939). Here, against a smugly Puritanical devil in human form, appears God Himself—also in human form—to side with a frail-fleshed preacher in his attempt to see justice done in a mill strike. Mary Barrow Linfield offers a direct and graphically telling interior portrait of a New Orleans salesmanager on his hour of business success in *Day of Victory* (1936) to expose his "sudden hideous aching" as he realizes that he has sold away his potential life of self-fulfillment.

The approaches of William T. Campbell, Foster Fitz-Simons, and Charles Wertenbaker place the reader in the heart of industry, a vantage point from which a liberal questioning of aims and methods appears as defection. Campbell's cola industry saga, *Big Beverage* (1952), adopts the method of ironic portraiture, and somewhat over-does it in his sprawling narrative. Much the same sort of scotching job is done with a Duke-like cigarette magnate in Fitz-Simons' *Bright Leaf* (1948), a more coherent and less caricatured account. Richer both in financial-industrial lore and in the treatment of human relationships are Virginian Charles Wertenbaker's two big novels: *The Barons* (1950), the saga of a DuPont-like powder family; and *The Death of Kings* (1954), the inside story of a *Time*-like magazine. Neither novel is Southern in setting; however, the power struggles they depict belong to industrial development in the South as elsewhere. Both books explore the capitalistic issues of an era, but *The Death of Kings* in particular, with its news-interpreting center seen through an original editor's honest humanitarian eyes, documents most effectively the gradual defeat of liberalism in the modern world.

There are a few more radical novels about big industry, like Robert Rylee's *The Ring and the Cross* (1947), which involves a complex alignment of Texas shipbuilders and politicians and sets forth its case strongly but too angrily. There are union-supporting but strongly anti-Communist stories like Elizabeth Coker's new South-old South mill town conflict, *The Day of the Peacock* (1952); effective liberal reporting jobs like that of John Downing Weaver's story of the Bonus March on Washington, *Another Such Victory* (1948); and even senti-mental treatments of mill problems like Edna Lee's *The Southerners* (1953). Still no properly so-called reactionary treatment of the South's growing industrial problems has appeared in fiction.

In an area of rapid industrial growth, new wealth, and shifting class structure, the battle for political power becomes a most obvious symptom of change. If its novelists may be trusted, the new South's alliances between industry and politics have bred a new caste of opportunistic demagogues. Thriving on the prejudices of their constituents and on rake-offs from businesses, legitimate and illegitimate, the fictional politicians are a sorry crew, whether descendants of the old aristocracy or ascendants from the red-neck mass. Opposed to them as a rule are crusading liberals, either too ignorant of political in-fighting or too upright to stoop to their opponents' methods.

The classic of Southern politics, Warren's *All the King's Men*, emphasizing demagogic tactics in a rich philosophic and symbolic context, has had the effect of dwarfing the considerable achievements of other writers in the genre. Hamilton Basso's earlier novels, particularly his treatment of the Louisiana dictator theme, *Sun in Capricorn* (1942), established him as the pioneer in the fictional exposure of Southern politics. Basso is something more than the competent reporter who produces the majority of the political novels. He writes well, conjuring up the atmosphere of New Orleans and Baton Rouge with graphic and sometimes poetic imagery and building scenes with dramatic skill. From a liberal point of view, Basso first in *Days before Lent* (1939) uncovered the hidden ties of influence and greed which made the politically controlled Board of Health a farce.

Most of the later political novels show a decided trend in style toward the school of tough writing exemplified most characteristically by John O'Hara in the North and James M. Cain in the South. They are peopled with ruthless politicians of easy morals, yes-men of no principles, and greedy business representatives. Wirt Williams' Hollywood-slanted *Ada Dallas* (1959), for example, contains all of these. The action crackles from page to page; there are shady deals, tumbled beds, rallies and speeches and violence. Red smears and black smears contend with personal scandal as the chief campaign issues. In all but a few cases, a young crusader is defeated, but beds the veteran politician's daughter or granddaughter.

The best of these fast-paced novels are Tom Wicker's *The Kingpin* (1953), involving smear tactics in a North Carolina campaign; Edward Kimbrough's *From Hell to Breakfast* (1941), story of a Mississippi Senatorial battle; Robert Wilder's *Flamingo Road* (1942), a local control fight, set in Florida; and George Garrett's *The Finished Man* (1959), a slower and more philosophical version of corruption in a Florida senatorial race. Of these, only Garrett's novel has symbolic pretensions and a diversified style. But his rather cynical story lacks the integration so evident in his short fiction. Philip Alston Stone's *No Place to Run* suffers from a lurid piling up of scandals and double-crossings. *Ada Dallas* and Francis Gwaltney's *A Step in the River* (1960) offer little but sensationalism and perverted character.

Two novelists have elected to treat politics lightly and have produced well-sustained amusing narratives. Berry Fleming's naive retired colonel in *Colonel Effingham's Raid* (1946) takes on the political organization in a Georgia city, only to be baffled by the complacency of business interests and the general public. Fred Ross's tall tale of a wild, good-natured and resourceful North Carolina hill youth, *Jackson Mahaffey* (1951), sustains its verve through a racy political campaign full of high gambles.

Serious political novels which shun the popular tough approach are rare. However, Pulitzer Prize winning newsman, Hodding Carter, and Evans Harrington treat Mississippi political situations soberly. Carter, who had introduced political complications in his earlier story of race prejudice, *Winds of Fear,* in *Flood Crest* (1947) concentrates on the political theme. His essentially liberal story, done with clarity and pace, expresses finally a concerned pessimism as it records a slipping demagogue's comeback through exploitation of a flood threat. Harrington confines his scene to a state prison in *The Prisoners* (1956), a strong book involving a warden's attempt to preserve his dignity in a struggle against political sadists. The most pretentious and the most impressive of later political novels, however, is Allen Drury's Pulitzer Prize winner of 1959, *Advise and Consent*. Drury, a Texas-born correspondent on the Congressional beat, manifests a convincingly detailed knowledge of Senatorial procedures, both in the public eye and behind the scenes. At the same time, he manages to keep a huge cast of characters in animated and suspenseful action. The curious mixture of idealism and cunning practicality, of demagoguery and compromise, honesty and ruthlessness—the essence of politics—has seldom been so fully exposed. If Drury stacks his cards for his tough-policy hero and resorts finally to a series of melodramatic climaxes to accomplish his end, he has provided so vivid a picture that it must inevitably color many an American's conception of his government's operations.

Still, the major preoccupation of the later sensitive town- or city-bred Southerner has been not the industrial nor yet the political problem, but the social situation which has been in part precipitated by the shift of wealth from an established group to the new Southern opportunist class and their Northern counterparts drawn Southward first by the industrial "invasion." The parvenu and the *nouveau riche* enter, in one capacity or another, a great many of the socially oriented stories. Their intrusion, or the intrusion of their sons and daughters, does not often comprise the major theme of the novels, but their presence is very generally one of the social elements to be reckoned with. And as often as not they are by implication championed by the younger writers.

In the main these novels represent the critical spirit of a generation dissatisfied with its parental attitudes, and by no means smug about its own. The core group is once again liberal, tolerant of everything but prejudice, snobbery, and pretense. It condemns or gently ridicules its elders often, but it can as well probe its own psychological dilemmas. Sometimes it broadens its critical perspective to expose the follies and hypocrises of whole communities; sometimes it concentrates on typical marital or pre-marital romantic problems. Chiefly the novels exhibit integrity and a sophisticated knowledge of the world. There are no truly major artists in this group, but there is a high level of literary competence on an astonishingly large scale.

The most extensive criticism in fiction of the South's manners and mores has been that of Hamilton Basso. Chronologically, Basso belongs to the first generation of Renaissance authors, but his career as a serious novelist began during the deep Depression years. All of his more important novels reflect his unwavering attachment to the South and, at the same time, his liberal-minded concern for its faults and follies. His typical story involves a professional man who is sufficiently detached to recognize the prejudices, the injustices, and the "Shinto-ism," or false pride, which he sees as the South's besetting vices, but who cannot escape his fascination for the country and its "unreal" inhabitants. Only *Cinnamon Seed* (1934) deals intensively with the Negro problem, and it is noteworthy rather for its liberal attitudes than for its art. Louisiana politics, also a factor in *Cinnamon Seed,* provides the major subject for *Days Before Lent* (1939), his most successful problem novel, and the Huey Long-inspired *Sun in Capricorn* (1942); and seldom has the cynical ruthlessness of bossism been so unsparingly exposed.

However, Basso's primary concern as it develops through all his novels and most centrally in *In Their Own Image* (1935), *Courthouse Square* (1936), *Wine of the Country* (1941), and *The View from Pompey's Head* (1954), is the analysis of Southern manners and morals. The pretensions of family and of wealth, the hypocrisies, intolerances, and inhumanities which an outworn caste-consciousness breeds appear constantly in these novels as the frustrations that inhibit and exasperate the protagonists. The charm remains for them all, however, something atmospheric and intangible, distilled out of landscape, buildings and monuments, instititions and manners. While Basso lacks the complexity and artistic distinction of the greater Southern novelists, he has been one of its most effective, because most loving, critics.

The portrait of a town may be painted through a series of separate brush strokes or graphic images, as Eugene Armfield presented Tuttle, N. C., or it may be gradually revealed as the impact of an important event, or a series of events, spreads out its waves of illumination. The former method serves Bernice Kelly Harris well in *Purslane* (1939), where she offers a complete picture of a North Carolina village through kaleidoscopic fragments. *Purslane* succeeds through its well-managed transitions and unified multiple story line, rather than through the depth of character portrayal. Its successor in the method, *Sweet Beulah Land* (1943), largely fails for lack of integration, and also from its author's tendency to indulge in sentimentalism—an unfortunate characteristic of her later novels. Margaret Long is anything but sentimental in her portrait of *Louisville Saturday Night* (1950), where the city is seen through briefly sustained looks into the sexual involvements of eleven quite different women. The view of a wartime, soldier-invaded city is inevitably a distorted one, but it has high color and sharp drawing.

The revelation of a town's emotional and intellectual temper by the ramification method has been most successfully employed by authors of liberal leaning bent on exhibiting humanity's frailties. Certainly the most moving of these exposés is Lillian Smith's *One Hour* (1959), a considerably more powerful book than her popular racist novel, *Strange Fruit*. *One Hour*, the story of a community's involvements springing from a little girl's false charge of molestation by a research scientist, achieves its strong effect through objective control and careful building of a mounting and widening tension. By employing the consciousness of a young Episcopal rector, Miss Smith is able to project without editorial intrusion the terrifying gullibilities and animosities through prejudice which lie crouched beneath the placid surface of a Southern city's life.

A similar technique is used by Bonner McMillion to uncover small-town cupidities and suspicions resulting from a lonely Texas wife's drowning in *The Lot of Her Neighbors* (1953); and also in Lonnie Coleman's lighter *Adam's Way* (1953), in which the snooping narrow-mindedness of an Alabama town's moral matrons all but destroys the life of an elderly liberal bachelor. W. L. Heath employs the basic technique also for his fast-paced semithrillers, *Violent Saturday* (1955) and *Ill Wind* (1957), in both of which a Southern town's integrity is challenged by untoward disruptions of its normal routines.

Several later authors have dealt with non-Negro race relations in much the same manner. Kathleen Crawford in *Straw Fire* (1947) and Burke Davis in *Whisper My Name* (1949) focus on Jewish problems in Virginia and North Carolina cities, respectively. Miss Crawford manages a nice discrimination between traditionally conservative and mildly liberal attitudes evolving from the affair of a deacon's daughter with a Jewish violinist. Davis uses a transplanted Jew's mercantile, banking, and social success under an assumed name to offer an outsider's view of the town, as well as to present an ironical portrait of the Jew himself, whose racial disguise has long been penetrated by his not too concerned fellow townsmen. Similarly, Claud Garner and Hart Stilwell, the latter more effectively in *Border City* (1945), dredge up latent hostilities toward the Mexican minorities in Southern Texas.

Two of the most interesting novels of this sort, both in structure and writing, are James Robert Peery's hard look at a Mississippi town in *Stark Summer* (1939), and Peggy Bennett's comprehensive view of a small Florida town in *The Varmints* (1947). No single crisis, but a series of developments involving a family and their Negro servants, compromises the town in Peery's novel. From shifting viewpoints as the intimate lives of one after another of the focal group impinge on others', we watch the town separate into its wholesome liberal element and its stronger sadistic and bigotedly religious faction. *The Varmints,* broken into small segments of narration and observation to detail the growing up of three partially orphaned siblings, makes its chief impression through its inclusive, sensitive, and wry awareness of the total community as it influences the children. Strangely mixing a hard eighteenth-century sort of realism and a Steinbeckian modernism, Miss Bennett displays a rarely original youthful talent—she wrote the book at twenty-one.

Edythe Latham and Speed Lamkin prove less interested in their industrialized towns themselves than in specific families which stand as representatives of the new and old South conflicts of our century. A great many of the problems of a changing society, particularly those of caste and custom, are intelligently discussed and handled in *The Sounding Brass* (1953) as a younger, artistically-minded generation of the town-controlling North Carolina family is forced to face them. A loose, somewhat overextended novel covering some forty years, *The Sounding Brass* has, nevertheless, solid substance and analytical perspicuity. Lamkin's *Tiger in the Garden* (1950) is all but pure allegory, with its aristocratic Louisiana family less real than a compendium of the weaknesses which have done much to doom the Old Order. As the Depression puts the final quietus on the clan, which had ironically put its trust in a hollow new South son-in-law, a cheap, codeless, money-minded class moves in to take over full control of the town's life.

Not all of the later talents dealing with the social scene in urban environments regard their subject with such serious mein. Social comedy and light satire of the sophisticated order initiated by Ellen Glasgow attract talents of the Forties and Fifties as economics had attracted those of the late Thirties. In particular, the novels of Josephine Pinckney and Robert Molloy of Charleston, of Herbert Lyons, Jennings Rice, Robert Tallant, and Lael Tucker display considerable abilities in witty observation of human foibles and in mastery of tempered irony. No earth-shaking themes, certainly, inspire these books; for the most part social rivalries animate the stories, though Tallant's *A State in Mimosa* (1950) turns on intolerance toward a D. P. couple. Miss Pinckney in *Three O'Clock Dinner*

(1945) and *Splendid in Ashes* (1958), even in her whimsy, *Great Mischief* (1948), exhibits her earlier poetic talent for evoking scene and mood, as well as a shrewd knowledge of human pretensions and hypocrises. Molloy, like Jennings Rice of Virginia, adopts a lighter tone as he treats with mild irony the idiosyncrasies of Charleston's elderly Catholics in a half-dozen novels. Rice's two small-town novels are cleverly contrived to expose the self-deceptions and absurd social ambitions among a circle of leading matrons. Herbert Lyons' *Other Lives to Lead* (1951) relates with sharp humor against a setting of Mobile's Mardi Gras the frantic, misguided efforts of spoiled children and dependent friends to thwart an aging widow's belated try for a little happiness on her own.

Lael Tucker's febrile, but often amusing, *Lament for Four Virgins* (1952) observes the lives of small-town Alabama girls, one from a parvenu family, as they find nothing better to do than fall in love with a harried young Episcopal minister, and settle for second bests. Tallant's series of New Orleans stories about decaying "Garden District" families, beginning with *Angel in the Wardrobe* (1948), maintain the lightest, most whimsical tone of all these productions. Mississippian George Patterson's satiric monologue, *Out of Egypt Ridge* (1959), is not, however, far behind. Adopting the technique of Eudora Welty's *Ponder Heart* to some effect, Patterson exposes both his socially pushing, inquisitive narrator and her better-class neighbors as a movie company invades the area to produce a film quite suggestive of Williams' *Baby Doll*. Frances Patton of North Carolina in two volumes of short stories and a light novel, *Good Morning, Miss Dove* (1954), brings her light humor and understanding to bear on minor domestic crises in middleclass families, occasionally on incidents involving Negroes, and on school situations. She often skirts the sentimental, but her feeling for the incongruous and her delicate comic touch keeps her always in control of her material.

The modern South, like the rest of the country, has produced a phlethora of novels dealing with romantic and marital problems at every level from the soap opera to probing psychological realism. The section has had and has its numerous popular purveyors of romance, like Peggy Gaddis, Temple Bailey, Sophie Kerr, and Fanny Hislop Lea, who can turn out plausible stories at whatever rate the market will absorb. At the same time, a number of thoroughly competent and seriously analytic writers of fiction have concentrated on these themes in the setting of the Southern town. Some, like Philip Atlee of Texas in his *The Inheritors* (1940) or the more recent Babs Deal of Alabama in *Acres of Afternoon* (1959), have turned their attention to an entire younger social set. Atlee's version of a young country club crowd is a harsh, tough, and often witty indictment of fast-paced and direction-less living; whereas Miss Deal's realism, though it also involves liquor, sex, and automobile accidents, is more deeply concerned with class, caste, and D.A.R.-type family protectiveness. Shelby Foote, in his *Love in a Dry Season* (1951), examines devastatingly an older set, the ambitious, wealthy, and socially prominent of a modern Mississippi cotton town, to discover only lust, greed, and frustration. The Georgia poet, Gilbert Maxwell, builds around a second wedding in *Sleeping Trees* (1949), and manages—or in a stricter sense, contrives—to tie into it the emotional entanglements of a whole group of disturbed and somewhat decadent small-town socialites.

The more impressive of these novels, however, are those which probe more deeply into the individual psychological problems of love and marriage. The authors, generally women, concentrate their analytical powers on dredging out from the emotional debris of lives the fundamental experiences which have dammed up or distorted their abilities to find satisfactory relationships. Worth Tuttle Heddon accomplishes the most difficult feat in her mature story of three funda-mentally disturbed lives, *Love is a Wound* (1952). Adopting in turn the points of view of an elder and a younger sister and the minister husband of the latter, she tells essentially the same story in three versions, and succeeds admirably in enlisting the reader's sympathy for each in turn as they try to recall "how it all began" and where the failure of the relationship lay. All three of the well-realized char-acters have serious flaws which result from or naturally accompany their chief virtues, and they all repress their emotional wounds until they fester and do irreparable harm.

Quite perceptively and intelligently done too are Mary Fassett Hunt's two Birmingham novels. *Family Affair* (1948) limits its com-pass to a wife's marital difficulties, but handles them with real insight through unsparing self-analyses and enlightening side views from the other principals. *Joanna Lord* (1954), a richer, more complex study of a physically and emotionally scarred woman, couples romantic problems with political and social issues. With rare effectiveness for its genre, this novel unites firm dramatic structuring, penetrating psychology and social analysis, a well-controlled variety of points of view, and even symbolic extension in images of fire and scars.

No other novels of this type rival those of Miss Hedden and Miss Hunt. However, John Hazard Wildman's ironic *Sing No Sad Songs* (1955) and Sarah Litsey's two Kentucky town stories possess real merits. Wildman's book purports to be the journal of a desperately frustrated woman attempting to understand and justify her desire to kill her husband. Wildman's mixture of several ironies and of serious themes involving political compromises and Catholic doctrines is not wholly successful, but he displays both intelligence and insight. Miss Litsey has a sensitive understanding of the romantic problems facing young girls, but in both her books she resorts to melodrama for her finales. In addition, Hollis Summers in his Kentucky town story, *City Limit* (1948), creates a plausible portrait of a narrow-minded high school dean who, on the verge of her menopause and psychologically unstable, transfers her troubles onto a wayward pair of students; Summers, however, does a much less persuasive job with his young couple.

The psychology of a student who killed a coed in an Iowa town fascinates Kentuckian Elizabeth Hardwick in her second novel, *The Simple Truth* (1955), but even more fascinating to her are the reactions of two trial spectators. Hardly a true novel, though it is, characteristically, quite well written, *The Simple Truth* is rather a record of a graduate student's largely social responses and a faculty wife's psychological theories as the case develops. There is no narrative movement, only discussion, and the verdict when it comes according to the hopes of both protagonists merely leaves both dissatisfied.

9

LATER FICTION:
A MISCELLANY

As Southern fiction of the Renaissance has developed since the pioneer phase of the Twenties, its writers have expanded their subject matter until their range has become no more limitedly provincial than that of New York's or San Francisco's authors. Southerners of the Forties and Fifties write intimately of psychoanalytic couches, of war islands in the Pacific, of Norman England, of expatriate colonies in Mallorca, and of life in French monasteries. They exhibit first-hand knowledge of Hemingway and O'Hara as well as Faulkner, of Sartre as well as Warren, of Steinbeck and Salinger and Mauriac as well as Wolfe and Welty. At the same time they continue, and in some cases develop, their specifically Southern literary heritages.

For all the adulation accorded him, Thomas Wolfe inspired relatively few direct followers. Wolfe is, of course, all but impossible of imitation; his success, however, might have been presumed to stimulate later sensitive youths to emulate his poetic self-preoccupation. A few, like Charles Mills of Georgia in *The Choice* (1943), and later J. R. Salamanca in *The Lost Country* (1958), quite evidently and quite disastrously did go directly to the Wolfean model. Mills, substantially lacking the necessary poetic flair as well as the gift for creating memorable character, takes the reader of his sprawling, though often sensitive, narrative from the confining home town situation to Florence among the early Fascists in a search for values. Salamanca, a rhapsodist of Virginia's Shenandoah Valley, describes a boy's growing up in exclamations.

The sensitive youth story, with or without model, is surely the almost inevitable recourse of the young first-novelist, so that the genre is in no danger of losing its popularity. Though it normally assumes a style of poetic romanticism, it may be told as pedestrianly as C. P. Lee's *The Unwilling Journey* (1940), an account of an Arkansas youth's attachment chiefly to the home scene. Harry Lee's story of art ambitions and early love in *The Fox in the Clock* (1938) is likewise told in more matter-of-fact language than its sensitive subject requires. Most commonly, of course, the weakness of these novels remains the Wolfean one of formlessness. For example, Julian Lee Rayford's *Cottonmouth* (1941), of a Mobile boyhood, develops much youthful enthusiasm, displays feeling for character and childhood's pangs, but has only biographical sequence for organization. Only a few of the Forties' novels escape this hazard, and they are those least indebted to Wolfe. *Hurricane Hush* (1941), a Florida pinelands story by Tennessee-born Laurie Havron, is a developed novel; what it lacks in character it compensates for in its intimate feeling for nature's moods and its success in conveying through its young girl protagonist the recognition of basic evils latent in human nature. Still more highly developed in form, Barbara Anderson's *The Days Grow Cold* (1941) exhibits sensitivity at an extreme in a twelve-year-old girl, and further pictures effectively her family life and her Southern town's profound aesthetic apathy.

The most interesting of the writers on sensitive youth since Wolfe is undoubtedly Robert Gibbons of Alabama, who made his fictional debut with a curiously mixed, but highly sensitive novel, *Bright Is the Morning* (1943). An exasperating sense of naïveté in handling of situations and in conversation comports strangely with sound perceptions and effective scenes which expose deep character conflicts. The story, essentially of two brothers, their mother and a wife, takes place almost in a vacuum, with no dependence on setting in time or place. The writing, at times excellent, often degenerates into a kind of poetic stuttering. But the problems, chiefly involved with morbid morality and sexual ignorance, are real and movingly dramatized.

Five years later Gibbons published one of the few experimentally conceived novels of the Renaissance in *The Patchwork Time.* Basically a new sort of *Pilgrim's Progress,* the book describes young Johnny Somers' course from shy, innocent, idealistic adventurer in Pineboro's Vanity Fair of temptations into a realist properly seasoned in sin and knowledge and ready to put solid ground under tempered ideals. Son of a father who sacrificed career to integrity, Johnny is caught in his first illicit love affair by news of his father's death and is overwhelmed with guilt. Only when he can repeat the offense on his own initiative is he able to recall his father's own trespasses, to accept human fallibility, his heritage, and himself.

Gibbons uses a variety of techniques and styles, some of them reminiscent of Joyce's *Ulysses*, as he shifts over the town and its lurid affairs. Johnny is harried by his own "agenbite of inwit" in the form of an inner "Heckler," who taunts his failures and reminds his guilt. But the author readily moves out from Johnny's consciousness to that of waitress Lurlene in her frightened pregnancy; to that of her tormented bastard seducer; to that of drunken unstable former football hero, Bill Boone, and his lush, free wife, Blackie, who seduces Johnny; and even outside the story to sections of author comment. *The Patchwork Time* is certainly uneven and at times overly lurid, but it remains one of the most interesting experiments in technique by a younger Southern writer.

The accomplished Elizabeth Hardwick of Kentucky, long associated with *The Partisan Review,* made her fictional debut with a novel of a sensitive girl's development, *The Ghostly Lover* (1945). It is an uneven performance in a variety of styles, almost as if the author were testing her potential literary range. She includes a strangely out-of-key Faulknerian episode, disturbing breaks in point of view, and a curiously unfunctional center section. Her story turns on escape from a decadent family heritage, but the break is accomplished only with a sense of "paralyzing regret," for the past itself proves finally the haunting "lover." Miss Hardwick's talents have been more satisfactorily exhibited in as yet uncollected short stories, several of them poignant episodes out of youth.

The history of this genre in the Fifties, though it is by no means meager quantitatively, lacks the distinction which has characterized so many aspects of the renewed Renaissance. Even the better novels, like Alice Fellows' sensitive story of a girl's preoccupation with an old estate in *Laurel* (1950); Eugene Walter's witty *The Untidy Pilgrim* (1954); John Hazard Wildman's ironic *Peter Marvell* (1952); Virginia Abaunza's compassionate and understanding *Sundays from Two to Six* (1956); Hamilton Maule's perceptive account of a boy's emotional life, *Jeremy Todd* (1959); John Craig Stewart's socially and racially involved *Through the First Gate* (1950); Thomas Sancton's class-centered *By Starlight* (1960); and Jessie Rehder's penetrating re-creation of a girl's guilts and failures in *Remembrance Way* (1956); all of them with considerable merits, offer talent but little that approaches genius.

Local colorists and regionalists have, during the forty-year prolongation of the Renaissance, searched out and turned to fictional ends not only all the mountain fastnesses of the lower continent, but most of its streams and bayous, islands and swamps. Mountain fiction enjoyed a burst of popularity in the late Thirties as a result of the extraordinary promotion of Jesse Stuart's homespun tales and Harriette Simpson Arnow's fine novel, *Mountain Path* (1936). Stuart, with the encouragement of Vanderbilt's Donald Davidson, published first a volume of poetic effusions in 1934, entitled *Man with a Bull-Tongue Plow*, straight hill stuff progressing from the naive to the sentimental to the unconsciously hilarious. His subsequent volumes of short stories, autobiographical pieces, and novels have won him a popular fame comparable to that of Grandma Moses in art, as the naive's naïf. Stuart's high point, both in popularity and in what may be loosely called sophistication, was reached with *Taps for Private Tussie* (1943). Here Stuart contrives that an officially dead World War II mountain soldier confoundingly returns after some forty-five of his kin have gaily and devastatingly gone through his G. I. insurance money. After this peak of inventiveness, Stuart's work falls off; *Hie to the Hunter* (1950), perhaps the most childishly incompetent novel ever published by a reputable American concern, is still thoroughly representative.

Harriette Simpson Arnow is quite a different matter. Her first novel, *Mountain Path* (1936), deserved the encomiums which reviewers heaped upon it, for it brought back vividly the honest objectivism of Tarleton's picture of people and custom while it carried through a clean, unified narrative development. Essentially a story of feuding families seen objectively but intimately through the eyes of a new teacher, *Mountain Path* paints in the local color richly, but keeps it properly subservient to the character problems which give the novel its substance. *Hunter's Horn* (1949) achieves a similar solidity in character presentation and depiction of setting, but lacks the unity and narrative pace of its predecessor. Miss Arnow's third novel, *The*

Dollmaker (1954), takes a mountain family to Detroit during war years and involves them tragically in a polyglot life of artificial values to which they cannot adjust. She tells a moving story but presses her simplistic thesis beyond fictional requirements.

Little of import has happened in the mountain novel since the advent of Stuart and Miss Arnow. There have been sensitive, competent stories of hill country youth like James Still's *River of Earth* (1940), John D. Weaver's *Wind Before Rain* (1942), and Henry Hornsby's *Lonesome Valley* (1949). An occasional volume like Mildred Haun's *The Hawk's Done Gone* (1940) stands out, in this case for the ironic self-exposure of narrating mother and grandmother, whose submissive and superstitious ministrations through these tales precipitate tragedies. The more colorful books of the genre are the fabulous stories of up-country eccentrics. Jack Boone, particularly, in his *Dossie Bell Is Dead* (1939) spins a skillfully managed yarn of a Western Tennessee hill community's wild night chases in search of a murderer, a seducer, and a bushwhacker. Fred Ross mixes an amusing brew of cock-fighting, gambling, whiskey, and politics in his un-restrained tale of a gifted North Carolina hillman, *Jackson Mahaffey* (1951). In *Satan's Rock* (1954), Kentucky's Carl Burton adds an elusive and beautiful Wild Girl to his melodramatic but well written story of mountain murders and pregnancies. Finally, Robert K. Marshall's queer but not ineffective mixture of eccentric protagonists, mystery, and sexual promiscuity in his North Carolina novels, *Little Squire Jim* (1949) and *Julie Gwynn* (1952), sustains interest without unduly challenging the reader's mental capacities.

The chief northern and western artery of the South, the Ohio-Mississippi, has supplied material for a group of inconsequential popular colorists: Ben Lucian Burman, Billy C. Clark, Harry Hamilton, Pat Smith, and Cid Ricketts Sumner. In the southernmost reaches of the bayou country, it has also stimulated the real talents of E. P. O'Donnell and Thad St. Martin, as well as the less effective ones of Cajun-born Charles Martin. Tidewater Georgia rivers have supplied the locale for Brainard Cheney's earlier novels, and the same state's Okefenokee Swamp served Vereen Bell for his Book-of-the-Month Club selection, *Swamp Water* (1941). Wilma Russ and Delight Youngs have drawn rather lurid material from the Florida Everglades,

James Street from the back-country area off the Mississippi Gulf Coast, Pat Carson and John Ehle from North Carolina's Outer Banks.

Kentucky's Ben Lucian Burman has unaccountably seduced a number of critics into dubbing him the "modern Mark Twain" and "the authentic voice of America" with his almost childishly crude stories of river folk on the Mississippi or displaced to the Congo. Burman has learned to insert a brief paragraph of description, complete with simile, between brief paragraphs of narration and conversation, all in the simplest sentences. Beyond that, he displays no knowledge of his craft or of people. He reaches such profound conclusions as that to *Rooster Crows for Day* (1945): " . . . 'the world's mighty fine. And the people in it's wonderful.'" Little better are Harry Hamilton's shanty-boat stories, Pat Smith's lower Mississippi novel, *The River Is Home* (1953), and Billy C. Clark's attempt to adapt some Hemingway themes and mannerisms to a Kentucky river family. Cid Ricketts Sumner manages to introduce a breath of freshness in her light, popular shanty-boat girl tales, *Tammy Out of Time* (1948) and *Tammy Tell Me True* (1959); while Brainard Cheney's two novels about logging on a Georgia river, *Lightwood* (1939) and *River Rogue* (1942) evidence close attention to authentic details of scene and speech, a feeling for texture, but very little for structure.

The Cajun country of Louisiana along the lower Mississippi delta streams and bayous offers a mixture of races, creeds, and customs more complex and democratic than that of any other Southern area. In literature it seems to lend itself best to the kind of treatment which John Steinbeck has accorded his Monterey fishing colony, the comedy of frustration. Like Steinbeck, E. P. O'Donnell of New Orleans and Thad St. Martin of Houma are not above introducing sentimental touches to sweeten their comic realism, but both authors create a lively sense of people and place. O'Donnell's "Delta comedy," *The Great Big Doorstep* (1941), followed his Literary Fellowship Prize novel, *Green Margins* (1936), a serious and colorful but episodic re-creation of highly complex Cajun-centered relationships. St. Martin's little story, *Madame Toussaint's Wedding Day* (1936), has less substance than the highly diverting *The Great Big Doorstep,* but it makes up in verve and its unique combination of the gay and the crude. Charles Martin's serious Cajun novel, *Unequal to Song* (1936), which alternates between Delta and Shreveport life, lacks real character and substance, despite some good color scenes.

The swamp, Everglades, and Outer Banks novel uniformly exhibits the local colorists' weakness in character portrayal along with his ability to depict scene and human idiosyncrasy. Of the fiction exploiting these regions, only Bell's *Swamp Water,* with its lush, deadly atmosphere and graphic description of human trials in the heart of Okefenokee arrives at any sort of distinction.

Southern religion, particularly that of the backwoods areas, has received little sympathy from the writers of fiction since the inauguration of the Renaissance. The country, or country town, preacher who appears in numbers of novels as a minor character is sometimes a subject of ridicule, often for criticism on the grounds of his bigotry and intolerance, seldom the sympathetic character. Among the later authors, several have concentrated their attention on individual preachers for comic and critical treatment. Jewel Gibson's Texas representative of the Church of Christ in *Joshua Beene and God* (1946) proves the most resourceful and inspired—at least by his own confidence—in his amusing and successful running war with Baptists and Holy Rollers. Charles Baker's Florida specimen, Love Gudger of *Blood of the Lamb* (1946), turns out the most flamboyantly hypocritical as he disguises his lust for female flesh in piety and engages in sex antics worthy of Erskine Caldwell's characters. Earl Hamner, Jr., combines lust and a true Christ-complex in his itinerant Virginia preacher of *Fifty Roads to Town* (1953), and produces a curious mixture of low comedy and serious criticism. More seriously, if less successfully, John Hewlett of Georgia in his *Cross on the Moon* (1946) strikes out in crudely guised anger at his whole hypocritical religious community.

James Peery provides the most complex of the revivalist preachers in his second Mississippi town novel, *God Rides a Gale* (1940). His self-made Holy Roller exhorter remains sincere in his fanaticism despite his highly developed consciousness of the monetary rewards available to the able religious promoter. Peery is careful to preserve his objectivity as he involves Newt Carter with the more enlightened elements of the town and finally precipitates tragedy when a tornado strikes Newt's revival meeting tent. The sceptical, pain-ridden doctor who becomes the hero of the emergency enlists sympathy and Newt antipathy, but only as Peery's controlled wide-ranging point of view exposes their actions and reactions.

On the positive side of Southern religious assessments, there appear a number of mildly sentimental novels, but only one first-rate story, Helen Norris's *For the Glory of God* (1958). In a brief, simple and poetic narrative, Miss Norris tells of a sincere young seminarist's attempt to win back the Episcopal congregation of a lovely church which had been built vindictively by the town's most egregious sinner. Hollis Summers' brightly told Kentucky Baptist story, presented from a child's view, in *Brighten Your Corner* (1952) possesses a measure of charm and liberal criticism; and Frank Clarvoe's North Carolina Episcopal novel, *The Wonderful Way* (1956), exhibits a ponderous sincerity in its description of a young minister's humanization.

The example of Margaret Mitchell's *Gone With the Wind*, with its tremendous popularity in an era of deep Depression, when fiction was providing solace for the discouraged as well as hope for the militant, encouraged a generation of Southern novelists to re-explore the dramatic possibilities of the past. Approximately a hundred new writers of historical fiction have appeared in respectable print since 1935. Far too many have deliberately sought popularity by exploiting the romantic and swashbuckling aspects of *Gone With the Wind*, and too many, like Alfred Crabb, LeGette Blythe, Frank Slaughter, Garland Roark, and Frank Yerby, have managed to win loyal audiences with shoddy formula productions turned out with assembly-line regularity. At the same time, however, a very considerable group of newer writers has seen the sounder side of Miss Mitchell's novel and been influenced to seek out and convey dramatically the truth and meaning of the past. Though none of this group has achieved the professional affluence of the popularizers, a number have made significant contributions to the literature of our age and to our understanding of the South's special heritages.

The more serious and accomplished of the younger generation have generally shied away from the War Between the States as the central focus of their fiction. So much has been written, and on the whole so badly written, that the young are understandably gun-shy. The few who merit special mention have shunned the broad canvas and the big issues, or have incorporated the war years in larger saga patterns.

Scott Hart of Virginia, for example, concentrates on the last days of the war in his *Eight April Days* (1949) and immerses us in the desolation with peddlars and strays. His subsequent *Stony Lonesome* (1954) generates a ballad-like atmosphere haunted by loneliness and violent feelings in bringing together a Northern captain and two Southern families shortly after the surrender. Mississippi's noted historian, Shelby Foote, concentrates in *Shiloh* (1952) on a single two-day battle as seen from a variety of subordinate points of view. With a similar concentration and a sure narrative ability, Robert Weekley of Alabama treats the same period in *The House in Ruins* (1958), concentrating on three Confederate veterans' attempt to continue the war on their return home. In contrast, Robert Richards' returning veteran in *I Can Lick Seven* (1942) is treated with an amused irony as he finds himself beset by predatory females, too long without men.

T. S. Stribling's multi-volume pattern for recounting the extended family saga has proved a congenial form for a number of later writers. Gwen Bristow of South Carolina has produced a social history of Louisiana from Colonial times to World War I by concentrating on a single family throughout her trilogy, *Deep Summer* (1937), *The Handsome Road* (1938), and *This Side of Glory* (1940). In addition, the versatile Miss Bristow has written a California story of early gold-rush days, *Jubilee Trail* (1950), and a Revolutionary tale about Swamp Fox Marion of South Carolina. From Alabama, Lella Warren has carefully and convincingly explored her heritage from 1823 to the '80's in two long volumes, *Foundation Stone* (1940) and *Whetstone Walls* (1952). In contrast, Charles Mills of Georgia compresses a full hundred years of a town's founding family into a huge overpeopled but quite solid single volume, *The Alexandrians* (1952). Hamilton Basso's span is shorter in *The Light Infantry Ball* (1959), but he builds slowly to and through the war years, documenting his thesis that the South largely defeated itself through political rivalries and corruption.

With the vogue of the historical novel firmly established, Southerners, like writers from other sections, have ranged farther and farther afield in search of unhackneyed material. Alice Walworth Graham, for example, after a Civil War novel and a better Reconstruction story, *Indigo Bend* (1954), both set, like her modern novels, in her native Mississippi, journeys back to thirteenth-century England in her soundly researched and flavorfully written, *Shield of Honor* (1957).

M. H. Davis journeys to eighth-century Britain in *The Winter Serpent* (1958), and Blair Niles takes us to Liberia of the 1840's in her well-told *East by Day* (1941). Still, it is American history which continues to attract most of the major talent. Jackson Burgess of Atlanta in his taut, well-paced *Pillar of Cloud* (1957) conducts a badly assorted group of pioneers on a harrowing trip from Kansas to Colorado. Antebellum Texas supplies Elythe Kirkland with material for a powerful character study and telling example of early intolerance toward Mexican and Indian in *Divine Average* (1952). Her somewhat less successful *Love is a Wild Assault* (1959) brings the checkered career of the famous Harriet Potter of Texas to bear on the love problems of her granddaughter. Bacon's Rebellion of 1676 furnishes both background and foreground for Virginian Philip Scruggs' solidly done study of self-seeking early Americans in *Man Cannot Tell* (1942), and Baltimore's Carlyn Coffin soundly and unspectacularly details the gradual Americanization of a German family immigrated to Maryland in *The Waltz is Over* (1943). One of the most thoroughly studied and impressive of the romantic historical novels, Welbourn Kelley's *Alabama Empire* (1957), tells of a Scotch doctor involved with plausibly portrayed Washington, Hamilton, Burr, and Knox, as well as with Creek Indians. In *The Ragged Ones* (1951) and *Yorktown* (1952), Burke Davis revives the slightly earlier Revolutionary War years, but does his most convincing re-creation in *To Appomattox* (1959). Kentucky's history from the 1770's through the Civil War has been exhumed in sets of novels by Janice Holt Giles, who excels at homely details and evocations of natural settings, and by Clark McMeekin, a team of two Louisville women. Don Tracy has done much the same sort of re-creation, but more luridly, for the Eastern Shore; Clifford Dowdey for Virginia and the Tidewater; and Elizabeth Boatwright Coker, more romantically, for South Carolina.

One further vein of historical fiction, that which was introduced in the first generation by James Stuart Montgomery, proved susceptible of later exploitation. The lightly told, burlesque or ironic romance owes its grandparentage to James Branch Cabell, and it is this older form which apparently inspired Josephine Pinckney to write her necromantic *Great Mischief* (1948), which culminates in the Charleston earthquake of 1886. Her story of an apothecary who deals successfully in black arts, visits Hell and loses his faith in it is replete with a sprightly irony, but lacks the romantic and sexual flair of a *Jurgen*. On the other hand, John Barth's seventeenth-century tale of England and Maryland has practically everything. This latter-day fleshed-out *Candide*, entitled *The Sot-Weed Factor* (1960), engagingly reproducing the style—as well as the frankness—of the period, carries a pure, idealistic "Poet Laureate of Maryland" through such a series of hijackings, Indian captures, mass rapes, disease, and mixed identities as would have delighted Voltaire. A master of invention as well as irony, Barth adds a brilliant command of hyperbole and epithet and distills from them a flavor unique in modern literature.

The traditional provincialism of the Southern writer is belied not only by the range of recent historical fiction but by the extent to which younger authors have undertaken serious interpretations of foreign peoples in a modern setting. Pati Hill's French village story, *Prosper*, William Styron's involved Americo-Italian tragedy, *Set This House on Fire*, Elizabeth Spenser's Italian piece, *Light in the Piazza*, as well as short stories by Katherine Ann Porter, Eudora Welty and others have been previously noted. A second World War, a rapidly shrinking globe, Fulbright, Guggenheim, and similar grants have rapidly multiplied opportunities for the novelist in search of a cosmopolitan understanding. There are cases, too, like that of Lettie Rogers, born of missionary parents in China; her first two novels, *South of Heaven* (1946) and *Storm Cloud* (1951), are soundly written and perceptive re-creations of life in foreign compounds during tumultuous periods in the history of modern China.

Occasional foreign travelers or part-time expatriates, however, make up the bulk of the Southern cosmopolitans in fiction. The novels they write vary as widely in the groups of people they choose to write about as in their settings. William Converse Haygood, for example, in his colorfully set out and many-angled story, *The Ides of August* (1956), confines himself to an expatriate group on the island of Mallorca. Lael Tucker's *roman à clef, Festival* (1954), exposes the intrigues among an international group of musicians and Casals worshippers in Prades. Robert Ruark shows us everything and everybody in Central Africa, including beddable airline hostesses and Mau Mau terrorists, in his opinionated, often intemperate *Something of Value* (1955). Leon Uris brings a limited reporter's talents to his stories of Greece and Israel, but his unprofessional biases give them considerable force.

Most impressive, however, is John Griffin's curious and emotion-wracked story of an American musicologist living in a French monastery, *The Devil Rides Outside* (1952). When the hard discipline and physical deprivations of the Benedictines prove unbearable, the town's cruelty, pride, possessiveness, and finally lust, as personified in the extraordinary landlady, Madame Renée, become finally an even more unbearable penance. Madame Renée, the utterly spiritual Dominican, Marie-Ornoux, and his lusty lay Christian companion, Dr. Castelar, form perhaps the most vivid trio of characters in recent fiction. In his second novel, *Nuni* (1956), Griffin deserts realism for allegory, offering a modern Crusoe story with an impractical professor cast ashore from a wrecked plane on a Pacific island, among true savages. As the protagonist is gradually initiated into the superstitious practices of the native savages in their slavery to "Elemental Nature," he and the reader gradually become aware of the parallel to modern man's slavery to "Mechanized Nature." One of the more original and thought-provoking of Southern novelists, Griffin undoubtedly has interesting surprises yet in store.

Most of the Southern literary travelers, however, were those who made their treks in uniform. The World War I contingent included Laurence Stallings of *What Price Glory?* fame; Major John W. Thomason, who wrote vigorous volumes of short stories about Marines and others, as well as two historical novels, from the Twenties until his death in 1944; and William March, whose series of Army sketches, *Company K* (1933), made a fresh, raw impact. The World War II and Korean War contingent picked up the new blunt realism of the elder generation, and often were able to add a fine command of pace and tension. Francis Gwaltney's *The Day the Century Ended* (1955) sets the pace for completely frank treatment of character and action, as well as taut combat drama. Gwaltney's Pacific jungle action contrasts graphically with the bitter cold Yalu retreat of Ernest Frankel's Korean War novel, *Band of Brothers* (1958). Though Frankel's story is less successful in character portrayal and overdoes its glorification of the G. I., it re-creates combat scenes and freezing marches with tension and highly graphic detail. A similar overglorification of the service mars General Robert L. Scott's suspenseful story of a flight to Okinawa, *Look to the Eagle* (1955).

The brutality of war and the rottenness it breeds are seldom the

Southern novelists' theme, but they have never received more vivid portrayal than William Hoffman of Virginia gives them in *The Trumpet Unblown* (1955). Essentially the account of a young idealist's indoctrination with Army sadism in England and on the European front, it develops all the vices bred by war and leaves its protagonists unfit for life at home. Joe David Brown's strong but ultimately melodramatic paratrooper novel, *Kings Go Forth* (1956), concentrates its evil influence in a V.M.I. graduate, native of Mississippi whose self-centeredness and scorn of Negro blood destroys a fine girl, his outfit's morale, and finally himself. It is the Pacific-based Marine's preoccupation with sex and brutality which receives the major emphasis in Lucy Herndon Crockett's story of a Red Cross unit, *The Magnificent Bastards* (1955). Miss Crockett respects the Marines as fighting men and even heroes at their duty, but her aristocratic Southern protagonist has much to learn before she can handle them in off-duty hours. For Wirt Williams in his submarine hunting story, *The Enemy* (1951), the shortcoming is cowardice, on the part of a cheap-commission officer. Williams' chief distinction is in re-creating the continuous strained monotony of a prolonged hunt for a hidden lethal foe. If he does not succeed entirely in escaping monotony in the telling, the authenticity of his record amply compensates.

A similar authenticity marks Douglas Kiker's story of the peacetime Navy, *Strangers on the Shore* (1959), but the offship life of his characters carries less conviction. More interesting and unusual is James Ballard's treatment of the peacetime Air Force in *The Long Way Through* (1959), the first-person account of a West Virginia mountaineer's career in and out of detention stockades. Spear's fundamentally simple honesty and limited sensitivity, as well as his too pure loyalty to a complexly corrupted service—or world—come through his strange grammar with effective moral force.

War as a subject for comic exaggeration seems to have a peculiar appeal for Southerners. First Marion Hargrove of North Carolina in *See Here, Private Hargrove* (1942), then Mac Hyman of Georgia in *No Time for Sergeants* (1954) jumped to the best-seller lists with their good-humored satires on Army life. In between these successes, William Bradford Huie, from Alabama, lightly pilloried the luxurious life of wine and women as led by the American high brass in wartime England. His *Revolt of Mamie Stover* (1951) provoked a lighter sequel in *The Americanization of Emily* (1959). Perhaps the least of these is Avery Kolb's Negro story, *Jigger Whichet's War* (1959).

As the Southerner's horizons have widened, his reading and hence his choice of models has been steadily enlarged. The influence of Hemingway, however perverted, created the beginnings of a "tough school" of Southern writing contemporaneous with John O'Hara's first novels in this vein. Maryland's James M. Cain, for example, produced his popular *The Postman Always Rings Twice* in the same year (1934) that saw O'Hara's first novel, *Appointment in Samarra* off the press; and Horace McCoy of Tennessee published *They Shoot Horses, Don't They?* a year later. Cain and McCoy have continued to produce and sell in the paperback market. Robert Wilder of Virginia and Florida soon picked up the style, as he has so many others, and James Ross of North Carolina transferred the setting to a roadhouse in his own state in his tensely written *They Don't Dance Much* (1940). Only with the Fifties and the enormous expansion of the paperback boom, however, have numbers of Southern authors been lured into the tough school. No Hemingways have appeared in the South—or elsewhere—but considerable fast hard writing has come from the pens of Tom Wicker of North Carolina, Donald Windham and Calder Willingham of Atlanta, and William Hoffman of Virginia. Francis Gwaltney of Arkansas in a first novel, *The Yaller-Headed Summer* (1954), has done an ironic version of the toughness-cum-sex potboiler with its center on an utterly stupid, blundering constable hired to protect the Good Families' interests.

The impact of Freud and the psychologically oriented novel, despite the early residence of Sherwood Anderson in the South, hardly occurs until the third generation of the Renaissance. Virginia's Blair Niles made a bold beginning in 1931 with her *Strange Brother,* a serious if not quite believable story of homosexual and interracial frustrations in and out of Harlem. She had no successors, however, until Hubert Creekmore's *The Welcome* (1948), which digs deeply into homosexual and kindred problems in a Mississippi town setting. Only Lonnie Coleman's *Sam* (1959), set in New York, takes up this theme, but Coleman's mixture of slickness and sensationalism serves only to underscore Creekmore's honesty and insight.

The inner workings of a psychiatric hospital are sensitively and dramatically exposed in Lettie Rogers' *Landscape of the Heart* seen through the eyes of a divorced girl patient. A somewhat similar, but more diffuse and complicated, treatment of a disturbed girl in a Swiss mental institution occurs in Gladys Baker's *Our Hearts Are Restless* (1955). Here the Catholic religion provides much of the complication, as well as the solution.

Only Robert Marks of South Carolina, however, brings the reader directly into the mind and onto the couch of the psychiatrist, in his *The Horizontal Hour* (1957). Mr. Marks' knowledge and insight are impressive, but he allows himself a considerable indulgence in sensationalism before he solves the complex sexual problems of patients and doctor, or simply disposes of them. William March manages his revelation of the emotionally disturbed in *The Bad Seed* (1954) with more sophistication, irony, and suspense. This skillfully contrived story of an eight-year-old girl addicted to murder builds chillingly through the mother's gradual realization of her child's depravity and her own involvement to a deft ironic conclusion. At the other end of the scale, Max Steele in *Debby* (1950) accomplishes well a difficult feat in portraying a feeble-minded old woman's perspective on the world of a family's relationships. Skirting the edges of sentimentality, Steele thoroughly involves the reader in Debby's emotional integrity and her intellectual bewilderment as she brings up a tolerant but nervous woman's children.

10

LATER POETRY AND DRAMA

The early Renaissance burst of poetic activity which produced three eventual winners of Pulitzer Prizes and three Bollingen Awards has abated little despite the fact that the American taste for poetry declined abruptly during the Depression years. Though many of those Southerners who had published poetry first turned exclusively to the popular medium of fiction, and most of the distinguished poets of later years have been forced to double as teachers and critics, the poetic urge remains compelling. Impressive talent continues to appear all over the Southern area and in great variety. No tradition has dominated poetry as it has fiction, but, as elsewhere, the influence of Eliot and Auden have been strongly felt. Only two of the later Southern poets have received major awards for poetic achievement, and none has arrived at the popular acclaim accorded in a more propitious era to Robert Frost, T. S. Eliot, Edna St. Vincent Millay, and others.

Karl Shapiro of Baltimore, with his *V-Letter* of 1944, came as close to popularity as any genuine modern poet, and he alone has won a Pulitzer Prize. In his 1935 *Poems* and especially in *Person, Place, and Thing* (1942), Shapiro had established himself as a sharp-eyed, surprisingly lucid, and technically accomplished poet. Owing little to Pound and Eliot or to the modern metaphysicals generally, Shapiro found more congenial models in Auden and MacNeice, with their mixture of eloquence and commercial jargon, their verbal energy and formal agility. But it is only in his technical equipment and his versatility that he suggests his models; in his conceptions, he appears rather an eighteenth-century rationalist than a "lunatic clergyman."

He is a common-sense rationalist but one endowed with sensibility, deep compassion and tenderness. Everything he sees, and he sees a great deal very acutely, becomes a subject for poetry: a buzzing fly, a soldier's burial, a letter, an auto crash, a cut flower, a gun, a new Buick, a "Nigger." Shunning the ellipsis and the allusive reference of the Eliotic tradition, he prefers full exposition and the images of everyday life. He writes a long *Essay on Rime* with all the aplomb and wit of a Pope or Dryden, but his verse always sounds with a modern accent. Equally at ease with swinging anapests or dactyls and with conventional iambic forms, he seems always fresh, always spontaneous.

Shapiro's universal sympathy for man, beast, insect, plant particularly distinguishes him from his contemporaries. With no lapses into sentimentalism and no shunning of the disgusting aspects, he can feel for that "hideous little bat," the housefly, the full pathos of its useless, hunted existence. He mourns an average soldier's death, "more than an accident, less than willed," but keeps a level tone as he reflects that "no history deceived him" in thus early cutting off his prospects. Despite their acuteness, he is never carried by his emotions into anger or hatred. A reasonable toughness underlies all his perceptions of life's pains and perplexities. He is a poet of heart as well as mind, but one without a trace of mysticism or romanticism.

Like Shapiro, Randall Jarrell of Nashville, who was to win a National Book Award in 1960 for his *The Woman at the Washington Zoo,* made his first impression as a war poet. Brought up, as it were, under the wing of Allen Tate, he has become one of the South's better critics as well as a novelist and poet. While he inherits some of the intellectual preoccupations of his mentor, his experience of war in the bomber command led him to concentrate most heavily on violence and death. Jarrell writes with compassion of the flyers, the gunners, the prisoners, the wives, and the German children. He can be brutal and colloquially hard, but most often he seeks intellectual understanding of the harsh realities he experiences. The anger and pity which most often inspire the war poems are turned into mental probing. He reflects on meanings, seldom arriving, however, at unqualified statement.

Jarrell's three earlier volumes, *Blood for a Stranger* (1942), *Little Friend, Little Friend* (1945), and *Losses* (1948), chiefly poems reflecting aspects of his war experience, contain his most intense and most moving verse. They exhibit his literary heritage in form, sometimes in density and obliquity, often in bookish reference; but the mind informing them and his more recent work shows no evidence of metaphysical orientation. On the other hand, none of Shapiro's lucid rationalism appears. Jarrell has frequent recourse to the realm of dream and fairy tale; his poems are often inhabited by spirits of the dead, the lost children and animals of the *märchen*. The preoccupation with mortality and creatures of the imagination does not exclude wit, however, which often flashes out in a phrase, sometimes informs a whole poem. Jarrell's gift for the striking epithet makes of his poetry a continual dance of the mind, rather than a logical progression. He is often led off the direct line of the poem's natural development into discursive movements which his agile mind suggests. Very few of his poems, therefore, have that firm definition which attracts the anthologist. Jarrell is an accomplished, sensitive poet, a serious, literary, clever poet; but he has written only a few memorable poems.

A number of skilled poets have kept alive the traditional forms and inspired them with somewhat modernized sensibilities. Georgia, for example, has produced such true, if not startling, talents as those of Gilbert Maxwell, Daniel Hicky, Florence Stearns, and Anderson Scruggs. Carlton Drewry of Virginia has won several prizes for his thoughtful, gracefully finished verse, and James V. Cunningham of Maryland has established a minor reputation for epigrams and wry verse comments on the passing scene. True originality appears more rarely, however. The South's two surrealist poets exhibit this commodity with notable effect. Charles Henri Ford of Mississippi and Parker Tyler of New Orleans, who collaborated on a novel published in Paris, made their chief reputations as magazine editor and as film critic. Influences of French poets like Cocteau and Eluard are evident in the image-glittering surfaces and the dream logic of their poetic structures. Ford presents the more dazzling display of verbal and visual pyrotechnics. Tyler, who seems more conscious of the symbolist heritage, provides greater density, if no less final obscurity.

Out of the common too is the group of poets from the hill and mountain regions of Georgia, Tennessee, Kentucky, and North Carolina. From his heritage of Georgian folk poetry, Byron Herbert Reece, also a fine novelist, spins out shortline ballads flavored with mysticism, but as readily writes deft lyrics which suggest Blake or Dickinson. George Scarbrough from the Cherokee country of Eastern Tennessee displays a similar control of ballad and narrative forms, as well as lyrics celebrating the homely scenes of his native area. Though he possesses a similar streak of mysticism, his verse is somewhat harsher and darker than Reece's, and more personal. James Still, a native of Alabama but an adopted Kentuckian, is less finished as a poet, but he records with spontaneous directness his feelings for the rugged coal-mining and hound-running country of the mountains. He accepts the shortness and harshness of hill life, the imminence of sudden death with stoic fortitude. No less spontaneous than Still, but embarrassingly crude, both in form and in sentiment, are Jesse Stuart's Kentucky mountain effusions. James Agee's early verse from the Tennessee hills often sinks to the Stuart level in his effusive treatment of religious and sentimental themes, but his burning honesty and compulsive drive indicate the power he was finally able to control as a novelist. One of the few dedicated narrative poets of our age, Frank Borden Hanes of North Carolina, after producing an often effective but uneven mountain novel in verse, turned to the West and the past in *The Bat Brothers* (1953). Of the three long and connected narrative poems which make up this volume, the first and third particularly prove Hanes a sensitive creator of lyric moods and an adept builder of heightened psychological tension.

In the main, those poets who have hewed closer to the neo-metaphysical tradition and to that established by Auden and his group have dominated the later Southern scene. Hubert Creekmore, Ben Belitt, and Kathryn Worth, all publishing first around 1940, illustrate various forms of mastery in the metaphysical vein. Creekmore, a Mississippian and a novelist, most clearly reflects the influence of Eliot, but he piles up imagery with the density of a Hart Crane and adds striking dissonances. His five volumes of verse prove him not only a skillful technician, but a thoughtful observer. His intense compression of thought and image, the sometimes tortured diction make for some obscurity, but his integrity is manifest. Ben Belitt in his two volumes of poetry has demonstrated his debt to the same tradition, especially in his imagetic density and compact diction. He has little of Creekmore's harshness, but piles up instead rich tonal effects. Whether he writes on war themes, his reading, on the scene before him, he weaves his thought and imagery in subtlely intricate patterns. Technically one of our most artistic poets, Belitt has yet to develop fully his personal voice and attitude. Kathryn Worth from North Carolina has published only a single volume of adult verse, but in it she shows complete familiarity with metaphysical practice. Sometimes she strains for the boldness of Donne in a too compact and allusive compound of thought and image, but in her readings of the world of childhood she is both sensitive and original.

Of the poets who have established themselves in the Fifties, Katherine Hoskins of Maryland most impressively cultivates the compactness and precision of the metaphysical tradition. She writes tensely, often dramatically, with emotional insight, but always under stern control of her effects. Hollis Summers, the Kentucky novelist, and William Jay Smith of Louisiana have little but a penchant for irony to ally them with the Eliot and Auden succession. Summers, who flowered as a poet only in 1959 with *The Walks Near Athens,* does possess the fine ear of an Auden and his occasional archness. But Summers, observing the smaller, more homely aspects of town life seizes on the wry, the tenderly amusing. And he is always lucid, always sceptic. A similar flair for the amusing, but also for the satiric and the brashly colloquial, distinguishes Smith's epigrammatic verse. He, like Auden, brushes often with the fantastic as he draws images and sounds out of a city world where the fantastic lives its own sort of normal existence. Donald Justice of Florida possesses all the virtuosity of Auden in established verse patterns, even in such intricate forms as the sestina, but he exhibits none of Auden's flare for histrionics and satire. There remain some touches of traditional Southern melancholy in Justice's quiet explorations of his personal experience. Never startling of image or thought, always lucid and perfectly controlled, he fully represents the accomplished products of the new Southern writing schools.

Five other poets who published first in the mid-Fifties demonstrate the continuing sway of tradition and its defiance, but more notably the new variety of approaches and effects. The most powerful of these, Vassar Miller of Texas, an accomplished virtuoso of form and sound effects, brings to her traditionally religious verse a Hopkins-like intensity of image and feeling. A poet of torn flesh and blood, of daily crucifixion, she displays the most unmodern of fervors, that of the true mystic-martyr. Adrienne Rich of Baltimore makes up for lack of emotional intensity with her sophistication. Her broad culture, her humor, her brilliant imagery combine with the control of a precise technician to make her one of the most appealing of contemporary poets. George Garrett of Florida, who has distinguished himself also as a writer of fiction, creates striking effects in his highly perceptive narrative poems and quick penetrations into human motivations. Traditional only in his preoccupation with the past is A. R. Ammons from North Carolina. Ammons' forms are uniformly free and his images verge often on the surreal, though he can descend abruptly to the dull commonplaces of modern life for contrast. Ammons' mild unorthodoxies pale, however, before the radical forms, the colloquial and literary "Beat" language of his fellow North Carolinian, Jonathan Williams, whose break with tradition is absolute. Williams' control of unpredictable verbal effects, his sharp and uninhibited wit, his scorn of marketplace America earn him distinction as the South's chief poet of the avant-garde.

Southern Negroes have contributed little indeed to the continuing Renaissance in poetry. In the Forties, volumes of undistinguished verse by Jonathan Brooks of Mississippi, H. Binga Diamond, Herbert Clark Johnson, and Naomi Witherspoon, all of Virginia, served only to break the general silence. One volume alone, Margaret Abagail Walker's *For My People* (1942), possesses originality and genuine feeling. Brought up in Alabama, Miss Walker is deeply concerned with racial problems, and speaks out her attitudes in long free-verse paragraphs, which carry something of the oratorical quality of Walt Whitman's social preachments. She is versatile, too; her colloquial ballads on historical themes, her sonnets and freely constructed nature lyrics, though less effective than her broadly conceived speeches to her people, prove her capable of handling traditional patterns and effects. Miss Walker remains the prime exception among recent Southern Negro authors, one who can find amid the clamorous calls for Negro social action a time and place for poetry.

The first two years of the Sixties have already unveiled at least four considerable new poetic talents from the South. The original and highly flavored Eleanor Ross and the painter-poet Barbara Guest, both from North Carolina, Marion Montgomery and James Dickey of Georgia have all been acclaimed for their first volumes. The

Renaissance in poetry, like that in fiction, has taken on new vitality in the last decade. As in fiction, it has as yet produced no new giants of literary pre-eminence, but again there is high promise for the future.

The American theatre, concentrated as it is in a single city and so largely subject to the critical judgment of seven men, has long offered the most precarious of careers to our creative talents. Success as a playwright has meant simply hits on Broadway, and Broadway has not always encouraged major new talents. More recently the expansion of the off-Broadway theatre and the summer theatre have provided less restricted arenas. For Southern playwrights brought up under the Koch influence, the outdoor historical drama in particular has offered scope and enormous popular audiences. Since Paul Green's initial success with *The Lost Colony,* produced on Roanoke Island since 1937, not only Green but Sam Byrd, John Ehle, Kermit Hunter, Hubert Hayes, and Robert Osborne have produced similar long-running spectacle plays for local historic sites.

For the most part, the history of the Southern Renaissance in drama after its early regional period is bound up with two names, those of Lillian Hellman and Tennessee Williams. Several of the novelists have tested Broadway, sometimes with adaptations of their novels, though only Carson McCullers' *The Member of the Wedding* (1950) achieved hit acclaim. Robert Wilder's *Flamingo Road* (1946) lasted seven performances, and Truman Capote's *The Grass Harp* (1952) nine. Novelist Noel Houston managed forty-four performances of a one-acter, "According to Law," dealing with a Negro rape case, and Donald Windham collaborated with Tennessee Williams on *You Touched Me!* (1945), a romantic comedy adapted from a D. H. Lawrence short story, for a run of 109 performances. Other dramatists have had their more or less successful flings at Broadway or off-Broadway without arousing critical enthusiasm. Robert Buckner of Arkansas and Tennessee collaborated on a mild hit, *The Primrose Path* (1939) but could show no other success in ten years with the theatre. Howard Richardson, a North Carolina Koch pupil, in collaboration with Alabaman William Berney, produced a successful poetic ballad-drama of the Smoky Mountains, *Dark of the Moon* in 1956, but his earlier plays failed of recognition. Another Koch graduate, Walter Carroll, has had well-received plays in the American Negro

Theatre and the Experimental Theatre; and Negro Theodore Ward
of Louisiana has won similar esteem in off-Broadway houses. A new
hope for the musical theatre has appeared in Jay Thompson of South
Carolina, principal collaborator in the off-Broadway hit of 1959-60,
Once upon a Mattress.

Only one other Southern playwright, John Patrick (J. P. Goggan)
from Kentucky through New Orleans, Harvard, and Columbia, has
made a conspicuous success on Broadway. Patrick, a versatile writer
for stage, screen, and radio, achieved his first success with *The Hasty
Heart* (1945), a comedy with serious overtones, set in a hospital on
the Burma front of World War II. Two years later a stage failure,
The Story of Mary Surratt, the grim tragedy of the woman condemned
for complicity in the shooting of Abraham Lincoln, won recognition
in Burns Mantle's *Best Plays of 1946-1947.* Three other relative failures preceded Patrick's immense hit of 1953, *Teahouse of the August
Moon.* If *Teahouse,* which ran over a thousand performances, was
no earth-shaking drama, it displayed wit and ingenuity, sufficiently
combined with pathos and satire, to make it one of the most appealing of modern light comedies. Playing skillfully on the differences
between East and West in an Okinawan village under American
occupation, *Teahouse* won critical as well as popular acclaim—both
Pulitzer and New York Drama Critics Awards.

Between 1941 and 1960, Miss Hellman and Williams have taken
five New York Drama Critics Awards or one quarter of those granted;
Williams has, in addition, won two Pulitzer Prizes. (If the news
reports are to be believed, Miss Hellman would have won a Pulitzer
Prize in 1935 but for some squeamishness in the Committee, and her
1939 entry tied for the New York Drama Critics Award.) Superficially, there seems little resemblance between the militant liberalism
which so often animates Lillian Hellman's exposures of greed and
malevolence and the often lyric treatment of twisted lives which gives
Tennessee Williams' best plays their power. Yet, underlying the
harsh dramatic effects which both playwrights know so well how to
achieve there lives untarnished a native romantic idealism which
speaks silently of its outrage at what it is compelled to portray. If
Miss Hellman's picture, especially of the South, has appreciably sof-
tened over the years and Williams' has grown harsher, it is not, apparently, that their basic visions have changed but that their senses

of effective theatre have been modified with the years of their successes.

Lillian Hellman crashed Broadway in her first effort with a sensational hit, *The Children's Hour* (1935). A tragedy turning on a malicious child's slander of her boarding school teachers, the play owed some of its initial success to the shock value of its lesbian suggestions. However, it was not its theme which kept it running through two seasons in New York and which led to uniformly successful revivals all over the country. The subject itself Miss Hellman handles with tactful discretion; the appeal of the play lies in its dramatic tensions, the unrelenting drive toward disaster which grows wholly out of human infirmities. In all her better plays, Miss Hellman displays truly vicious characters activated by greed, need for power or for recognition, but not until another Southerner, William March, brought his *The Bad Seed* to the stage has such a vicious child as Mary Tilford been exposed by the footlights. Miss Hellman never revels in the evil she recognizes; she pinpoints the insecurites which underlie the cruelties and always opposes them by determined forces of light and good will. She consistently reveals herself as a fighting liberal of the post-Depression generation, never a chronicler of decadence.

When, after a strong but unsuccessful labor problem play, she turned to her native South in *The Little Foxes* (1939), the portrayal of viciousness multiplies, while the forces of decency suffer subtraction. Here evil is adult in form and in power; good is weak or sick or young. Alexandra's victory over the family foxes is only one of rejection and escape, but it is, for the audience at least, a true victory, carrying with it a true comic catharsis. When later Miss Hellman returns to the Hubbard family to elucidate the background of their viciousness in *Another Part of the Forest* (1946), she can afford no such alleviation. The untempered dog-eat-dog plot in this moderately successful play approaches most closely those of the later Williams. But Miss Hellman does not complicate her stories with depravities and perversities of Gothic proportions. Her analysis of the South's condition is relatively simple: the consuming greed for money and power of the new-moneyed classes is completing the destruction of the already defeated weak and proud old aristocracy. And her answer is nothing more complex than Alexandra's escape.

In her treatment of the Fascist-Nazi menace in her two plays of the early Forties, *Watch on the Rhine* (1941) and *The Searching Wind* (1944), Miss Hellman is ready with positive, militant answers. The former, almost classic in its singleminded directness and firmness of control, argues cogently that the meek must adopt the weapons of the strong, even to killing, in order to preserve civilized values. The latter, primarily denouncing the compromises that lead to such betrayals as that at Munich, insists that the youth which suffered for those compromises in a World War will have no more of such mistakes in the future. Both of these plays clearly follow leftist propaganda lines, and risk all the hazards of topicality and tendentiousness, but *Watch on the Rhine,* at least, retains its vigor in posing the archetypal pattern of human resistance to imposed power.

In her later plays, *The Autumn Garden* (1951) and *Toys in the Attic* (1959), Miss Hellman has returned to the South, but with a new temperateness and even compassion for human frailty. Her characters are indeed frail, but there is little or no bitterness left in them. Victims of frustration or vanity or misunderstanding or of sheer stupidity, they blunder into disruptive actions which destroy the fragile relationships that have preserved them. These plays are neither comedies nor tragedies, but slowly building studies of human character and of the tenuous webs by which men and women are connected to others. There is satire certainly, directed at human inadequacies, but the spirit is less that of Voltaire himself than that of Miss Hellman's 1956 musical version of *Candide,* in which the teeth of Ferney's Patriarch are not drawn but half veiled by an indulgent smile. The fiery social liberalism which gave power, sometimes an all but melodramatic power, to Miss Hellman's plays has been lost, but it has been replaced by a more balanced, more delicate sense of human motivations and involvements.

Tennessee Williams' development, through eleven major plays, has been an almost uninterrupted movement from compassion and poetry to harshly dramatic exposure of twisted and perverted lives. The one constant in his plays since the unusually staged *The Glass Managerie* (1945) has been his sense of dramatic form. Whether his subject is frustration, violence, or self-deceit—and these are his major problems— whether his plots are simple or multiple, he builds his scenes of revelation or clash with a sure sense of their cumulative effect. Though his characters often strain the limits of credibility, they speak and act always with a compelling consistency, which renders them theatrically acceptable. Furthermore, Williams' range, encompassing the lyric effusions of youth, the stormy eloquence of the demagogue, the coarseness of sexual perverts, the tough talk of the factories, and the delicate hysterias of the gently bred, is surprisingly broad and, in all its tones, convincing.

Glass Menagerie is all poetry, gossamer and fragile as the gauze curtains which veil the memory action of the play and as Laura's symbolic collection of glass animals. Substantial realism and substantial drama in the forms of pathos and revolt move behind the transparencies and through them, but Williams' theatric devices are employed constantly to create and sustain mood. The realism and the drama manage their effects against and despite the suffusion of poetic nostalgia, which constantly muffles their voices. The result is one of the rare achievements of modern drama, a convincing illusion of truth and of emotion built by means of illusions, of symbols, the stuff of poetry itself.

Williams' second play, though the third in date of production, *Summer and Smoke* (1948), continues the strain, though now in a metaphysical, rather than a lyric, style. Set rather vaguely in the past under the aegis of a statue of Eternity, this drama of too prudish Alma and too realistic John is boldly but still humanly symbolic. Williams' basic thesis, that of the modern "dissociation of personality," in Eliot's phrase, has become a predominantly Southern one through its extensive use by John Crowe Ransom and Robert Penn Warren. Here the life-alienated soul is garbed in Alma's traditionally Southern idealism and maidenly reticence, which fails of proper integration with the body, represented by physical John, despite their mutual yearning together. The dialogue at times reaches the poetic proportion of one of Yeats' "Dialogues of Soul and Body," but Williams, by involving the families, precipitates the poetry into dramatic action, finally a tragedy of frustration.

The last of the plays to embody a large element of poetry, *A Streetcar Named Desire* (1947), won Williams his first Pulitzer Prize and his second New York Drama Critics Award. Here, on a broader scale and in naturalistic terms, Williams presents the conflict between the decadent and pathetic old South survival and the brash new elements of the modern world. Blanche Dubois, a victim of the new order of power, is also a victim of her own schizophrenic weakness, for in her reside both Alma and John in their most irreconcilable aspects. Pitifully spiritual and lost in her attachment to her old ideal of Southern life, she is also compulsively nymphomaniac. If her poetry is literally false, it rings emotionally true with tragic nostalgia. Against the violent new reality of the Stanley Kowalskis, with which her down-to-earth sister had made her peace by embracing it, Blanche is brutally exposed and helplessly caged. Perversion and violence have entered importantly into Williams' interpretation of the South, but they remain tempered by the healthy union of Stella and Stanley, the adaptable old and still crude new.

With *The Rose Tattoo* (1951), Williams makes violence and extreme sexuality, if not perversion, his central focus. Enlisting a group of Sicilian refugees settled on the Gulf Coast, he plays a series of variations on a central symbol, the rose, and on the passion it represents. This lurid comedy suggests that Williams, wishing to explore further the nature of sexual passion and finding its manifestations in the traditional South cramped and perverted by social pressures, as with Blanche, found it necessary to create a new cultural milieu for displaying its full natural development. The result is a bravura offering, with the wildly emotional, earthily admirable Serafina sweeping play and audience before her. If the roses are laid on too thickly and the passions somewhat overheated, the playwright manages to create a mood in which they are not taken too seriously.

After *Rose Tattoo,* however, Williams takes his violence, as well as his perversions and frustrations, very seriously indeed. Indeed, they preoccupy him to the point that they become obsessive, even obsessively repellent. *Camino Real* (1953) parades a long series of cynical opportunists, homosexuals, escapists, and various flotsam across its Latin American scene through sixteen episodes of initiation for his young American protagonist. Williams supplies no relief nor suggestion for relief from this maimed world. Fascinatingly written and vividly produced in antirealistic fashion, the play nevertheless seemed to open the floodgates for the mentally and morally crippled, who engage the playwright all but exclusively from this time through 1959.

Cat on a Hot Tin Roof (1955) explores sex and greed in the South, the Hellman subject, but does it at a lurid and theatrical pitch which convinces only in the theatre under the immediate spell of Williams' imaginative flair. *Orpheus Descending* (1957) and *Sweet Bird of Youth* (1959) continue and deepen the preoccupation with violence and perversion, as well as with greed and sex, until the suspicion begins to form that Williams is simply exploiting a theatrical formula, has abandoned life and poetry for the tested ingredients of past successes. Yet, the one-act play of 1958, *Suddenly Last Summer,* shows the artist at his poetic and symbolic best, albeit the symbolism is of a quite horrible sort. Here again perverted sex is the issue and an operation to cure an apparent psychosis is threatened. But the play is clothed in a terrible beauty which carries it in unity to the violently emotional climax. No other American playwright has approached such effects.

Williams' promise: "From now on I want to be concerned with the kinder aspects of life," was only partially redeemed in his 1960 "serious comedy," *Period of Adjustment.* Though it was praised by the opening night critics as "warm" and "touching," its lasting effect is hardly that. The play is often funny, but a touching warmth is not what exudes from complications which essentially expose the absurdities and psychological dilemmas of the leading characters. The four principals are living over a gradually collapsing cavern, both literally and psychologically, and though they literally escape in the end, one can hardly believe in their psychological escape, however sincerely they intend their "starting over." The ending is finally a sorry joke on them.

Night of the Iguana (1961), while it contains at its heart a touching scene between spinster and old lecher, hardly concentrates on the "kinder aspects" either. The characters, with various perversions and idiosyncrasies, resemble those of the middle period plays; twisted love and guilt are the primary themes. If the playwright allows a bittersweet kind of rapport to develop, he does not allow redemption. Williams' power, as well as his theatrical sense, have enabled him to stay on top of the most unpromising material. His poetic gifts and the deeply ingrained moral sense which drives him are still evident, but his concern with misplaced, frustrated, and distorted love cannot be exorcised. And his promise still awaits fulfillment.

11

CONCLUSIONS

The Southern Renaissance continues to flow fresh and abundant after forty years. The surviving major authors of the first generation remain active and, what is more, new. Katherine Anne Porter has produced her long-awaited novel, and critics have been all but unanimous in calling it her masterpiece. William Faulkner's final work proves to be his first all-comic novel. The latest offering of Robert Penn Warren reaches into European backgrounds to involve an immigrant protagonist, and in many ways reverses the tendencies of his later novels. Even Upton Sinclair, in his middle eighties, gives us something different, a light epistolary satire. Of the later authors discussed in previous pages, more than forty have published new volumes during the subsequent two years, including Carson McCullers, Ann Hebson, George Garrett, William Goyen, Lucy Daniels, Julian Mayfield, Babs and Borden Deal.

More remarkable still are the young, who have already proved the intense fecundity of Southern letters in the Sixties. Fifteen first novelists have been hailed as highly promising new talents. These include a Pulitzer Prize winner for 1960, Harper Lee, for her *To Kill a Mockingbird*; a recipient of the National Book Award in 1961, Walker Percy, for his existentialist novel, *The Moviegoer;* a young man whose novel was printed complete in an issue of *Harper's Magazine,* Reynolds Price's *A Long and Happy Life* (1962). Others who clearly deserve citation are Ellen Douglas for *A Family's Affairs* (1962), Jesse Hill Ford for *Mountains of Gilead* (1961), Norris Lloyd for *A Dream of Mansions* (1962), Guy Owen for *A Season of Fear* (1960), Louis Rubin for *The Golden Weather* (1961), Joan Williams for the *The Morning and the Evening* (1961). Evidently the South means to perpetuate its latter-day reputation as the literary center of America.

Seldom in literary history has a movement so broad as the Southern Renaissance continued to perpetuate itself, to evolve, and to retain its vitality over so long a period. It may be argued that the incidence of genius has declined with the later generations, for no Faulkners, Warrens, Porters, Ransoms, Tates, or Wolfes have appeared to command universal acclaim. The fact is, however, that more highly talented writers have been produced by the younger generation and far more have won wide recognition for their early works. Only Wolfe of the first era was pronounced a genius when his first major book appeared—and his reputation has proved the least secure. Among the younger, first Welty and McCullers, then Styron, O'Connor, Jones, Taylor, Spencer, Capote, Goyen, Grau, Williams, Shapiro, Jarrell, to name a few, have been hailed as potential geniuses in the Fifties, and already in the Sixties four or five more have received like tribute. Time is necessary for the evaluation, as well as for the development, of a major talent. The odds would appear to favor the young, for never has the incidence of high quality approached its present level. The potential among the younger Southern writers is tremendous. What they will finally achieve cannot be predicted; one suspects it will be considerable.

In seeking an explanation for this prolonged creative activity, critics have emphasized the South's continuing sense of the past, its agrarian tradition, and its lingering heritage of family solidarity. All of these factors have weighed heavily, certainly, in lending depth and fullness to the literary interpretations of Southern life. A Faulkner without the funded history, the land-based values, and the feeling for family integrity would be a mere rhetorician or what modern French writers have found him to be, an experimenter in *anti-roman* techniques. But a Wolfe burgeoned substantially without these fertilizing elements, and a considerable number of the modern generation ignore or repudiate them. Factors such as these do not stimulate men and women to write, however valuable they may prove as literary equipment.

Southerners in the 1920's turned to artistic forms of expression under the pressure of social change and with a distinct consciousness of the literary backwardness of their native regions. The pattern of

change or threatened change or need for change has continued un-
broken to this moment, and has indeed been constantly accelerated.
The great economic shift from the culture of cotton and the exploitation of lumber resources to cattle breeding, textile and chemical manufacture, and the oil industry was largely a post-Depression development, which brought with it new social alignments and new outlooks.
The desegration decision of 1954 was only a larger step in a direction
in which change had been occurring steadily since the Depression.
The Negro's virtual peonage, which only a cotton culture could justify,
no longer had even an economic sanction. The drive for equality
of opportunity, given new impetus by World War II and the Korean
War, was again accelerated by international developments in the post-
wars world. New nationalistic movements sprang up everywhere
among the colored races, and were almost everywhere successful in
their demands for independence. The national government in America, standing in world councils for independence of all peoples and
races, could hardly afford to tolerate officially a policy of inequality
within its own borders.

The educated Negro in the South, supremely aware of all these
forces and spurred by his Northern neighbors, black and white,
doubled and redoubled his pressure for a new social status. All of
Southern society, therefore, has been kept continuously aware of the
impending revolution. Change has become the order of life for the
Southerner, in the recent past, the present, and the foreseeable future.

A further major reason for the continued and accelerated activity
on the part of Southern authors has been a matter of literary consciousness. It is a notable fact that nothing resembling a renaissance has
occurred in painting, sculpture, architecture, or music, though interest
in all these fields has been demonstrated in the rapid expansion of
facilities in schools, museums, and concert halls. The challenge in
the Twenties had been almost wholly a literary one, and the first
generation of writers, highly conscious of their function, met it with
enormous success. By the time the later generations had reached
maturity, not only had the reputations of the prime authors been
established, but the South had come to look on itself as a true literary
center. Furthermore, the critical theories of its Fugitive group had
begun to permeate the colleges and universities, writing courses were
established, literary societies formed, and Southern magazines pro-

vided immediate outlets. This process has been cumulative over the years, until now established Southern writers teach the ambitious young, and publishing houses employ writing scouts in Southern cities.

All of this stimulation has built an atmosphere of literary consciousness without parallel on so wide a scale. Every area has sufficient talent latent within it to produce a renaissance in almost any field of human endeavor. It requires only a special concentration of stimuli to focus it in a given direction. The case of Nashville's little renaissance of the early Twenties is instructive. There with only one man, John Ransom, a dedicated poet, but with a sense of challenge in the air, occurred the Fugitive phenomenon, which drew to it teachers, students, and businessmen in a fever of poetic activity. So with the whole South today. The talents were always there, but they trained as lawyers, journalists, or as scholarly dilettantes and planters. Furthermore, the artistically-minded women, raised on sentiment and shielded against hard facts, were not encouraged to exercise their talents except in decorous verse or moral romance. Independent bachelor women like Ellen Glasgow and Elizabeth Maddox Roberts pioneered the break from a sheltered tradition. Their success and the widespread feminine revolt of the Twenties stimulated the Evelyn Scotts, the Katherine Anne Porters, the Frances Newmans, Carmen Barnes, and Edith Popes to assert their individual creativity in defiance of their heritages. Since the Forties, the emancipated Southern girl goes to college, takes writing courses, gets newspaper, radio, and advertising experience, goes into social work, goes to war—and adumbrates a first novel.

In view of the wide range of Renaissance literary activity, it becomes all but impossible to generalize on the attitudes which it has exhibited. Primarily, the writers demonstrate their developed sense of literature as art, not as simply a vehicle for expressing pious sentiments, nostalgia, and romantic dreams. With the Fugitive writers, Faulkner, and Porter setting the standards, they have long recognized the modern truisms of criticism, that "art is life at the remove or meaning," and that only technique can develop meanings. In addition, they are realists. They have learned that only the concrete image, sharply evoked, carries the immediate conviction they seek, that the generalization, the abstraction, saps life from the work. In novel after novel, poem after poem, play after play, it is the feeling for the living detail, what Ransom called the "texture" of "the World's body," which vitalizes the illusion. If most of the more accomplished authors add symbolic extensions to their immediate observations, they have learned to develop the symbols directly and unobtrusively out of the imagetic reality itself, rather than to impose them arbitrarily.

Philosophically and sociologically, Southern authors remain divided into the agrarian-minded conservatives and the forward-looking liberals and humanitarians, with the latter more and more in the preponderance. But even these groups unite in their animosity toward the encroachments of finance capitalism into the region. For the traditionists, like Donald Davidson, who has waged a long literary battle from Nashville against the "Leviathan"; or like Faulkner, who offers their Southern image in the Snopes family, the banker and industrialist represent the prime agency destroying sound Southern values. For the liberal, they and their system embody the principles of exploitation and perpetuation of caste and money privilege. Both of the groups see the old aristocracy as doomed, either from its inability to fight with the opponents' crude weapons, or from its degeneracy and refusal to face fact. While the traditionist deeply laments the loss, the liberal is, like Basso, torn between regret and impatience, or simply impatient for the end.

The Agrarian issue which so excited the early generation of Renaissance writers has finally worn itself out, but the attitudes which lent it urgency remain. No longer a source of economic disagreement, traditional agrarian values still provoke highly divergent social views among the creative authors. In their interpretations of the proletariat, "red neck" or Negro or even Mexican, the traditionist and the humanist exhibit in common only a feeling ranging from distrust to anger at its mass manifestations. As a mob, as a political assembly, even as a congregation at times, the Southern poor white frequently acts violently, is easily aroused to many forms of emotional excess, which counterbalance his habitual lack of display in private life. His chief agitators, the preachers and the politician risen from his own ranks, elicit both amusement and contempt. In particular, the upstart, rabble-rousing politician finds unanimous condemnation. In book after book he appears as greedy and corrupt, trailing along with him an unprincipled gang of henchmen and secretaries. Even the occasional old aristocratic senator or the young crusading idealist seeking to gain or retain office is forced to compromise with the corruptive elements or with the demogoguery which his "red neck" opponent employs against him. There is no instance in modern Southern literature where the Huey Long, Talmadge, or Bilbo type of politician is condoned. His constituency, therefore, largely the poor white country man, is, by implication at least, roundly censured by all the literati of the area.

The major divergence between the tradition-minded author and the humanitarian occurs in his attitude toward the individual poor white and the Negro. The conservative generally, recognizing the fact of unequal treatment, resorts to paternalistic attitudes and even, in the case of the Negroes, to a doctrine of inferiority, for which he resurrects the Old Testament story of Ham's sin, giving it a black twist. This traditional view, or, if you will, excuse, is now constantly and strongly refuted by many Southern white writers who evidently know their subjects intimately. The individualistic treatment of the poor white from Edith Kelley and Elizabeth M. Roberts on has insisted on his personality, his solidly human aspirations, and his economic frustrations. Even more insistent has been the recognition of the Negro as a suffering member of the human race. The most remarkable development of the Southern Renaissance, aside its from its growth in artistic consciousness, has been its matured understanding of the Negro viewpoint. While the conservative continues to see the Negro's progress as subversive of traditional values, his humanitarian neighbor has first sympathetically observed him, then sided with him, and finally entered fully into his life as a fellow being.

Southern literature, despite its recent expansion in settings, has remained in its most important manifestations a regional literature. Never has an extensive and diversified area been so thoroughly explored in all its natural and human variety. Its mountains and bottoms, its rivers, lakes, bayous, and bogs have been richly detailed in all their charms and menaces. The inhabitants, from raggedest Negro farmhand, slum dweller, or swamp fugitive to its proudest D.A.R., F.F.V., or industrial mogul, have been offered up living for examination and assessment. Though the Southern author himself surprisingly often has become a dweller in the asphalt jungles of the metropolis or in suburbia, his fascination with his native soil and the variety of its people has not left him. He retains freshly the images of sight and sound and smell, and he has learned consummately well the art of reproducing them vividly. He has created, therefore, a body of literature unrivaled in our century for its variety, its abundance, and its quality.

APPENDIX

It is a manifest impossibility to list here all those Southerners who have printed stories, verse, and drama. All of the authors here included have published book-length volumes which have been issued by reputable publishers of more than local prestige. All of those whom I have been able to authenticate as Southern writers under my definition appear here. If there are omissions, I apologize and should be happy to know of them.

SOUTHERN RENAISSANCE AUTHORS BY STATES

ALABAMA
Fiction
Robert Bell
Jack Bethea
Wyatt Blasingame
Joe David Brown
James Saxon Childers
Marian Cockrell
Paul Cook
Babs Deal
Alice Fellows
Zelda Sayre Fitzgerald
Robert Gibbons
William Howard Harris
Harriet Hassell
Annette Heard
William L. Heath (b. Ark.)
George W. Henderson (N.)
William Bradford Huie
Mary Fassett Hunt
Caroline Ivey
Welbourn Kelley
Harper Lee
Eloise Liddon
Herbert Lyons

J. Max McMurray
William March (Campbell)
Sarah Haardt Mencken
Charles Curtis Munz (b. Mo.)
Albert Murray (N.)
Helen Norris
George S. O'Neal
Florence Glass Palmer
Julian Lee Rayford
Catherine Rogers
Thomas Rowan
Elise Sanguinetti
Marie Stanley
John Craig Stewart
James Still
Frances Tillotson (b. Ark.)
Lael Tucker
Anne Tyson
Howell Vines
Eugene Walter
Lella Warren
John Weld
John H. Wildman
Clement Wood
Julia Yenni

Drama
William Howard Harris
Kate Porter Lewis

Poetry
Sarah Henderson Hay
Louise Crenshaw Ray
James Still
Anne Southerne Tardy
Margaret Abagail Walker (N.)
Clement Wood

EASTERN ARKANSAS
Fiction
Karle Baker
Janice Holt Giles
Francis Gwaltney
C. P. Lee
May Mellinger
Charlie May Simon (Fletcher)
David Thibault
Francis Tillotson
Everett Webber (b. Miss.)

Drama
Robert L. Buckner

Poetry
Karle Baker
C. T. Davis
John Gould Fletcher
Charlie May Simon
Don West

FLORIDA
Fiction
Charles Baker
Gladys Baker
Peggy Bennett (b. N.C.)
Wesley Ford Davis
George Garrett
Mercedes Gilbert (N.)
Hazel Gobay
Edwin Granberry (b. Miss.)
Leon O. Griffith
Rubylea Hall

Zora Neale Hurston (N.)
James Weldon Johnson (N.)
Edith Pope
Marjorie Kinnan Rawlings (b. D.C.)
Lillian Smith
Mary-Elizabeth Witherspoon
Delight Youngs (b. Ind.)

Poetry
George Dillon
George Garrett
James Weldon Johnson (N.)
Donald Justice
Majorie Meeker
Edith Taylor (Pope)

GEORGIA
Fiction
Annulet Andrews
Vereen Bell
Jackson Burgess
Erskine Caldwell
William T. Campbell
Harriet Gift Castlen
Brainard Cheney
Mary Cobb
Lonnie Coleman
Donald Corley
Roxanne Cotsakis
LeGarde Doughty
Julian Drake
Willie Snow Ethridge
Foster Fitz-Simons
Berry Fleming
John Porter Fort
Peggy Gaddis
Isa Glenn
Arthur Gordon
Mary Granger
John Temple Graves
Ward Green (b. N.C.)
Tom Ham
Evelyn Hanna
William C. Haygood
John Hewlett

Mac Hyman
Arthur Crew Inman
Sara Jenkins
Douglas Kiker
John O. Killens (N.)
Mary Jackson King
Elizabeth Kytle (b. S.C.)
Margaret Rebecca Lay
Edna Lee
Celeste Lindsay
Norris Lloyd
Betsy Lochridge
Margaret Long
Carson McCullers
Gilbert Maxwell
Caroline Miller
Charles Mills
Margaret Mitchell
James Stuart Montgomery
Marion Montgomery
David Morrah
Eleanor Nash (b. Ky.)
Frances Newman
Howard Odum
Flannery O'Connor
Edwin Peeples
Louis B. Pendleton
Byron Herbert Reece
Robert L. Scott
Marian Sims
Laurence Stallings
Nan Bagby Stephens
Davenport Steward
Christine Teague
Sam Tupper
Nedra Tyre
Walter F. White (N.)
Calder Willingham
Donald Windham
Frank Yerby (N.)

Drama

Rietta Bailey
Daniel Hicky
Carson McCullers

Ward Morehouse
Laurence Stallings
Donald Windham

Poetry

James Dickey
Ernest Hartsock
Daniel Hicky
Nelle Irwin Horkan
Arthur Crew Inman
Georgia Douglas Johnson (N.)
Gilbert Maxwell
James Stuart Montgomery
Marion Montgomery
Roselle Montgomery
Byron Herbert Reece
Anderson Scruggs
Florence Stearns
James E. Warren, Jr.
Mary V. Womble

KENTUCKY

Fiction

Juliet Alves
Barbara Anderson (b. Mass.)
Harriette Arnow
Wendell Berry
Ben L. Burman
Carl Burton
William W. Chamberlain
John Clagett
Billy C. Clark
Irvin S. Cobb
Alfred Crabb
Olive Dargan (Fielding Burke)
Frances Fox
Henry Giles
Durwood Grinstead
Elizabeth Hardwick
Harlan Hatcher (b. Ohio)
Ann Hebson
Henry Hornsby
Carter Brooke Jones
Edith Summers Kelley
Wallace McElroy Kelly

John Kennedy
Sarah Litsey
George Looms
Laetitia McDonald
Charles R. McDowell
Clark McMeekin
George Madden Martin
Jane Mayhall
Eldred Means
Eli Millen
Jane Morton
Frances Ogilvie
Elizabeth Maddox Roberts
Emanie Sachs
Ann Steward (b. Ohio)
Jesse Stuart
Hollis Summers
Allen Tate
Jean Thomas
Charles H. Towne
Robert Penn Warren
Leane Zugsmith

Drama

LeGette Blythe
Olive Dargan
Abbie C. Goodloe
Laetitia McDonald
Jane Mayhall
Frances Ogilvie
John Patrick
Stewart Walker

Poetry

Gertrude Nason Carver
Joseph S. Cotter, Jr. (N.)
Olive Dargan
George Elliston
Mary C. Eudy
Henry Fuson
Hortense Flexner
Jesse Lemont
Sarah Litsey
William McCreary
David Morton

Jessie Murton
Elizabeth Maddox Roberts
Jesse Stuart
Allen Tate
Robert Penn Warren

LOUISIANA

Fiction

Virginia Abaunza
James Aswell
Hamilton Basso
Sallie Lee Bell
Arna Bontemps (N.)
Truman Capote
Mentis Carrere
Hodding Carter
Harris Downey
Alexander Federoff
James Feibleman
Peter Feibleman (b. N.Y.)
Zas Fortmayer
George F. Gibbs
Barbara Giles
Emily Godchaux
Arthemise Goertz
Shirley Ann Grau
Georgette Hall
Clelie Huggins
Charlotte Johnson
Harnett Kane
Robert E. Kennedy
Grace King
Speed Lamkin
Myrick Land
Fanny Heaslip Lea
Leroy Leatherman
Mary Barrow Linfield
Charles Martin
Alfred Maund
Mary Morgan
E. P. O'Donnell
Walker Percy
Hertha Pretorius
Dalton Reymond
Thad St. Martin

Thomas Sancton
Lyle Saxon
Robert Tallant
Fiswoode Tarleton
Carlyle Tillery (b. Miss.)
Jean Toomer (b. D.C.) (N.)
Augusta Tucker
Parker Tyler
Helen Upshaw

Drama
Truman Capote
Lillian Hellman
Theodore Ward (N.)

Poetry
Oliver Evans
James Feibleman
Mae Winkler Goodman
John E. Hardy
Robert Emmett Kennedy
Richard Kirk
Gordon Lawrence
Charles Quirk
William Jay Smith
Rosa Coates Richards
Jean Toomer (N.)
Parker Tyler

MARYLAND
Fiction
Barbara Avirett
John Barth
Gilbert Byron
James M. Cain
Carlyn Coffin
J. V. Cunningham
Daniel McIntyre Henderson
Victor H. Johnson
Sophie Kerr
Alexander Key
Frederic Kummer
Fulton Oursler
Frances Hopkinson Smith
Don Tracy (b. Conn.)

Augusta Tucker (b. La.)
Waters E. Turpin (N.)
Leon Uris
Robert Van Gelder
Jere Wheelwright

Drama
Thomas Cole
Robert Garland
Frederic Kummer
Fulton Oursler
Adrienne Rich
Rida Young

Poetry
Gilbert Byron
Thomas Cole
J. V. Cunningham
Daniel McIntyre Henderson
Dorothy Hobson
Katherine Hoskins
Audrey McGaffin
Frank O'Hara
Adrienne Rich
E. Merrill Root
Karl Shapiro
Eli Siegel
Eleanor G. Wallis

MISSISSIPPI
Fiction
William Attaway (N.)
Katherine Bellamann
Maxwell Bodenheim
Ada Jack Carver
Ed Louis Cochran
Hubert Creekmore
Louise Crump
Reuben Davis
Borden Deal
Ellen Douglas
John Faulkner
William Faulkner
Lucille Finlay
Shelby Foote

Charles Henri Ford
Frances Gaither (b. Tenn.)
Alice Walworth Graham
Evans Harrington (b. Ala.)
Edward Kimbrough
Avery Kolb
George Lee (N.)
Walter Lowrey
Virginia Oakey (b. Va.)
George Patterson
James Peery
W. T. Person
Thomas Hal Phillips
Clark Porteous (b. La.)
William Russell
H. A. Shands
Pat Smith
Elizabeth Spencer
Philip Stone
James Street
Cid Ricketts Sumner
Mildred Topp (b. Ill.)
Evans Wall
Ben Wasson
Everett Webber
Robert S. Weekley (b. Ala.)
Eudora Welty
Annie Lucile White
Tennessee Williams
Wirt Williams
Richard Wright (N.)
Jefferson Young
Stark Young

Drama

Thomas D. Pawley (N.)
William Russell
Tennessee Williams
Stark Young

Poetry

Charles G. Bell
Katherine Bellamann
Maxwell Bodenheim
Jonathan Brooks (N.)

Hubert Creekmore
Henry Dalton
William Faulkner
Charles Henri Ford
Jamie Sexton Holme
Muna Lee
Louise Moss Montgomery
George Marion O'Donnell
William Alexander Percy
Joseph B. Roberts
Tennessee Williams
Stark Young

NORTH CAROLINA

Fiction

Paul Ader
Eugene Armfield
Anne W. Armstrong
Agnew Bahnson
Rose Batterham
Doris Betts
Mary Bledsoe
William LeGette Blythe
James Boyd (b. Pa.)
Mathis Boynton-Hamilton
Evan L. Brandon
Russell Brantley
Zoe Kincaid Brockman
Julia Canaday
Pat Carson
Emily Clark
Frank Clarvoe
E. Wade Cranford
Rebecca Cushman
Jonathan Daniels
Lucy Daniels
Burke Davis
Paxton Davis
John Ehle
Ernest Frankel (b. N.Y.C.)
Adelaide Fries
Daisy Gold
Paul Green
Ben Haas
Marion Hargrove

Bernice Kelly Harris
R. P. Harriss
Worth Tuttle Heddon
Walter P. Henderson
Jesse Hollingsworth
Noel Houston (b. Okla.)
Edith W. Huggins
Gerald W. Johnson
Joe Knox
W. Frank Landing
Edythe Latham
Laurette McDuffie
Robert K. Marshall
Joseph Mitchell
Kathleen Morehouse
David Morrah
Hoke Norris
Stanley Olmsted
Guy Owen
Frances Patton
James Larkin Pearson
Josephine A. Peck
Ovid Pierce
William T. Polk
Reynolds Price
Tim Pridgen
Jesse C. Rehder
Peirson Ricks
Joseph B. Roberts (b. Miss.)
Lettie Rogers (b. China)
Fred Ross
James Ross
Robert Ruark
Phillips Russell
Frank G. Slaughter (b. D.C.)
Jan Cox Speas
Julia Montgomery Street
Orren Jack Turner
John Van Alstyn Weaver
Thomas G. Wicker
Thomas Wolfe
Charles B. Wood

Drama
Sam Byrd
Walter Carroll

John Ehle
Foster Fitz-Simons
Frances Goforth
Paul Green
Hubert Hayes
Bertha Hester
Edward P. Harris
Noel Houston
Hatcher Hughes
Kermit Hunter
Henry McIver
Robert Osborne
Howard Richardson
Walter Spearman (b. S.C.)
Julia Montgomery Street
George Tidd
Lula Vollmer
Thomas Wolfe

Poetry
A. R. Ammons
James Boyd
Lucy Crisp
Charles Eaton
Barbara Guest
Frank Borden Hanes
Francis Pledger Hulme
Sneed Ogburn
Anne B. Payne
James Larkin Pearson
Eleanor Ross
Phillips Russell
Thad Stem, Jr.
Gertrude Vestal
John Van Alstyn Weaver
Jonathan Williams
Thomas Wolfe
Kathryn Worth

SOUTH CAROLINA
Fiction
Edward C. L. Adams
Lillian Alexander
Glenn Allan
Havilah Babcock
John Bennett III

Benjamin Brawley
Gwen Bristow
Octavus Roy Cohen
Elizabeth Boatwright Coker
Richard Coleman (b. D.C.)
Samuel Arthur Derieux
Ann Head
Dubose Heyward
M. A. Johansen
Margaret Law
Alice A. Lide
Grace Lumpkin
E. C. McCants
William F. McIlwain
Robert Marks
Julian Mayfield
Robert Molloy
C. S. Murray
Julia Peterkin
Josephine Pinckney
Katherine Ball Ripley
Ben Robertson
Louis Rubin
Archibald Rutledge
Herbert Ravenel Sass
Katherine Simons (Mayrant)
Elliott Springs
Max Steele
Samuel G. Stoney
Vinnie Williams
William Woodward

Drama

Octavus Roy Cohen
Dubose Heyward
Jay Thompson

Poetry

Bertie H. Clinkscales
Dubose Heyward
Helen Von Kolnitz Hyer
Margaret Law
Clelia P. McGowan
Mary Owings Miller
Josephine Pinckney
Beatrice Ravenel

Archibald Rutledge
Katherine Simons
Elizabeth Charles Welborn

TENNESSEE

Fiction

James Agee
Anne Armstrong
Carmen Barnes
Frank Lee Beals
Thomas E. Bell
Jack Boone
Roark Bradford
Maristan Chapman
Wilma Dykeman
Francis Eisenberg
Sara Pett Fain (b. Tex.)
Jesse Hill Ford
Charles Givens
Caroline Gordon
Christine Govan (b. N.Y.)
Emmett Gowen
Harry Hamilton
Mildred Haun
Laurie Havron
Edwin Huddleston
Bowen Ingram
Randall Jarrell
Stanley Johnson
Madison Jones
Harry Kroll (b. Ind.)
Elery Lay
John A. Leland
Andrew Lytle
Thomas Mabry
Horace McCoy
J. Walker McSpadden
Gilmore Millen
Sonia Novak
Edd Winfield Parks
Jennings Perry
Robert Ramsey
Robert Richards
Charles B. Roberts
Gene Robinson

Adelaide Rowell (b. Ohio)
Robert Rylee
Evelyn Scott
T. S. Stribling
Walter Sullivan
Peter Taylor
Denton Whitson
Joan Williams
Ridley Wills
Anne Winslow

Drama

Charles Givens
Adelaide Rowell
Evelyn Scott
Peter Taylor
Denton Whitson

Poetry

James Agee
Robert Avrett
Mary McD. Axelson
Donald Davidson
Meade Harwell
Randall Jarrell
Violet McDougal
Jeanette Marks
Abby C. Milton
Merrill Moore
Sonia Novak
Edd Winfield Parks
John Crowe Ransom
Isla P. Richardson
George Scarbrough
Evelyn Scott
Nell Thompson-Miller
Robert S. Walker
Anne Winslow

EAST TEXAS

Fiction

Philip Atlee
Barry Benefield
Sigman Byrd
Walter Clemons
Madison Cooper

Ruth Cross
Cleo Dawson
Allen Drury
Frank Elser
Zena Garrett (b. Ala.)
Jewel Gibson
Aubrey Goodman
Marcus Goodrich
William Goyen
John Howard Griffin
Harry Hervey
Margaret Bell Houston
William Humphrey
Jack Jones
Donald Joseph
Harry Kidd (b. Va.)
Elithe Kirkland
Laura Krey
Edwin Lanham
Mary Lasswell (b. Scotland)
Bonner McMillion
Emma Louise Mally
Hamilton Maule (b. Fla.)
Mary King O'Donnell
Cothburn O'Neal
William A. Owens
Marion Parker
Norma Patterson
George Sessions Perry
James Young Phillips
Evelyn Pierce
Katherine Ann Porter
Elinor Pryor
Garland Roark
Dorothy Scarborough
Hart Stilwell
Alma Stone
John W. Thompson
John Cherry Watson
David Westheimer
Elizabeth Wheaton
Willson Whitman
John W. Wilson
Vurrell Yentzen

Drama
Frank Elser
John William Rogers
Arthur Sampley
Poetry
Walter R. Adams
Frances Alexander
John Houghton Allen
Robert Avrett
Stanley E. Babb
William E. Bard
William Burford
Irene Carlyle
Thelma Cash
Hilton Ross Greer
Margaret Bell Houston
Siddie Joe Johnson
Therese Lindsey
Lilith Lorraine
Tom H. McNeal
Vassar Miller
Patrick D. Moreland (b. **N.C.**)
Lexie Dean Robertson
Grace Ross
David Russell
Arthur Sampley
Dorothy Scarborough
Goldie Capers Smith (b. **La.**)

VIRGINIA

Fiction
Havilah Babcock
Temple Bailey
James Ballard
Mary Beechwood (b. D.C.)
Arthur H. Bryant
Robert Buckner
Thomas Bowyer Campbell
Helena Caperton
John Bell Clayton
Kathleen Crawford
Lucy Herndon Crockett
   (b. Hawaii)
Foxhall Daingerfield

M. H. Davis
Samuel Arthur Derieux
Clifford Dowdey
Hamilton Eckenrode
Murrell Edmunds
William F. Fitzgerald
Roy Flannagan
Ellen Glasgow
Earl Hamner
Scott Hart
Pati Hill
William Hoffman (b. W.Va.)
Pendleton Hogan
Claudia Holland
Stanley Hopkins
Aline Kilmer
Ronald C. Lee
Morris Markey
May Davies Martenet
Julian Meade
Virginia Moore (b. Neb.)
Blair Niles
Myra Page
Blanche Perrin
Green Peyton (Wertenbaker)
Martha Byrd Porter
Jennings Rice
J. R. Salamanca
Glenn Scott
Philip Scruggs
Herbert Silvette
Bart Spicer
William Styron
Beverley Randolph Tucker
Nancy Bird Turner
Virginia Cruse Watson
John Downing Weaver
Charles Wertenbaker
Robert Wilder

Drama
Randolph Edmonds (N.)
Beverley Tucker
Robert Wilder

Poetry

Ben Belitt	Mary Leitch
Gertrude Boatwright Claytor	Virginia Taylor McCormick
Julia Johnson Davis	Virginia Moore
H. Binga Diamond (N.)	John Moreland
Carlton Drewry	Edwin Quarles
Leigh Hanes	Nancy Ransom
Leslie Pinckney Hill (N.)	Coleman Rosenberger (b. D.C.)
William Hull	Lucia Trent
Cary Jacob	Emma G. Trigg
Herbert C. Johnson (N.)	Virginia L. Tunstall (b. Ky.)
Sallie Bruce Kinsolving	Nancy Bird Turner
Lawrence Lee	Naomi Witherspoon (N.)

INDEX